University Success

READING

INTERMEDIATE TO HIGH-INTERMEDIATE

Carrie Steenburgh

Series Editor: Lawrence Zwier

Authentic Content Contributors: Ronnie Hess II
and Tim McLaughlin

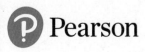

University Success Reading, Intermediate to High-Intermediate Level

Copyright © 2018 by Pearson Education, Inc.

Pearson Education, 221 River Street, Hoboken, NJ 07030

Staff credits: The people who made up the *University Success* team, representing content development, design, manufacturing, marketing, multimedia, project management, publishing, rights management, and testing, are Pietro Alongi, Stephanie Callahan, Kimberly Casey, Tracey Cataldo, Sara Davila, Dave Dickey, Gina DiLillo, Warren Fischbach, Nancy Flaggman, Lucy Hart, Sarah Henrich, Gosia Jaros-White, Niki Lee, Amy McCormick, Jennifer Raspiller, Robert Ruvo, Katarzyna Skiba, Kristina Skof, Katarzyna Starzynska-Kosciuszko, Joanna Szyszynska, John Thompson, Paula Van Ells, Joseph Vella, Rebecca Wicker, and Natalia Zaremba.

Project coordination: Lawrence Zwier

Project supervision: Debbie Sistino

Contributing editors: Lida Baker, Eleanor Barnes, Andrea Bryant, Barbara Lyons, Leigh Stolle, and Sarah Wales-McGrath

Cover image: Oleksandr Prykhodko / Alamy Stock Photo

Video research: Constance Rylance

Video production: Kristine Stolakis, assisted by Melissa Langer

Text composition and illustrations: EMC Design Ltd

Library of Congress Cataloging-in-Publication Data

A catalog record for the print edition is available from the Library of Congress.

Printed in the United States of America

ISBN-10: 0-13-465322-X

ISBN-13: 978-0-13-465322-8

1   18

Contents

Welcome to *University Success*

INTRODUCTION

University Success is a new academic skills series designed to equip intermediate- to transition-level English learners with the reading, writing, and oral communication skills necessary to succeed in courses in an English-speaking university setting. The blended instructional model provides students with an inspiring collection of extensive authentic content, expertly developed in cooperation with five subject matter experts, all "thought leaders" in their fields. By utilizing both online and in-class instructional materials, *University Success* models the type of "real life" learning expected of students studying for a degree. *University Success* recognizes the unique linguistic needs of English language learners and carefully scaffolds skill development to help students successfully work with challenging and engaging authentic content.

SERIES ORGANIZATION: *THREE STRANDS*

This three-strand series, **Reading**, **Writing**, and **Oral Communication**, includes five distinct content areas: the Human Experience, Money and Commerce, the Science of Nature, Arts and Letters, and Structural Science, all popular fields of study among English language learners. The three strands are fully aligned across content areas and skills, allowing teachers to utilize material from different strands to support learning. Teachers can delve deeply into skill development in a single area, or provide additional support materials from other areas for richer development across the four skills.

THE *UNIVERSITY SUCCESS* APPROACH: *AN AUTHENTIC EXPERIENCE*

This blended program combines the utility of an interactive student book, online learner lab, and print course to create a flexible approach that adjusts to the needs of teachers and learners. Its skill-based and step-by-step instruction enables students to master essential skills and become confident in their ability to perform successfully in academic degree courses taught in English. Students at this level need to engage with content that provides them with the same challenges native speakers face in a university setting. Many English language learners are not prepared for the quantity of reading and writing required in college-level courses, nor are they properly prepared to listen to full-length lectures that have not been scaffolded for them. These learners, away from the safety of an ESL classroom, must keep up with the rigors of a class led by a professor who may be unaware of the challenges a second-language learner faces. Strategies for academic success, delivered via online videos, help increase students' confidence and ability to cope with the challenges of academic student and college culture. *University Success* steps up to the podium to represent academic content realistically with the appropriate skill development and scaffolding essential for English language learners to be successful.

PUTTING STUDENTS ON THE PATH TO *UNIVERSITY SUCCESS*

Intensive skill development and extended application—tied to specific learning outcomes—provide the scaffolding English language learners need to become confident and successful in a university setting.

Global Scale of English	10	20	30	40	50	60	70	80	90
CEFR		<A1	A1	A2 +	B1 +	B2 +	C1	C2	

INTERMEDIATE TO HIGH-INTERMEDIATE LEVEL B1–B1+ | 43–58	ADVANCED LEVEL B2–B2+ | 59–75	TRANSITION LEVEL B2+–C1 | 68–80
Authentic content with careful integration of essential skills, the Intermediate to High-Intermediate level familiarizes students with real-world academic contexts.	Challenging, authentic content with level-appropriate skills, the Advanced level prepares students to exit the ESL safety net.	A deep dive for transition-level students, the Transition level mirrors the academic rigor of college courses.
INTENSIVE SKILL PRACTICE	**INTENSIVE SKILL PRACTICE**	**INTENSIVE SKILL PRACTICE**
Intensive skill practice tied to learning objectives informed by the Global Scale of English	Intensive skill practice tied to learning objectives informed by the Global Scale of English	Intensive skill practice tied to learning objectives informed by the Global Scale of English
AUTHENTIC CONTENT	**AUTHENTIC CONTENT**	**AUTHENTIC CONTENT**
■ Readings: 200–2,000 words ■ Lectures: 15–20 minutes ■ Multiple exposures and chunking	■ Readings: 200–3,000 words ■ Lectures: 20 minutes	Readings and lectures of significant length: ■ 200–3,500-word readings ■ 25-minute lectures
EXPLICIT VOCABULARY INSTRUCTION	**EXPLICIT VOCABULARY INSTRUCTION**	**CONTENT AND FLUENCY VOCABULARY APPROACH**
■ Pre- and post-reading and listening vocabulary tasks ■ Glossing of receptive vocabulary ■ Recycling throughout each part and online	■ Pre- and post-reading and listening vocabulary tasks ■ Glossing of receptive vocabulary ■ Recycling throughout each part and online	■ No direct vocabulary instruction ■ Online vocabulary practice for remediation
SCAFFOLDED APPROACH	**MODERATELY SCAFFOLDED**	
Multiple guided exercises focus on comprehension, application, and clarification of productive skills.	Guided exercises focus on comprehension, application, and clarification of productive skills.	
VOCABULARY STRATEGIES	**VOCABULARY STRATEGIES**	
Vocabulary strategy sections focus on form, use, and meaning.	Vocabulary strategy sections focus on form, use, and meaning to help students process complex content.	
GRAPHIC ORGANIZERS		
Extensive integration of graphic organizers throughout to support note-taking and help students process complex content.		

Key Features

UNIQUE PART STRUCTURE

University Success employs a unique three-part structure, providing maximum flexibility and multiple opportunities to customize the content. The series is "horizontally" aligned to teach across a specific content area and "vertically" aligned to allow a teacher to gradually build skills.

Each part is a self-contained module allowing teachers to customize a non-linear program that will best address the needs of students. Parts are aligned around science, technology, engineering, arts, and mathematics (STEAM) content relevant to mainstream academic areas of study.

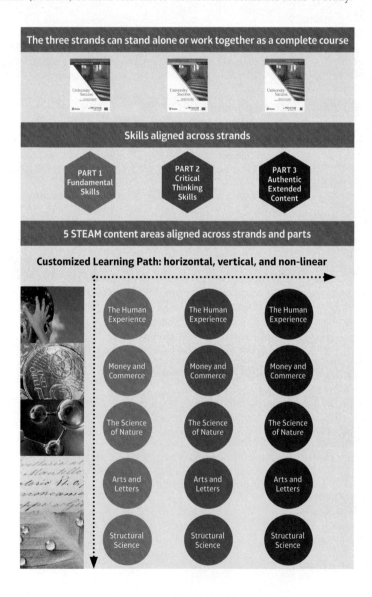

The three strands can stand alone or work together as a complete course

Skills aligned across strands

PART 1
Fundamental
Skills

PART 2
Critical
Thinking
Skills

PART 3
Authentic
Extended
Content

5 STEAM content areas aligned across strands and parts

Customized Learning Path: horizontal, vertical, and non-linear

The Human Experience

Money and Commerce

The Science of Nature

Arts and Letters

Structural Science

THE THREE PARTS AT A GLANCE

 Parts 1 and 2 focus on the fundamental reading skills and critical thinking skills most relevant for students preparing for university degrees. In Parts 1 and 2, students work with comprehensive skills that include:

- Being an active reader
- Working with main ideas and details
- Managing multiple sources
- Becoming a more fluent reader
- Engaging in processes

 Part 3 introduces students to extended practice with skills. Content created by top university professors provides students with a challenging experience that replicates the authentic experience of studying in a mainstream university class.

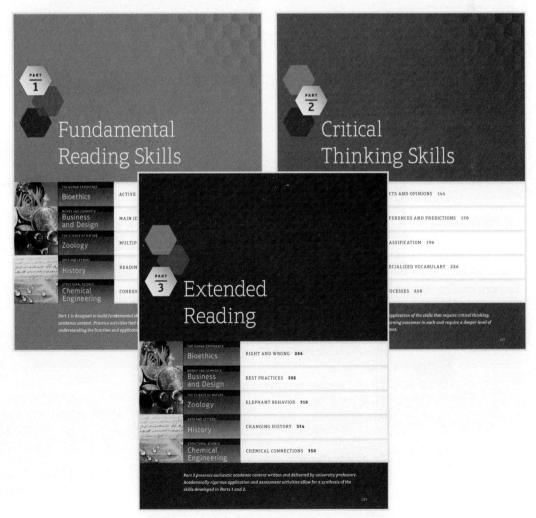

Student Book

MyEnglishLab

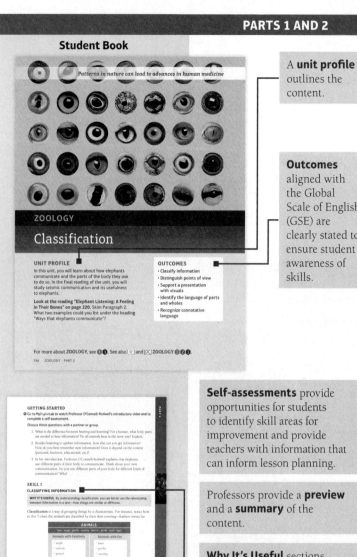

A **unit profile** outlines the content.

Outcomes aligned with the Global Scale of English (GSE) are clearly stated to ensure student awareness of skills.

Self-assessments provide opportunities for students to identify skill areas for improvement and provide teachers with information that can inform lesson planning.

Professors provide a **preview** and a **summary** of the content.

Why It's Useful sections highlight the need for developing skills and support transfer of skills to mainstream class content.

A **detailed presentation** demonstrates the skills' value in academic study.

A **variety of reading types**, including magazine articles, journal passages, and textbook excerpts, represent "real-life" university experiences.

Visuals on the page support information in the readings.

Student Book

MyEnglishLab

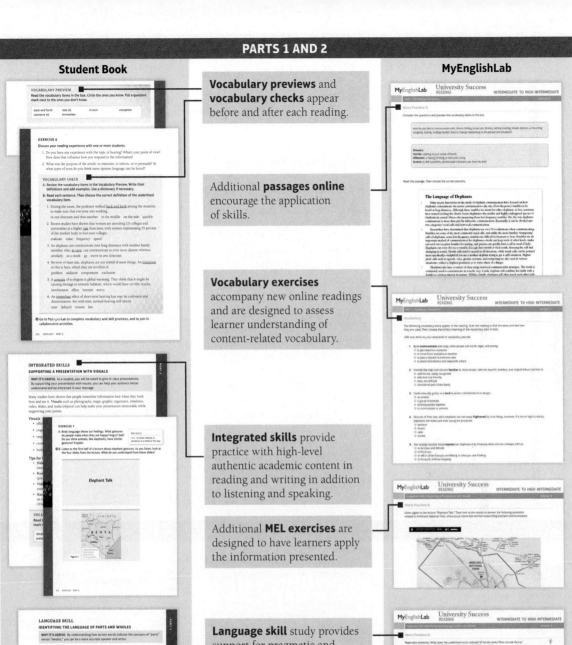

Vocabulary previews and **vocabulary checks** appear before and after each reading.

Additional **passages online** encourage the application of skills.

Vocabulary exercises accompany new online readings and are designed to assess learner understanding of content-related vocabulary.

Integrated skills provide practice with high-level authentic academic content in reading and writing in addition to listening and speaking.

Additional **MEL exercises** are designed to have learners apply the information presented.

Language skill study provides support for pragmatic and grammatical skills.

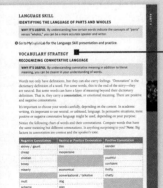

Vocabulary strategies offer valuable means for recognizing and retaining vocabulary, such as guessing meaning from context, analyzing word families, and identifying collocations.

Student Book

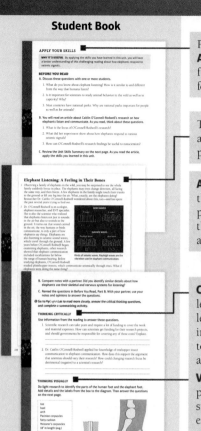

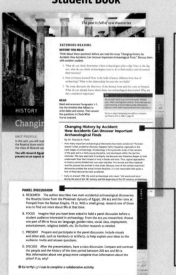

MyEnglishLab

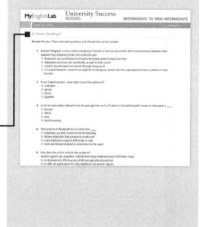

Parts 1 and 2 end with an extended **Apply Your Skills** section that functions as a diagnostic or formative assessment.

This longer **reading passage** allows students to apply skills practiced in the unit.

A closer reading gives students the opportunity to read the passage again, answer critical thinking questions, and complete a summarizing activity.

Critical thinking activities ask learners to engage at a deep level with the content, using information from the reading to address specific real-world applications.

Visually thinking sections provide an opportunity for students to analyze and create or expand upon charts, graphs, and other visuals.

Student Book

MyEnglishLab

Students read an **authentic essay** written by a professor working in a specific STEAM field. The essays are presented in sections, to allow for clarifications and comprehension checks.

Students use critical thinking skills to consider a **situation** related to the essay and record their thoughts.

A **related extended reading**, written by the same professor, gives students another opportunity to practice their reading skills and check comprehension.

As a **final project**, students prepare and participate in a presentation or discussion.

STRATEGIES FOR ACADEMIC SUCCESS AND SOFT SKILLS

Strategies for academic success and soft skills, delivered via online videos, help increase students' confidence and ability to cope with the challenges of academic study and college culture. Study skills include how to talk to professors during office hours and time management techniques.

TEACHER SUPPORT

Each of the three strands is supported with:

- Comprehensive **downloadable teaching notes** in MyEnglishLab that detail key points for all of the specialized, academic content in addition to tips and suggestions for how to teach skills and strategies.
- **An easy-to-use online learning management system** offering a flexible gradebook and tools for monitoring student progress.
- Essential tools, such as **audio and video scripts** and **course planners**, to help in lesson planning and follow-up.

ASSESSMENT

University Success provides a package of assessments that can be used as precourse diagnostics, midcourse assessments, and final summative assessments. The flexible nature of these assessments allows teachers to choose which assessments will be most appropriate at various stages of the program. These assessments are embedded in the student book and are available online in MyEnglishLab.

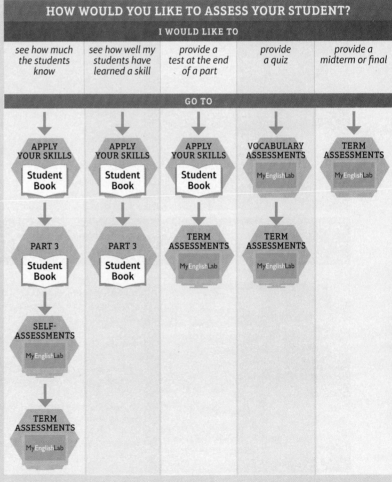

Scope and Sequence

PART 1 Fundamental Reading Skills is designed to build fundamental skills step-by-step through exploration of rigorous, academic content.

		Fundamental Skills	Integrated Skills	Language Skills
	BIOETHICS **Active Reading**	Skimming to survey a text Scanning to discover specific information	Annotating to identify key information	Choosing effective search terms
	BUSINESS AND DESIGN **Main Ideas and Details**	Identifying main ideas Identifying supporting details	Paraphrasing	Using synonyms and equivalent expressions
	ZOOLOGY **Multiple Sources**	Making associations Synthesizing information	Writing quotations to support ideas	Expressing contrast and concession
	HISTORY **Reading Fluency**	Increasing smoothness and pace to build fluency Developing accuracy	Reading aloud to build fluency and comprehension	Identifying thought groups
	CHEMICAL ENGINEERING **Cohesion**	Identifying cause and effect Examining examples	Summarizing	Working with pro-forms

PART 2 Critical Thinking Skills moves from skill building to application of the skills that require critical thinking.

		Critical Thinking Skills	Integrated Skills	Language Skills
	BIOETHICS **Facts and Opinions**	Identifying facts Identifying opinions	Fact-checking	Examining language for subjectivity
	BUSINESS AND DESIGN **Inferences and Predictions**	Making inferences Predicting	Identifying parts of a lecture	Interpreting hedging language
	ZOOLOGY **Classification**	Classifying information Distinguishing points of view	Supporting a presentation with visuals	Identifying the language of parts and wholes
	HISTORY **Specialized Vocabulary**	Finding definitions and explanations in a text Dealing with specialized vocabulary	Responding in an online forum	Demonstrating civil discourse online
	CHEMICAL ENGINEERING **Processes**	Analyzing time and space descriptions Examining conditions	Using passive voice	Making use of conditionals

PART 3 Extended Reading presents authentic content written by university professors. Academically rigorous application and assessment activities allow for a synthesis of the skills developed in Parts 1 and 2.

		Readings
	BIOETHICS **Right and Wrong**	Whole Genome Sequencing: Uses and Challenges Considering Cognitive Enhancement
	BUSINESS AND DESIGN **Best Practices**	So What Is a Business Model? Branding 101
	ZOOLOGY **Elephant Behavior**	For Elephants, Being Social Has Costs and Benefits The Role of Ritual in Male African Elephants
	HISTORY **Changing History**	Changing History by Accident: How Accidents Can Uncover Important Archaeological Finds Seeking Discoveries: The Intentional Quest for Archaeological Finds
	CHEMICAL ENGINEERING **Chemical Connections**	Physics of Scale: How are Candle Flames, Lake Flow, and Continental Drift Related? From Molecules to Materials: The Whole Is Greater Than the Sum of the Parts

Vocabulary Strategy	Apply Your Skills
Utilizing a dictionary to strengthen vocabulary	Read "How Useful Is Genetic Mapping and Sequencing?" Explain and defend your position on genetic mapping. Draw conclusions from a line graph about the cost of genome sequencing, and make predictions about the future of the practice.
Building word families	Read "The Secret to a Successful Crowd-Funding Campaign." Evaluate the advantages and disadvantages of crowd-funding. Interpret a map showing trends in crowd-funding worldwide and make predictions about the future of crowd-funding.
Improving receptive and productive vocabulary	Read "The Long-Term Effects of Poaching." Predict the impact of poaching on future animal populations and discuss what can be done to stop the practice. Evaluate a map showing the illegal trade of ivory and create a visual based on statistics from the unit.
Recognizing collocations	Read "Who Owns the Rosetta Stone?" Choose and defend a position on who should own the Rosetta Stone and other relics like it. Identify trends about location from a list of historically important sites and draw conclusions about the dates.
Utilizing the Frayer model	Read "How Land Moves." Defend your position on the reception of Alfred Wegener's theory and whether plate movement is a real concern today. Evaluate images showing Pangaea and then imagine how gravitational spreading might affect the world in the future.

Vocabulary Strategy	Apply Your Skills
Guessing meaning from context	Read "Reversing the Aging Process." Explain your position on reversing the aging process and whether you think aging is a "problem" that needs to be fixed. Predict the impact of CRISPR on aging trends.
Compiling a vocabulary journal	Read "Working Together for a Better World." Explore and explain why a deadline is important for development goals and what can be done to ensure quality education for everyone. Assess participation in the UN's Global Compact, based on a map, and make predictions about future participation.
Recognizing connotative language	Read "Elephant Listening: A Feeling in Their Bones." Choose and defend a position on whether scientific research should receive government funding. Evaluate the similarities and differences between the same body part of two different species.
Using graphic organizers	Read "The Influence of History on Pop Culture." Examine whether cultural values inform pop culture and whether accuracy is important in retelling history. Infer patterns from a timeline about historic events and make predictions about future rises and falls.
Identifying collocations	Read "Ice, Eggs, and the Second Law of Thermodynamics." Explain how examples from the reading illustrate entropy, and use ice cream to explain it and the second law of thermodynamics. Analyze the relationship between temperature and entropy, and create a visual showing change with another substance.

Research / Assignment

Small group presentation: Research the Precision Medicine Initiative, and then choose and support a position on the program.

Small group presentation: Choose and research a real company's business plan to evaluate, and then complete a Business Model Canvas with your findings.

Pair presentation: Choose and research an animal group that lives in a matriarchal society and an animal group that lives in a patriarchal society, and then compare and contrast their social structures.

Panel discussion: Choose and research the culture of either the Ptolemaic dynasty of Egypt around 196 BCE or the Roman Empire around 79 CE, and then discuss an aspect of the culture, using visuals.

Small group presentation: Research gravity density flow and then choose an example that can best explain it, using visuals or realia.

A Note from Lawrence Zwier

Series Editor for *University Success Reading*

Our intermediate to high-intermediate ESL reading students at Michigan State University are eager to explore real academic English. They have already been taught all the basics of English grammar, have heard a lot about text structure and cohesion, and have built vocabularies that allow them to read texts of moderate complexity. They need instruction that will help them step beyond the relatively straightforward discourse of low-intermediate readings. Above all they need more practice and broader exposure to academic readings.

It is important for them to work with serious, substantive reading material that is of a decent length and vocabulary level. They need to build fluency, for large volumes of academic reading await them in discipline-area classes only a few months from now. Vocabulary development is critical. Vocabulary that is roughly in the range of the Academic Word List (AWL) is one appropriate target (some students may already be strong in much of it). We also have to move beyond the AWL and bring them up to real strength with vocabulary up to about the 3.5K level (roughly, the 3,500 most common words in English). Much of my work involves, as the cliché goes, helping them help themselves. The development of both fluency and vocabulary must be up to them, because there is not enough class time in an entire year for me to put them through the necessary paces. All I can do is provide practice and explain things to the best of my ability.

The intermediate to high-intermediate level of *University Success Reading* is perfect for them. It offers serious, informative, expertly calibrated texts with which to practice. There is instruction in basic and higher-level reading skills, along with academic tasks that are well scaffolded but still leave plenty of room for individuals to stretch. The readings are of various lengths, including some long ones for practice with extended discourse. This volume has a personality—direct, mature, eager to explore difficult topic realms, challenging, and proud of it.

PART 1—FUNDAMENTAL SKILLS

In the first five units of *University Success Reading,* each of the five main subject areas (Bioethics, Business and Design, Zoology, History, and Chemical Engineering) is introduced. The most fundamental aspects of structure and approach in academic texts—such as main ideas, cohesive patterns, and fluency-building strategies—are featured and practiced in ways appropriate for intermediate to high-intermediate readers. The Stanford University professors who are the thought leaders for all three strands introduce themselves and their fields. This part of the text presents academic discourse in accessible yet challenging ways. Students encounter thematically related yet diverse reading passages that demonstrate fundamental text features. They get some scaffolding as they tackle the passages, but they still have a lot of independence as readers.

PART 2—CRITICAL THINKING SKILLS

In these units, each main subject area is explored in greater depth, with reading passages that demand more sophisticated processing and analysis. Critical thinking is more directly elicited. Students engage in such processes as evaluating the quality of evidence, drawing inferences, and understanding classifications. As in the Part 1 units, here the Stanford thought leaders have informed the content so that the reading passages are accessible and appealing yet rock-solid in their factuality and field-specific relevance.

PART 3—EXTENDED READING

University Success Reading opens up and brings the Stanford thought leaders front and center. Each of the readings in this part is serious, and substantive—penned by the professor and testing the frontiers of thought in his or her academic specialization. The Part 3 questions operate on a global scale of comprehension. They are high-interest and meant to promote lively discussion among readers. In Part 3, *University Success* does something no other intermediate to high-intermediate ELT text does: It dives deep into the work of high-prestige professors and researchers. This helps students take a large step toward facility with real academic English.

SUBJECT MATTER EXPERTS

Henry T. (Hank) Greely is the Deane F. and Kate Edelman Johnson Professor of Law and Professor by courtesy of Genetics at Stanford University. He directs Stanford's Center for Law and the Biosciences and its Program on Neuroscience in Society. The author of *The End of Sex*, he serves as president of the International Neuroethics Society; on the Committee on Science, Technology, and Law of the National Academy of Sciences; and on the NIH Multi-Council Working Group on the BRAIN Initiative.

Juli Sherry is the Design Lead at Worldview Stanford, where she develops hybrid courses and learning experiences for professionals. She facilitates sessions on Design Thinking, creating visualizations and experiences to communicate complex ideas and expose students to potential futures including drones, food substitutes, and wearable technologies. As a business strategist, designer, and entrepreneur, she develops strategic brands for small businesses and startups to help drive her clients' businesses into the future.

Caitlin O'Connell-Rodwell is an adjunct professor at Stanford University School of Medicine. She has studied elephants for the last 25 years, authored seven popular books and dozens of scientific papers and magazine articles about elephants, and was the focus of the award-winning Smithsonian documentary *Elephant King*. She taught creative science writing for Stanford and *The New York Times*, and has won numerous awards for her writing. She currently blogs for National Geographic from her field site in Namibia.

Award-winning archaeologist and author **Patrick Hunt** has taught at Stanford University for 25 years. He directed the Stanford Alpine Archaeology Project from 1994 to 2012 and continues to conduct research in the region. Hunt is a National Geographic Expeditions Expert and a National Lecturer for the Archaeological Institute of America as well as an elected Fellow of the Royal Geographical Society. In addition to publishing over 100 articles, he is the author of 20 published books including the bestseller *Ten Discoveries That Rewrote History* and most recently, *Hannibal*.

Andrew Spakowitz is a professor in the Department of Chemical Engineering at Stanford University, where he established a theoretical and computational lab that develops physical models to understand and control critical biological processes and cutting-edge materials applications. In 2009, he was awarded the NSF CAREER Award in 2009 for work in modeling DNA in living cells. In addition to his research and teaching programs, Professor Spakowitz established an outreach program that developed a comprehensive science lab curriculum for high school students who are being treated for cancer or other illnesses.

SERIES EDITORS

Robyn Brinks Lockwood teaches courses in spoken and written English at Stanford University in the English for Foreign Students graduate program and is the program education coordinator of the American Language and Culture undergraduate summer program. She is an active member of the international TESOL organization, serves as Chairperson of the Publishing Professional Council, and is a past chair of the Materials Writers Interest Section. She is a frequent presenter at TESOL regional and international conferences. Robyn has edited and written numerous textbooks, online courses, and ancillary components for ESL courses and TOEFL preparation.

Maggie Sokolik holds a BA in Anthropology from Reed College, and an MA in Romance Linguistics and PhD in Applied Linguistics from UCLA. She is the author of over 20 ESL and composition textbooks. She has taught at MIT, Harvard, Texas A&M, and currently UC Berkeley, where she is Director of College Writing Programs. She has developed and taught several popular MOOC courses in English language writing and literature. She is the founding editor of *TESL-EJ*, a peer-reviewed journal for ESL / EFL professionals, one of the first online journals. Maggie travels frequently to speak about grammar, writing, and instructor education. She lives in the San Francisco Bay area, where she and her husband play bluegrass music.

Lawrence J. Zwier is an Associate Director of the English Language Center, Michigan State University. He holds a bachelor's degree in English Literature from Aquinas College, Grand Rapids, MI, and an MA in TESL from the University of Minnesota. He has taught ESL / EFL at universities in Saudi Arabia, Malaysia, Japan, Singapore, and the US. He is the author of numerous ELT textbooks, mostly about reading and vocabulary, and also writes nonfiction books about history and geography for middle school and high school students. He is married with two children and lives in Okemos, Michigan.

Acknowledgments

Writing a textbook is a herculean task and this one couldn't have been created without the exceptional team at Pearson: Sarah Hand, Gosia Jaros-White, Niki Cunnion, Amy McCormick, and untold others involved in creating an innovative series like *University Success*. Tim McLaughlin and Ronnie Hess deserve much credit for crafting accessible readings from the challenging materials. Special thanks to Debbie Sistino for her guidance and levity throughout the process and for pairing me with Leigh Stolle as an editor. Leigh's creativity, attentiveness, wit, and expertise created an ideal space for writing and revising, and I was extremely fortunate to have her guidance.

I am indebted to the students at Union County College in New Jersey for inspiring me to create materials that are both engaging and challenging, and to my colleagues who enrich my practice with their collective wisdom, skill, and laughter. Writing takes up a lot of time, and I'm thankful to my friends and family—near and far—who understood, and pitched in when I couldn't. And finally, to Carlos, Sophia, and Lucas—I am tremendously appreciative that you allowed the space and time for me to write. None of this would have been possible without your love, support, and patience. —*Carrie Steenburgh*

Reviewers

We would like to thank the following reviewers for their many helpful comments and suggestions:

Jamila Barton, North Seattle Community College, Seattle, WA; **Joan Chamberlin**, Iowa State University, Ames IA; **Lyam Christopher**, Palm Beach State College, Boynton Beach, FL; **Robin Corcos**, University of California, Santa Barbara, Goleta, CA; **Tanya Davis**, University of California, San Diego, CA; **Brendan DeCoster**, University of Oregon, Eugene, OR; **Thomas Dougherty**, University of St. Mary of the Lake, Mundelein, IL; **Bina Dugan**, Bergen County Community College, Hackensack, NJ; **Priscilla Faucette**, University of Hawaii at Manoa, Honolulu, HI; **Lisa Fischer**, St. Louis University, St. Louis, MO; **Kathleen Flynn**, Glendale Community College, Glendale, CA; **Mary Gawienowski**, William Rainey Harper College, Palatine, IL; **Sally Gearhart**, Santa Rosa Junior College, Santa Rosa, CA; **Carl Guerriere**, Capital Community College, Hartford, CT; **Vera Guillen**, Eastfield College, Mesquite, TX; **Angela Hakim**, St. Louis University, St. Louis, MO; **Pamela Hartmann**, Evans Community Adult School, Los Angeles Unified School District, Los Angeles, CA; **Shelly Hedstrom**, Palm Beach State University, Lake Worth, FL; **Sherie Henderson**, University of Oregon, Eugene, OR; **Lisse Hildebrandt**, English Language Program, Virginia Commonwealth University, Richmond, VA; **Barbara Inerfeld**, Rutgers University, Piscataway, NJ; **Zaimah Khan**, Northern Virginia Community College, Loudon Campus, Sterling, VA; **Tricia Kinman**, St. Louis University, St. Louis, MO; **Kathleen Klaiber**, Genesee Community College, Batavia, NY; **Kevin Lamkins**, Capital Community College, Hartford, CT; **Mayetta Lee**, Palm Beach State College, Lake Worth, FL; **Kirsten Lillegard**, English Language Institute, Divine Word College, Epworth, IA; **Craig Machado**, Norwalk Community College, Norwalk, CT; **Cheryl Madrid**, Spring International Language Center, Denver, CO; **Ann Meechai**, St. Louis University, St. Louis, MO; **Melissa Mendelson**, Department of Linguistics, University of Utah, Salt Lake City, UT; **Tamara Milbourn**, University of Colorado, Boulder, CO; **Debbie Ockey**, Fresno City College, Fresno, CA; **Diana Pascoe-Chavez**, St. Louis University, St. Louis, MO; **Kathleen Reynolds**, William Rainey Harper College, Palatine, IL; **Linda Roth**, Vanderbilt University ELC, Greensboro, NC; **Minati Roychoudhuri**, Capital Community College, Hartford, CT; **Bruce Rubin**, California State University, Fullerton, CA; **Margo Sampson**, Syracuse University, Syracuse, NY; **Sarah Saxer**, Howard Community College, Ellicott City, MD; **Anne-Marie Schlender**, Austin Community College, Austin, TX; **Susan Shields**, Santa Barbara Community College, Santa Barbara, CA; **Barbara Smith-Palinkas**, Hillsborough Community College, Dale Mabry Campus, Tampa, FL; **Sara Stapleton**, North Seattle Community College, Seattle, WA; **Lisa Stelle**, Northern Virginia Community College Loudon, Sterling, VA; **Jamie Tanzman**, Northern Kentucky University, Highland Heights, KY; **Jeffrey Welliver**, Soka University of America, Aliso Viejo, CA; **Mark Wolfersberger**, Brigham Young University, Hawaii, Laie, HI; **May Youn**, California State University, Fullerton, CA

Fundamental
Reading Skills

Part 1 is designed to build fundamental skills step by step through exploration of rigorous, academic content. Practice activities tied to specific learning outcomes in each unit focus on understanding the function and application of the skills.

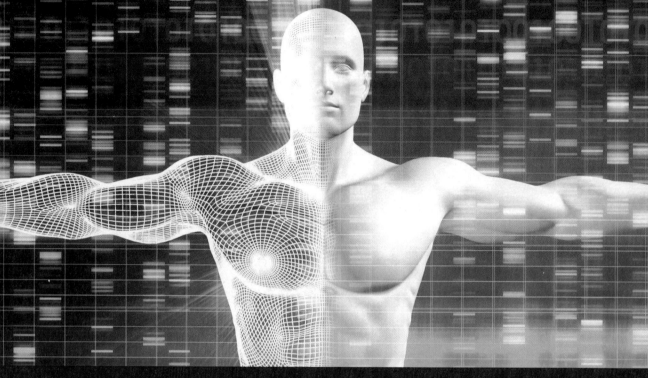

BIOETHICS

Active Reading

UNIT PROFILE

In this unit, you will read about genes and DNA—the biological "instructions" passed from parents to children. Specifically, you will read about the human genome project and new gene technologies. In the final reading of the unit, you will learn how useful studying your own map is or isn't.

Look at the reading "How Useful Is Genetic Mapping and Sequencing?" on page 24. Quickly read the first sentence of each paragraph. As you read, underline keywords and phrases about DNA. Then try to answer the question "What is DNA and why is it important?"

OUTCOMES

- Skim to survey a text
- Scan to discover specific information
- Annotate to identify key information
- Choose effective search terms
- Utilize a dictionary to strengthen vocabulary

For more about **BIOETHICS**, see ❷❸. See also ⬛W⬛ and ⬛OC⬛ **BIOETHICS** ❶❷❸.

GETTING STARTED

⟐ Go to MyEnglishLab to watch Professor Greely's introductory video and to complete a self-assessment.

Discuss these questions with a partner or group.

1. Genetics is a growing field of science. What do you already know about things like DNA, genetic testing, and genetic mapping?

2. In your everyday life, how important are new genetic treatments and practices?

3. In his introduction, Professor Greely explains that the DNA in our body makes up our genome. What is a genome? What are some difficulties that scientists have when studying a genome?

SKILL 1

SKIMMING TO SURVEY A TEXT

> **WHY IT'S USEFUL** By skimming a text, you can get a quick idea of the main idea. Improving your skimming skills can help you manage the large amount of reading expected in academic classes.

What do you do to get the general idea of a reading? Skimming—running your eyes over a passage—is a quick way to understand what it is generally about. After a skim, you will probably know the topic, the main idea, possibly the attitude of the writer, the type of language he or she uses, and some of the details.

Techniques for Skimming

- Read key parts of the text, such as the title and headings.
- Read the first and last sentence of each paragraph.
- Read the first paragraph and the last paragraph.
- Notice the images.
- Move your eyes quickly over the reading. Do not read each word.

VOCABULARY PREVIEW

Read the vocabulary items in the box. Circle the ones you know. Put a question mark next to the ones you don't know.

study (n)	decides	combined	specific	section	identify

EXERCISE 1

A. Skim the article on the next page. Specifically, read the title and the first sentence of each paragraph. Check (✓) what the article is generally about.

☐ A criminal who was put in jail because of his DNA

☐ A description of DNA and why DNA is important

☐ How children inherit DNA from their parents

TIP

When skimming, scanning, or reading for speed, don't stop to look up words you don't know. You can mark them and look them up later.

B. Think about your skimming experience. What did you learn about DNA from reading the first sentence of each paragraph? Write three things and discuss with a partner.

1. ....

2. ....

3. ....

EXERCISE 2

A. Answer these questions.

1. What do you know about DNA? Is understanding DNA important? Why?

....

2. Think about the title "DNA: What It Is and What It Does" and what you know. Predict what the author will explain in the article.

....

B. Skim the information in the diagram in the article. How does it add to what you already know about DNA?

....

....

Glossary

Disease: an illness that affects a person, animal, or plant, with specific symptoms

Characteristic: something that makes someone or something different from others

Cell: the smallest part of any living thing except a virus

Chromosome: the part of a cell that houses genes

Gene: the central part of an atom; controls things like eye color and height

Inherit: to get a quality, type of behavior, appearance, etc., from one of your parents

TIP

Add this vocabulary and any other useful items from the article to your vocabulary flashcards, journal, or study list.

C. Now read the article. Then read the statements that follow. Circle *T* (True) or *F* (False). Correct the false statements.

DNA: What It Is and What It Does

1 The study of DNA was one of the biggest scientific advances of the 20th century. Since then, it has helped doctors understand how to fight disease and assisted researchers in the development of better medicine. It has also been used in criminal investigations to both imprison guilty individuals and release people who are not guilty. A simple DNA "spit test" can give a lot of information about a person—from the chance of developing a disease to where family members originally came from. So, what exactly is DNA?

2 Deoxyribonucleic acid (DNA) is the genetic information that decides almost every physical characteristic of all life on this planet. It is found in nearly every cell—inside the cell's nucleus, located inside the cell—of all living things. DNA is packed inside chromosomes and is the shape of a double helix—think of a long ladder that has been twisted. Inside these so-called "strands" of DNA are different pairings of four types of chemical bases: cytosine (C), guanine (G), adenine (A), and thymine (T). See Figure 1.

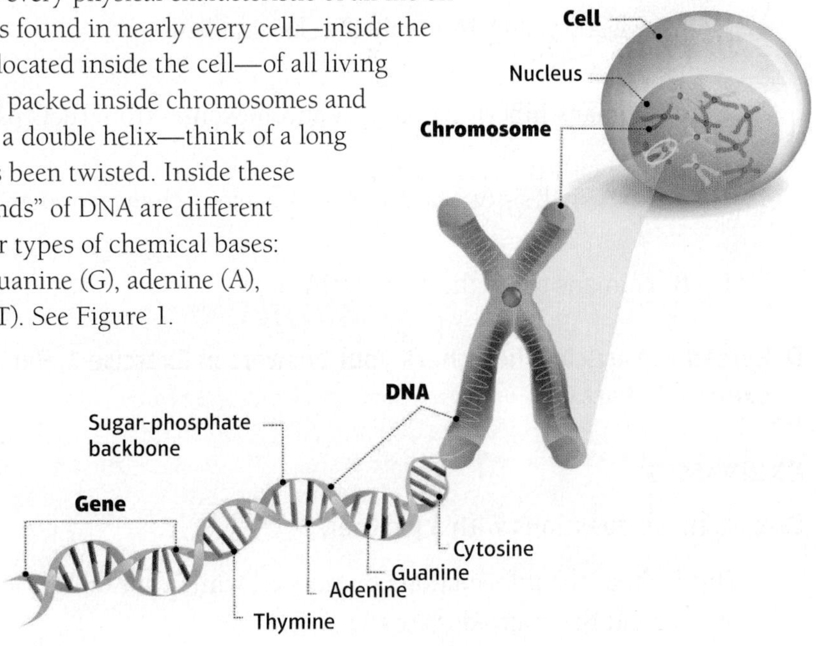

Cell
Nucleus
Chromosome
DNA
Sugar-phosphate backbone
Gene
Cytosine
Guanine
Adenine
Thymine

Figure 1

(Continued)

3 These chemical bases are combined into very specific pairs: normally A with T, and C with G. Within a single cell, a DNA strand can be millions of letters long, with each section of that strand acting as a code. The strand is a set of instructions that decides a characteristic—for instance, eye color. A section of the DNA strand is called a *gene,* and genes tell a cell how to make a protein. It is those proteins that are the building blocks of the human body. In fact, everything in a body—hair, bones, blood—is made up of those proteins. Genes decide, for example, a person's height or how likely he or she is to get a disease.

4 Organisms—plants, animals, and humans—inherit their DNA from their parents. Most get a near photocopy of their parents' DNA. Each human cell has 23 pairs of chromosomes, having received one set of 23 chromosomes from the mother, and one set of 23 chromosomes from the father. This inheritance explains why children often look like their parents. Nearly 99.9 percent of DNA is the same for everybody. But that .1 percent makes individuals unique and can be used to identify someone.

T / F   1. Investigators have used DNA evidence to imprison criminals.

T / F   2. DNA helps decide the appearance of all living things.

T / F   3. The nucleus is located inside each chromosome.

T / F   4. Chromosomes are made up of strands of DNA.

T / F   5. A section of DNA is called a *chemical base.*

T / F   6. Humans inherit 24 pairs of chromosomes from their parents.

T / F   7. DNA analysis can help predict a person's chance for developing a disease.

T / F   8. Humans share the same DNA.

D. **Reread the article. Then check your answers in Exercise 1, Part A and Exercise 2, Part C.**

EXERCISE 3

Discuss these questions with a partner.

1. Think about the information you noticed while skimming. How did it help you understand the main ideas of the article?

2. In what other situations do you use skimming? Why?

VOCABULARY CHECK

A. Review the vocabulary items in the Vocabulary Preview. Write their definitions and add examples. Use a dictionary if necessary.

B. Read each sentence. Then choose the correct definition of the underlined vocabulary item.

1. The <u>study</u> was led by two researchers who recorded how the new drug affected 100 patients.

   a. the presentation of something in a drawing or diagram
   b. a careful look at something in order to understand it

2. The father's genes <u>decide</u> the gender of the child: boy or girl.

   a. to be the reason something has a particular result
   b. to create a living organism

3. If you <u>combine</u> unrelated gene pools, you can avoid some hereditary diseases.

   a. to split something into two or more categories
   b. to mix two or more things together

4. The weight loss study participants were given <u>specific</u> instructions: to walk 20 minutes before breakfast, cut out all salt and sugar, and get eight hours of sleep.

   a. unusual
   b. particular

5. The most interesting <u>section</u> of the bioethics article was the first half.

   a. a part of something
   b. the beginning of something

6. Through a series of tests, the doctors <u>identified</u> a torn shoulder muscle as the cause of pain.

   a. to recognize something or discover exactly what it is
   b. to find the solution to a problem, such as a disease

⬤ Go to MyEnglishLab to complete vocabulary and skill practices, and to join in collaborative activities.

SKILL 2

SCANNING TO DISCOVER SPECIFIC INFORMATION

WHY IT'S USEFUL By scanning, you can find specific information quickly, saving you time.

To **scan** is to look at a text, searching for specific information. You work quickly, without stopping to read each word.

Techniques for Scanning

- Decide what information you need to find, for example: a name (of a person, place, or event), a date, or a keyword.

- Look for **capital letters** (for names of people, places, and things) or **numbers** (for times, dates, and amounts).

- Move your eyes quickly over the text to help you find the needed information. Don't read every word.

> **TIP**
> A **keyword** might be a question word (for example, *when*, to indicate a date or time) or a specific noun (for example, *genome*). This will help you look for only the information you need.

VOCABULARY PREVIEW

Read the vocabulary items in the box. Circle the ones you know. Put a question mark next to the ones you don't know.

approximately	contained	despite	enormous	multiple	researched

EXERCISE 4

A. Read the questions. Then scan the reading on the next page to find the information. Try to do this as quickly as possible. Then compare answers with a partner.

1. How many genes are in the human body? ....

2. What does *HGP* stand for? ....

3. What are the names of the two US agencies that established the HGP?

   ....

4. When was the HGP officially established? ....

The Human Genome Project

1 **The task seemed impossible: Map and analyze the human genome, which has over 3 billion nucleotide base pairs (adenine-thymine, guanine-cytosine) that make up the body's approximately 20,000 genes. The information contained in the genome tells cells how to build and grow an organism. Despite the enormous size of the task, the reward of finishing was even bigger. Scientists would have a much better understanding of genes and possibly be able to develop better technologies to fight genetic diseases—for example, certain cancers, heart disease, and Alzheimer's (a disease that damages memory). From this task, the Human Genome Project (HGP) was born.**

> **Glossary**
>
> Analyze: to study carefully
>
> Human genome: all of the genetic information in people
>
> Cancers: a group of serious diseases that make cells in the body sick
>
> Sequence: (v) to put in order

2 In the 1980s, advances in molecular biology and computer science were creating a lot of excitement in the scientific community about the benefits of fully understanding the human genome. This led the US Department of Energy (DOE) and the National Institutes of Health (NIH) to coordinate a plan and officially establish the HGP in 1990. The project's budget was $3 billion, and scientists from the United States, the United Kingdom, France, Australia, and China were involved. Its goals were: 1) to develop technology for mapping and analyzing DNA in order to create a map of multiple organisms' genomes, 2) to sequence their base pairs, and 3) to study the social, legal, and moral issues of mapping the human genome.

3 Nine years later, in 1999, scientists mapped and sequenced Chromosome 22, one of the smallest human chromosomes. At the time, it was the longest piece of genetic material ever to be mapped. In 2000, they fully sequenced the genome of the fruit fly, one of the other organisms being researched. The HGP came to a finish in 2003 after scientists had sequenced nearly all human genes. Amazingly, it was completed in 13 years—ahead of schedule and under budget.

> **CULTURE NOTE**
>
> Chromosome 22 was mapped by researchers at the Sanger Centre near Cambridge, England; the University of Oklahoma, Norman, OK; Washington University, St. Louis, MO; and Keio University in Japan.

4 The HGP is one of humanity's greatest scientific achievements. By mapping the genome, not only have we learned more about our own genes and their history but also technologies have been developed to map and sequence other organisms' genomes more quickly. The knowledge that is gained from this work allows us to better understand genetic diseases and medicine, helping people to live longer and healthier lives.

B. Think about your scanning experience. What questions did you find challenging? Which were easy? Why?

EXERCISE 5

A. The reading "The Human Genome Project" is about the impact that the HGP achievement has had on the scientific community. What might be one benefit of mapping the human genome?

....

B. Read each question and underline the keyword(s). Then scan "The Human Genome Project" to find the answer. Remember to move your eyes quickly over the text. Do not read every word.

1. What is a genome? ....

2. What is an example of a genetic disease? ....

3. How much money was budgeted for the Human Genome Project? ....

4. What countries were represented in the project? ....

   ....

5. When was Chromosome 22 mapped and sequenced? ....

6. When was the fruit fly's genome sequenced? ....

7. When was the HGP finished? ....

8. How many years did it take to complete the HGP? ....

CULTURE NOTE

Gene mapping and *gene sequencing* are familiar terms to many people, thanks to news stories and gene analysis services like 23andMe. However, few outside the medical field could explain the difference. Here's a simple way to think of it: Picture one of those amusement park maps, with big arrows and paths showing you how to get from one place to another, like from the ice-cream stand to the new triple-loop roller coaster. That's a gene map, an overview of the place. A gene sequence, on the other hand, is much more personalized, like the photos you take at the park—close-ups that show details.

C. Now go back and read the whole passage. Then choose the correct answers.

1. A genome is _____ .

   a. the process of copying a cell's DNA
   b. a plan for repairing a cell
   c. a map of base pairs
   d. all of the genetic information inside a living thing

2. The reading suggests that the Human Genome Project was _____ effort.

   a. an international
   b. an easily accomplished
   c. a short-term
   d. an ethically questionable

3. _____ was NOT mentioned as one of the main goals of the HGP.

   a. Studying the social and legal issues of mapping the human genome
   b. Writing scientific articles about the human genome project
   c. Developing technologies to map organisms' genomes
   d. Sequencing organisms' base pairs

4. Chromosome 22 is one of the _____ human chromosomes.

   a. longest
   b. most complicated
   c. smallest
   d. oldest

5. In Paragraph 3, the phrase "at the time" suggests that _____ .

   a. since 1999, longer genetic material has been mapped
   b. before 1999, longer genetic material had been mapped
   c. Chromosome 22 is the longest genetic material ever mapped
   d. Chromosome 22 took very little time to map

6. The benefits of the Human Genome Project include a better understanding of our genes and genetic diseases, and _____ .

   a. the ability to research the common housefly
   b. the elimination of some genetic diseases
   c. the prevention of heart disease
   d. the development of medical technologies

D. Reread the passage. Then check your answers in Parts B and C.

EXERCISE 6

Discuss your reading experience with one or more students.

1. Did scanning—looking quickly for specific information—give you enough information to answer the questions before you read? Was looking for keywords a helpful strategy for scanning?

2. Scanning is, of course, an important academic reading skill. But it's also a skill used in everyday life. List three situations in which you would use scanning.

   • ....

   • ....

   • ....

VOCABULARY CHECK

A. Review the vocabulary items in the Vocabulary Preview. Write their definitions and add examples. Use a dictionary if necessary.

B. Complete each sentence using the correct vocabulary item from the box. Use the correct form.

approximately	contain	despite	enormous	multiple	research

1. The doctor .... the disease by reading textbooks and talking to other doctors.

2. The cancer study took .... a dozen years to complete.

3. .... the high price tag, the government funded the project because of its importance to human health.

4. Because of the growing number of Alzheimer's patients, researchers are under a(n) .... amount of pressure to find more effective drugs for the disease.

5. There are .... possible causes of lung cancer, not just one.

6. A DNA sample can .... a wealth of information to both medical researchers and criminal investigators.

➊ Go to MyEnglishLab to complete vocabulary and skill practices, and to join in collaborative activities.

INTEGRATED SKILLS
ANNOTATING TO IDENTIFY KEY INFORMATION

WHY IT'S USEFUL By annotating and taking notes while reading, you can become more deeply involved with the text. Taking notes makes you an active reader, which can help you remember the information better. In academic classes, you will be expected to read and remember a lot of information.

One way to take notes is to **annotate** a text. Annotations are brief notes that you make within a text, almost as if you are having a conversation with the author. These notes can be written between the lines or in the margins of the text.

How to Annotate

There are many kinds of **key information** you may want to annotate, depending on your reading purpose. For example:

- Note the **definitions** of **key terms** or expressions.

- Record **opinions** and emotions you have while reading.

- Ask **questions** about information that you find unclear or incomplete.

- **Make connections** between the information you are reading and something you have read, heard, or experienced.

- Identify **important details**.

- **Summarize** sections of the text.

> **TIP**
>
> Readers will often highlight key information as they annotate. *Highlighting* means "to underline, use a symbol, or mark with a special color." Key information may be a name, a date, a place, a main idea, or a definition. It's a good idea to 1) think about your purpose for reading, 2) read the text, and 3) then go back to highlight only the information that is useful for your purpose.

After you finish annotating a text, you may want to transfer some of those ideas to a notebook. In this **note-taking** step, consider doing the following:

- Think about your reading purpose and take notes on relevant information.

- Put the information in your own words (paraphrase). Use quotation marks for language that is taken directly from the reading.

- Note where you found the information (the source).

- Use headings to organize your information.

- Keep your notes organized for future use.

Although annotating and note-taking may slow down your reading speed, it will increase your recall of the information.

TIP

In addition to annotating a text, you may want to record your notes in a **graphic organizer**. These are what they sound like: graphics that help organize your thoughts. You can create these yourself.

One example is an **outline**:

I. (Main Idea 1)
   A. (Detail)
   B. (Detail)
II. (Main Idea 2)
   A. (Detail)
   B. (Detail)

Another example is a **mind map** (also called a *cluster diagram*):

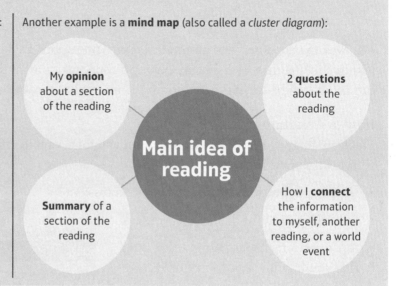

My **opinion** about a section of the reading

2 **questions** about the reading

Main idea of reading

Summary of a section of the reading

How I **connect** the information to myself, another reading, or a world event

VOCABULARY PREVIEW

Read the vocabulary items in the box. Circle the ones you know. Put a question mark next to the ones you don't know.

unusual	removed	variety	permission	decades	patients

EXERCISE 7

A. How can everyday people contribute to medical research? Give an example.

B. Read the passage on the next page and look at the annotations. What types of annotations did the reader make? Match the annotations (a–d) to the types (1–4).

.... 1. definition   .... 3. question
.... 2. opinion   .... 4. connection

Glossary

Cervix: the narrow opening into a woman's womb

Survive: to live through a difficult situation, such as a disease

Cloning: making copies

Ethical: relating to principles of what is right and wrong

C. Reread the passage and make annotations about important information or questions. Then read the statements that follow and circle *T* (True) or *F* (False). Correct the false statements.

Henrietta Lacks and Her Contribution to Medical Research

1 On a wintery morning in January of 1951, Henrietta Lacks a poor African-American farmer, went to Johns Hopkins Hospital in Baltimore, Maryland, because of bad stomach pains. At the time, Johns Hopkins was <u>the only hospital near Lacks's home that treated African Americans.</u> While Lacks was there, doctors noticed an unusual group of cells in her cervix. They performed a biopsy—a procedure in which cells are taken from the body to test for diseases. The biopsy results showed that Lacks had a <u>malignant</u> form of cancer in her cervix.

a. *Reminds me of articles about how African Americans were denied basic services in the 1950s*

b. *deadly*

2 The biopsy also showed something unusual about Lacks's cancer: The cells were able to survive longer than any cancer cells the doctors had seen before. Because of this, the doctors later removed two more cell samples from Lacks 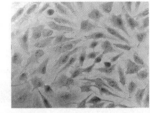 for research. The cancer cells that so interested her doctors could not be treated. On the night of October 4, 1951, Henrietta Lacks died at the <u>age of 31.</u>

c. *Sad—she was so young*

3 But her story does not end there. Soon after her death, researchers removed many more cancer cells from her body because they believed that they would be useful for a variety of studies. The head of the research, George Otto Gey, decided to create a cell line—a group of cells that continue to divide without dying—and named it the HeLa cell line after the first two letters of Lacks's first and last name. The HeLa cell line would become the most important cell line in history; HeLa cells have been used in developing vaccines, in cloning, and in gene sequencing. HeLa cells are used in medical research today.

4 The experience of Henrietta Lacks and the use of HeLa cells raises a number of ethical issues for science and medicine. First, Lacks's cells were taken from her, both before and after her death, without her permission, and not as part of her treatment. Then, over the next few decades, her cells were grown, sold, and

(Continued)

used for thousands of different research studies, which earned millions of dollars for the medical industry. <u>However, neither Lacks nor her family received any money from this</u>. In fact, courts in the United States have decided that patients do not own their cells after they are taken from their bodies. Cells like these are considered "medical waste," courts say, and scientists are free to use them in their research.

d. *Has the Lacks family ever asked for $ or recognition especially since companies made millions of $ from the cell line?*

5 A second ethical issue involving the Lacks family came in 2013. A team of researchers in Germany published details of the HeLa genome, again without asking the Lacks family for permission. Her family worries that this information could negatively affect them if it is used in the wrong way. In the United States, cells from hundreds of millions of people are kept in labs and are available for use in research. Many of these were taken without permission and could be used to develop profitable cell lines and technologies, for example. This might be great for science, but it creates problems for people who want their health to be kept private. In the years to come, debate about the ethical use of genetic material will surely continue.

CULTURE NOTE

Henrietta Lacks's story is told in the 2010 prize-winning book *The Immortal Life of Henrietta Lacks,* written by Rebecca Skloot. Since the time of publication, the Lacks family and the National Institutes of Health have reached an agreement about the HeLa cells. It says the family will receive acknowledgment in scientific studies that use the line. Also, the family will be on the committee that controls access to the genetic code.

T / F   1. Henrietta Lacks was a wealthy woman.

T / F   2 Lacks allowed the doctors to use her cells for research

T / F   3. Lacks lived for many years after the biopsy was performed.

T / F   4. HeLa cells have been used in the development of vaccines.

T / F   5. HeLa cells are no longer used today.

T / F   6. The use of the HeLa cells has been very profitable for the Lacks family.

T / F   7. Once a patient's cells are removed, the patient no longer owns them.

D. With a partner, compare annotations you each made. Explain each type of annotation (opinion, definition, etc.).

E. Discuss these questions with a partner.

1. Did the annotations help you understand the passage? Why or why not?

2. Do you usually annotate when you read? If so, what information do you annotate?

3. Do you usually take notes on a separate piece of paper or do you use a device? How do you organize your notes?

4. When would it be helpful to review your annotations or notes? Think of at least two situations when you might review them.

VOCABULARY CHECK

A. Review the vocabulary items in the Vocabulary Preview. Write their definitions and add examples. Use a dictionary if necessary.

B. Complete each sentence using the correct vocabulary item from the box. Use the correct form.

decade	patient	permission	remove	unusual	variety

1. Emergency room doctors treat a(n) .... of problems, from broken toes to heart attacks.

2. The cells were .... because they grew faster than ordinary cells.

3. By signing the agreement, we gave them ....

4. A(n) .... is a lifetime to a ten-year-old.

5. Anyone receiving medical treatment from Dr. Lee is a lucky ....

6. After the doctors .... the cancer, it never returned.

◊ Go to MyEnglishLab to complete a skill practice and to join in collaborative activities.

LANGUAGE SKILL
CHOOSING EFFECTIVE SEARCH TERMS

WHY IT'S USEFUL By carefully selecting search terms, you can save time and get the exact information you need.

◊ Go to MyEnglishLab for the Language Skill presentation and practice.

VOCABULARY STRATEGY
UTILIZING A DICTIONARY TO STRENGTHEN VOCABULARY

WHY IT'S USEFUL By knowing how to use a dictionary, you can strengthen your vocabulary and improve your accuracy.

Dictionaries are best known for listing a word's spelling, pronunciation, and defition. But dictionary entries also include a word's **word class** (also called *part of speech*), such as noun, verb, adjective, or adverb. Word class information usually appears at the top of the entry.

Consider the word *study*, which can be used as a noun or verb. Look at these two entries:

---

stud·y¹ /stʌdi/ ••• *noun* (*plural* **studies**) ◀))

| WORD ORIGIN | COLLOCATIONS | THESAURUS |

1 [countable] **a piece of work that is done to find out more about a particular subject or problem, and that is usually written in a report:**
◀)) *Several* **studies showed** *the drug can cause birth defects.*
◀)) *Researchers did a* **study on/of** *100 patients.*

2 [uncountable] **the process of learning about a subject:**
◀)) *The course focuses on the* **study of** *ancient history.*
◀)) *The workshop will show students ways to improve* **study skills/habits***.*

3 [countable] **a room in a house that is used for work or study**

4 **studies** [plural] **the work you do in order to learn about something:**
◀)) *She began graduate* **studies** *at Berkeley.*

study² /stʌdi/ ••• *verb* (**studied, studies**) ◀))

| VERB TABLE | COLLOCATIONS | THESAURUS |

1 [intransitive, transitive] **to spend time going to classes, reading, etc., to learn about a subject:**
◀)) *I need to* **study for** *a midterm.*
◀)) *She* **studied at** *Harvard.*
◀)) *I'm* **studying English/psychology/medicine, etc.**

2 [transitive] **to examine something carefully to find out more about it:**
◀)) *An accounting firm is* **studying** *the problem.*
◀)) *Dr. Brock is* **studying how** *the disease affects children.*

In addition to word class, a good dictionary will include **collocations**, or word combinations typical of that word. For example, it may show if a preposition combines with the noun form of the word (***the study of*** + *something*), or if, as a verb, the word is followed by an object or infinitive (***study*** + ***to be*** + *something*).

COLLOCATIONS WITH *STUDY*

VERBS

to do/conduct a study
🔊 *Researchers conducted a study on the effects of the drug on soldiers suffering from depression.*

to release/publish a study (=to make it be known)
🔊 *A study of hospitals released last week shows that the number of these dangerous infections are rising.*
🔊 *The organization published a study that said that people who practice yoga have less pain than those who don't.*

to participate in a study
🔊 *The medical team is looking for teens to participate in a study on diet and exercise.*

ADJECTIVES/NOUNS + *STUDY*

a case study (=a study of a person, group, or event over a period of time)
🔊 *The case study examined preschool children who were overweight.*

a research study
🔊 *The national research study is trying to find out why the insects are disappearing.*

a scientific study (=one that is done using scientific methods)
🔊 *This is not a scientific study—the company just asked a sample of its customers some questions.*

a detailed/comprehensive/in-depth study
🔊 *We will need to do a more comprehensive study to be sure of our results.*

Knowing the word class and the common combinations of a word can help you strengthen and expand your English vocabulary.

EXERCISE 8

A. Review the dictionary entries for *research* and then complete the chart on the next page.

---

re·search¹ /rɪˈsɜːtʃ, ˈriːsɜːtʃ/ ••• AWL *noun* [uncountable] ◀))

COLLOCATIONS   THESAURUS

serious study of a subject, which is intended to discover new facts about it:
- ◀)) *The team is conducting scientific* **research on/into** *heart disease.*
- ◀)) *Holmes is* **doing research** (=finding information) *for a book on the Middle Ages.*

COLLOCATIONS

VERBS

to do research *also* **to conduct research** *formal*
- ◀)) *The university is paying him to do the research he has always wanted to do.*

to publish your research
- ◀)) *The team will publish their research in the journal Science.*

research shows/indicates/suggests something
- ◀)) *Research shows that medical treatment improves when the patient feels it is OK to ask questions.*

ADJECTIVES

scientific/medical/historical, etc., research
- ◀)) *Her new book is a piece of historical research that is as entertaining as a novel.*
- ◀)) *Some of the best medical research into the causes of the disease has been done at this hospital.*

RESEARCH + NOUNS

a research project/program/study
- ◀)) *The military conducted a research program on chemical weapons.*

research findings (=the things that are discovered by research)
- ◀)) *They published their research findings on the effects of secondhand smoke in a scientific journal.*

a research grant (=money for doing research)
- ◀)) *There are several research grants that you could apply for.*

---

re·search² /rɪˈsɜːtʃ, ˈriːsɜːtʃ/ ••• AWL *verb* [intransitive, transitive] ◀))

VERB TABLE

to study a subject in detail, in order to discover new facts about it:
- ◀)) *She has been researching her family's history for several years.*

---

research		
Word class	noun (*uncountable*)	verb ( )
Definition	*serious study of a subject, intended to discover new facts about it*	
Prepositions used with *research*	*on, into*	
Verb collocation that means to "have your study printed or posted"		
Adjective collocation that means "research related to health"		
Can the verb form take an object? How do you know?		
An original sentence using *research*		

TIP

Use the information from a dictionary entry to create vocabulary cards. Decide what features of the word to include. Then write the same features in the same places on the card: the front, back, upper-left corner, across the bottom, etc.

B. The following excerpts are from readings in this unit. Circle the word class of the bolded word. Then write an original sentence using the bolded word. Use the correct word class.

> 1. The task seemed impossible: Map and analyze the human genome, which has over 3 billion nucleotide base pairs (adenine-thymine, guanine-cytosine) that make up the body's approximately 20,000 **genes**.

noun / verb / adjective / adverb

2. Technologies have been developed to map and sequence other organisms' genomes more **quickly**.

noun / verb / adjective / adverb

3. In fact, courts in the United States have decided that **patients** do not own their cells after they are taken from their bodies.

noun / verb / adjective / adverb

4. For centuries medical doctors and scientists have been developing new ways to treat their patients and **prevent** disease.

noun / verb / adjective / adverb

5. These chemical bases are combined into very **specific** pairs.

noun / verb / adjective / adverb

6. Sometimes an A is **switched** with a C, T, or G, or sometimes an extra T might be added in.

noun / verb / adjective / adverb

C. Look up each word from Part B in your dictionary, or refer to your vocabulary flashcards. Check the word class. Compare your example sentences with the examples in the dictionary. Discuss with a partner.

🔊 Go to MyEnglishLab to complete a skill practice.

APPLY YOUR SKILLS

WHY IT'S USEFUL By applying the skills you have learned in this unit, you can gain a better understanding of this challenging reading about the usefulness of gene mapping.

BEFORE YOU READ

A. Discuss these questions with one or more students.

1. Genomic research can be costly. Money is needed to pay for researchers, laboratory materials, and space. Why do you think governments, companies, and individuals are willing to finance this research?

2. What are some pros and cons of having your genome sequenced? Explain.

3. If you discovered that you had a gene that made you more likely to get a disease, what would you do? Explain.

B. You will read an article about the usefulness of gene mapping. As you read, think about these questions.

1. How are genetic maps used?

2. What are some reasons to support gene mapping?

3. What are some of the concerns about gene sequencing?

C. Review the Unit Skills Summary. As you read the article, apply the skills you learned in this unit.

UNIT SKILLS SUMMARY

BECOME A MORE ACTIVE READER BY USING THESE SKILLS:

Skim to survey a text

- Look at key parts of the text, such as the title and headings, read the first and last sentence of each paragraph, and notice the images to help you get a quick idea of the main ideas.

Scan to discover specific information

- Decide what information you need and then quickly look at the text to find it. Move your eyes quickly over the text to look for capital letters, numbers, and keywords.

Annotate to identify key information

- Write key terms and definitions, note opinions, jot down questions, connect the information to what you already know, mark important details, and summarize main ideas.

(Continued)

Choose effective search terms

• Use 3–6 focused content words to find the information you need.

Utilize a dictionary to strengthen vocabulary

• Examine not only the definition of a new word but also the word class and the list of collocations.

READ

A. Read the article. Annotate as you read. Then summarize your thoughts in the mind map that follows.

How Useful Is Genetic Mapping and Sequencing?

1   In 2007, James Watson, the scientist who helped first discover DNA's double helix structure, was one of the first people to have his genome sequenced, at a cost of around $1 million. Since those early years, the cost of genome sequencing has fallen greatly as technology has improved. But at around $1,000, the service is still not cheap.

2   The price tag is not surprising, however, considering the time and effort involved in developing gene mapping. Gene mapping is the process that identifies where genes are located on chromosomes and the effects they have on an organism. The earliest gene mapping was done in the 1910s by American scientist Thomas Hunt Morgan. In his work with fruit flies, Hunt found that genes are located on chromosomes. This opened the door to many other scientists interested in genes, starting the field of what's called "modern genetics."

Glossary

Trait: characteristic

Sensitive to: easily affected, hurt, or damaged by

Carry a mutation: to have in your body a gene that isn't normal

Surgery: medical treatment in which a doctor cuts open your body to fix something

Ovaries: the part of a female that produces eggs

Percentage: a certain number out of 100

3   The mapping of *human* genes began around the second half of the 20th century as technology improved. Now genetic maps allow researchers to look for differences between the DNA of healthy and unhealthy family members, and once found, the location of the different, or mutated, gene can be mapped. Researchers can then find the sequence of the gene in the unhealthy person. Sequencing can be done for almost any trait that varies among a group of people, not only diseases. When someone has his or her genome sequenced, genetic maps are important because they can help experts understand the data of the sequencing. But as with any new product, people are right to ask: Is it worth it?

4   Through sequencing, James Watson, the scientist, learned that his genes made him sensitive to his blood pressure medication, so his doctors reduced his prescription. This made him feel better. However, he did not learn much else about his chances of developing genetic diseases.

5   For others though, the results can be significant. Actor Angelina Jolie received troubling news from her genetic tests: Results showed that she carried a mutation in her BRCA1 gene, which, for women, greatly increases the chance of developing breast and ovarian cancer (see Figure 1). Having surgery to remove the breasts (a mastectomy) and ovaries greatly reduces the risk of developing these cancers. Based on this information, Jolie decided to have these surgeries as a preventative measure—an effort to stop cancer from developing.

Chance of Developing Breast Cancer by Age 70

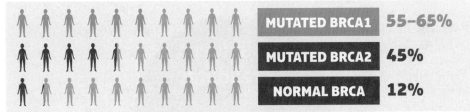

MUTATED BRCA1	55–65%
MUTATED BRCA2	45%
NORMAL BRCA	12%

Figure 1

6   Jolie's case is a good example of how genetic maps help experts understand data from genome sequencing. The BRCA1 gene mutation is unusual, however: Women who have the BRCA1 gene mutation are much more likely to develop certain types of cancer. Other cancer-related genes show much smaller percentages. In many cases, having a certain gene only increases the chance for disease by 1 or 2 percent. The reason for this is that multiple genes are often involved in coding for a disease. Some scientists warn that as genome sequencing becomes more common, people will focus on these "weak signals"—small increases in the chance of developing a disease. This may not only cause unnecessary stress for individuals but could also cause problems for healthcare: People might worry too much about a small increase in cancer risk and ask for medical treatment unnecessarily. There is also an issue with medical insurance: Will companies make people pay more if they have a gene that puts them at risk for a deadly cancer? Some argue that it is unfair to charge more if a person is only *more likely* to develop a disease.

7   On the other hand, there are many reasons to support continued use of genetic mapping and sequencing research. By collecting data through these methods, science can gain important knowledge about the causes of and treatments for diseases. Like James Watson, some people react poorly to medication because of their genes. With a better understanding of genetics, doctors can give their patients more effective medicines. And of course, there is already the known benefit of gene mapping and genome sequencing: For people like Jolie, early treatment greatly reduces the chance of developing cancer. This benefits individuals' health and can certainly reduce healthcare costs.

(Continued)

8 As genome sequencing becomes cheaper and more common, genetic mapping is sure to improve. This will allow more people to unlock their genetic information and make better decisions about their health.

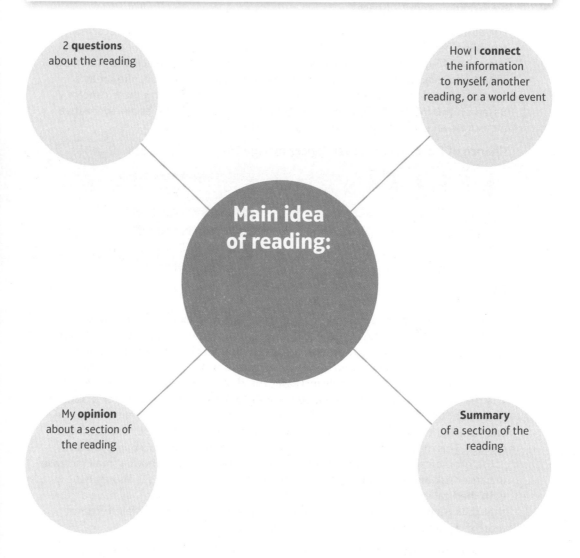

2 **questions** about the reading

How I **connect** the information to myself, another reading, or a world event

Main idea of reading:

My **opinion** about a section of the reading

Summary of a section of the reading

B. Compare notes with a partner. Did you have similar opinions or ask similar questions? What skills from this unit can help you identify key ideas?

C. Reread the questions in Before You Read, Part B. With your partner, use your notes and opinions to answer the questions.

⊙ Go to MyEnglishLab to read more closely, answer the critical thinking questions, and complete a summarizing activity.

THINKING CRITICALLY

Use information from the reading to answer these questions.

1. Do the concerns about genetic mapping outweigh the benefits? Why or why not?

....

....

2. Do you think preventative surgery should be performed if there is only a small chance that the patient will develop the disease? Explain.

....

....

THINKING VISUALLY

Use information from the reading and this line graph to answer the following questions.

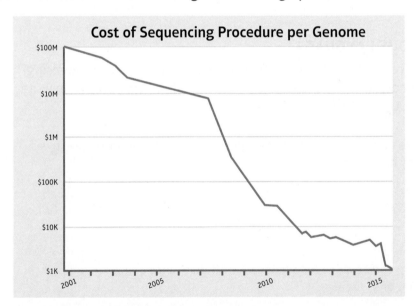

1. Look at the line graph and consider what you have read. What does this information suggest about the cost of genome sequencing in the next few years? What effect might that have on demand?

....

....

2. Record your knowledge and predictions about genome sequencing in the chart.

	What I Know	What I Predict Will Happen
About the costs of genome sequencing		
About the demand for genome sequencing		

THINKING ABOUT LANGUAGE

A. Read these excerpts from "How Useful Is Genetic Mapping and Sequencing?" Using a dictionary, write the word class of each underlined word. Then write the definition. Use a dictionary if necessary.

1. Since those early years, the cost of genome sequencing has fallen <u>greatly</u> as technology has improved.

Word class: ....

Definition: ....

2. Sequencing can be done for almost any trait that varies <u>among</u> a group of people, not only diseases.

Word class: ....

Definition: ....

3. Jolie's case is a good example of how genetic maps help experts understand <u>data</u> from genome sequencing.

Word class: ....

Definition: ....

4. Some scientists warn that as genome sequencing becomes more common, people will <u>focus</u> on these "weak signals"—small increases in the chance of developing a disease.

Word class: ....

Definition: ....

5. Some <u>argue</u> that it is unfair to charge more if a person is only *more likely* to develop a disease.

Word class: ....

Definition: ....

6. By collecting data through these methods, science can <u>gain</u> important knowledge about the causes of and treatments for diseases.

Word class: ....

Definition: ....

7. With a better understanding of genetics, doctors can give their patients more <u>effective</u> medicines.

Word class: ....

Definition: ....

B. Check (✓) the question that you would like to learn more about. Then create a list of effective search terms to find the information. Share results with a partner.

☐ Are there genetic diseases that only men get, and what are they?

☐ What are the various treatments for women who have breast cancer?

☐ What are the specific costs associated with having my genome sequenced, and who profits from my business?

For help with choosing effective search terms, go to MyEnglishLab, Bioethics, Part 1, Language Skill.

....

⬥ Go to MyEnglishLab to watch Professor Greely's concluding video and to complete a self-assessment.

Design principles help create business innovation

BUSINESS AND DESIGN

Main Ideas and Details

UNIT PROFILE

In this unit, you will consider the subject of business—specifically the ideas of value propositions and business-model designs. You will also hear an interview about a popular crowd-funding website. In the final reading of the unit, you will follow the story of a successful crowd-funding campaign.

Look at the reading "The Secret to a Successful Crowd-Funding Campaign" on page 50. Skim the title, image, and first paragraph. What do you think the topic and main idea are?

OUTCOMES

- Identify main ideas
- Identify supporting details
- Paraphrase
- Use synonyms and equivalent expressions
- Build word families

For more about **BUSINESS AND DESIGN**, see ❷❸.
See also Ⓦ and ⓄⒸ **BUSINESS AND DESIGN** ❶❷❸.

GETTING STARTED

◐ Go to MyEnglishLab to watch Juli Sherry's introductory video and to complete a self-assessment.

Discuss these questions with a partner or group.

1. *Entrepreneurs* are people who start their own business. Describe the kind of person who becomes a successful entrepreneur—the personality, behavior, etc.

2. Imagine a business you would like to start. What are your start-up costs—the things your business needs? Where or how do you get the money to pay for them?

3. In her introduction, Juli Sherry describes designing a business model as an "awesome" (really good, important) experience. Why is business model design an important part of running a business? What components do you think make up a successful business model?

SKILL 1

IDENTIFYING MAIN IDEAS

WHY IT'S USEFUL By identifying the main idea, you can get a better understanding of the topic, specifically what the writer is trying to express.

The **topic** of a text is what the text is generally about. The **main idea** expresses a particular idea or thought about that topic. Essentially, the main idea is the most important idea about the topic. The main idea is usually found in the first paragraph of a reading. It may also be repeated in the last paragraph, as part of the conclusion.

Steps for Identifying the Main Idea

1. Read the whole text to determine the general topic.

2. Ask yourself what point the writer is trying to make about the topic.

3. Reread the text, focusing on the beginning paragraphs. Authors generally mention the main idea near the beginning.

4. Read the title and see if it gives a clue about the main idea.

The following example is the introduction to an article titled "How to Start a Business." Below are three students' idea of the main idea. Which is best?

What to sell? Where to open? What financing is available? Starting a business involves answering a lot of questions, putting in a lot of time, and dealing with stressful situations. However, there is hope. The stress can be managed by following ten basic steps. ...

Student A: *Starting a business involves a lot of issues and stress.*

Student B: *If you want to start a business, you need money.*

Student C: *Follow some basic steps to help you start a business in a stress-free way.*

Student A focuses on only the problems. Student B is too general. Student C is the best choice. It reflects the main idea, which is also expressed in the title.

TIP

In traditional academic writing, students are taught to express the main idea in a topic sentence. This usually comes at the beginning of each paragraph. In essay writing, students are taught to include the main idea in a thesis statement. This usually comes at the end of the introductory paragraph. However, in academic articles, writers don't always follow these rules.

VOCABULARY PREVIEW

Read the vocabulary items in the box. Circle the ones you know. Put a question mark next to the ones you don't know.

profit (n)	qualities	includes	appropriate (adj)
market (n)	brand (n)	dozens	

EXERCISE 1

A. Skim the article on the next page. Look at the title and image, and read the first paragraph. Then mark your answers.

Topic of Article: business   value proposition   profits   customers

Main Idea of First Paragraph:

☐ A value proposition is similar to a slogan because it is trying to sell a product.

☐ A value proposition includes the product as well as many intangible qualities.

☐ A value proposition is only concerned with making money.

B. Before you read something, do you anticipate the main idea? How can that be helpful? As you read, does your understanding of the main idea change? Why?

EXERCISE 2

A. From the title of the article and the visual, check (✓) what the author might explain.

☐ the characteristics of a value proposition

☐ the problems of a value proposition

☐ how to create a value proposition

B. Read the article. Then read the statements that follow. Circle *T* (True) or *F* (False). Correct the false statements.

The Value of a Value Proposition

1   In business, what does every person, idea, and system work toward? Most would answer, "Profit." But this is too easy. Actually, a business's *value proposition* is what the various qualities and parts of a business must support. Otherwise there will be no way for that profit to be made! Simply stated, the value proposition includes everything that is being offered to the customer. A well thought-out value proposition can tie together every process and part of a business, while a poorly considered value proposition may doom the business before it begins. Far beyond the product itself, the value proposition also includes intangible qualities—things like style, time saved, safety, and trust.

Glossary

Value proposition: a written statement that explains to a potential customer how a product (or service) solves a problem or improves his or her situation, what the specific benefits are, and why the product is different and better than what is offered by the competition

Intangible: having no physical qualities

Endorse: approve

Slogan: a memorable phrase used in an ad

Perk: benefit

Manufacturing: the making of something by a machine, usually in a large amount

2   A value proposition is more than the intangibles, though. Consider the difference between a coach plane ticket and a first-class plane ticket. Both tickets let you travel from one place to another, but the value proposition of one ticket is very different from the other. Understanding value proposition lets a business owner target appropriate groups of customers and work well in each market.

(Continued)

3 Also, don't mistake a company's value proposition for the actual product or service itself. Often, the value proposition is much more complicated than "Product A at Price B." This will be easier to understand by comparing two similar products. Imagine two pairs of shoes: one, an off-brand pair of sneakers priced at $20; the other, a brand-name pair of basketball shoes endorsed by a famous athlete, accompanied by a slogan, and priced at over $100. These shoes have *very* different value propositions.

4 The first value proposition promises you a pair of shoes. The shoes will cover your feet … and that's about it. The second pair promises you not only a pair of shoes but also dozens of other perks: unusual and expensive shoes, a sporty design, connection to a famous athlete, and fashionability. The brand-name pair's value proposition offers much more to the customer—*even if* the cost of manufacturing, materials, and shipping are almost the same as the other shoe! This is one example of how a clearly stated value proposition can attract customers and result in enormous profits for a business.

T / F   1. A value proposition is the same as a company's slogan.

T / F   2. A value proposition is concerned with the product as well as the benefits that the product provides.

T / F   3. Style, safety, and trust are qualities that a value proposition might include.

T / F   4. In business, a *brand* is a product given a specific name.

T / F   5. Connecting the product with a famous person can be part of a value proposition.

T / F   6. A successful value proposition can result in higher profits for a company.

T / F   7. A company that doesn't think about its value proposition will probably not do as well as one that does.

C. Reread the passage. Then check your answers in Parts A and B.

D. Discuss these questions with a partner.

1. What is the main idea of the passage? Use your own words.
2. Does the title reflect the main idea? If so, how? If not, suggest a title.
3. Why does the author compare pairs of shoes in Paragraphs 3 and 4?
4. What is the main idea of Paragraph 4?

EXERCISE 3

Discuss these questions with a partner.

1. Did identifying the topic and the main idea before you read the whole article help you understand the article?

2. Did the writer of this article have a clearly written topic sentence that introduced each paragraph?

VOCABULARY CHECK

A. Review the vocabulary items in the Vocabulary Preview. Write their definitions and add examples. Use a dictionary if necessary.

B. Read each sentence. Then match the underlined vocabulary item with the correct definition. With a partner, explain what the vocabulary item means.

.... 1. Good finanical leadership has resulted in huge <u>profits</u> this year.

.... 2. When choosing a phone, consumers think about <u>qualities</u> such as design, usability, prestige, and cost.

.... 3. Some companies <u>include</u> a one-year warranty with the purchase of an item. Others require you to buy a warranty separately.

.... 4. The movie was not <u>appropriate</u> for a young audience because of the violence.

.... 5. If gasoline becomes more expensive, the <u>market</u> for electric and hybrid cars will grow.

.... 6. Some customers buy a certain <u>brand</u> because a famous person backs it.

.... 7. Eggs are usually sold by the <u>dozen</u> although they can also be found in half-dozen cartons.

a. to be part of

b. twelve

c. money made by selling things, after expenses are paid

d. suitable or good

e. features typical of one thing (size, color, etc.)

f. a particular group of people that a company sells to

g. a specific type of product, with a specific name

⯈ Go to MyEnglishLab to complete vocabulary and skill practices, and to join in collaborative activities.

SKILL 2

IDENTIFYING SUPPORTING DETAILS

WHY IT'S USEFUL By identifying supporting details, you can better understand the information that supports the main idea.

Supporting details give readers more information, allowing them to go deeper into their experience of a text. Supporting details come in a variety of forms, including:

anecdote	definition	description	example
fact	quotation	reason	statistic

How to Identify Supporting Details

1. Read the text to understand the topic and the main idea.

2. Turn the main idea into a *wh-* question. For example, if the main idea of a text is that businesses need a good value proposition in order to succeed, ask yourself, "*Why* does a business need a good value proposition?"

3. Reread the text to find the answers (supporting details).

Look for signal words like *first*, *also*, *additionally*, *next*, and *finally*. Writers may use these when introducing details.

In this example, the main idea is underlined. By turning the main idea into a question—"What are the steps to starting a business?"—we can identify the major supporting details and the minor supporting details.

Starting a business can be easy if you follow these steps. First, write a business plan. A business plan will explain what the business hopes to achieve from a marketing, financial, and operational viewpoint. Then prepare yourself financially. It's important to separate your personal finances from the business, so open up a bank account for the business, and arrange financing through loans or business partners. Additionally, make sure you meet all the legal requirements. You might need special licenses or business permits and a tax identification number, and you might have other legal requirements if hiring employees. Finally, the right attitude is important. Persistence, confidence, patience, and creativity are important characteristics to have as a business owner. Seeing your business become profitable may take time, but if you follow these steps, success will be much closer.

VOCABULARY PREVIEW

Read the vocabulary items in the box. Circle the ones you know. Put a question mark next to the ones you don't know.

operate (v)	achieve	evaluated	advantages	adapt	constructing

EXERCISE 4

A. Read each main idea and supporting detail. Underline the supporting detail. Then write the kind of detail it is. Use the words from the box.

anecdote	definition	description	example
fact	quotation	reason	statistic

1. Nowadays, watching movies is not only done in movie theaters. In 2015, the annual number of DVD rentals in the US was 120 per adult, on average.

   ....

2. Movie theaters are noticing a decline in attendance. Most of the people I know don't go to theaters; in fact, my parents watch movies on their home televisions, and most of my friends stream them on their phones.

   ....

3. In order for a business to make a profit, it must do many things. For instance, it must offer a wanted product or service; it must advertise that product; and it must make sure that product or service will be reliable and meet the customer's needs.

   ....

4. Apple is an example of a company that has changed over the years. At the beginning, it focused solely on computers but now sells a variety of products including phones, watches, and music.

   ....

5. Entrepreneurs must be persistent. As Winston Churchill once said, "Success consists of going from failure to failure without loss of enthusiasm."

   ....

B. Think about the supporting details that were used in Part A. Do you think the main idea influences the type of supporting detail? Explain.

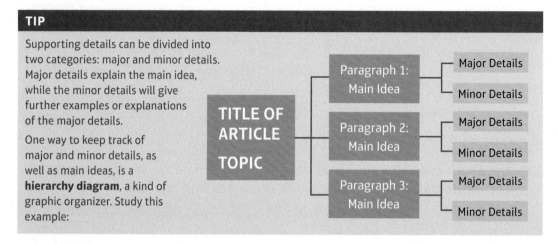
EXERCISE 5

A. Think of a company that you buy goods or services from. Who would you say are that company's "target" customers, or customer base? What's the connection between the product and the base?

B. Read the passage. Then answer the questions that follow.

The Importance of a Business Model

1   The main document of any business is the *business model*. This document explains how a business is supposed to operate. The business model outlines things like sources of revenue and customer interactions. Think of a business model as something that helps a business provide the value proposition it promises. A business model should not be confused with a business strategy. The *model* explains how the business works, while the *strategy* outlines the business's approach to a competitive market. For instance, if you opened a café near a university, the details of buying and selling of coffee drinks and baked goods would be your business model. Your business strategy would be something your business does that is special—say giving discounts to students. This is your unique selling point (USP).

2   So what makes a business model different from an ordinary plan? First, a business model outlines practices and makes clear that these practices can be

Glossary

Revenue: money that is earned by a company

Discount: lower price

Unique selling point (USP): the thing about your product or service that makes it special

Brick and mortar: a business that is operated out of a building, not online

Subscription: an amount of money you pay regularly to receive something

changed as needed to achieve specific ends. A business model should be evaluated in terms of available data—like customer information, profit, performance, and so on. Also, a business model shouldn't be set in stone—it should be changed and improved regularly, to help a business achieve its value proposition profitably. Finally, improvements to a business model can give a company many advantages over the competition.

3 One example of a business model making enormous profit through innovation involves the movie rental company Netflix. Netflix was able to compete with Blockbuster, a long-time brick-and-mortar movie rental company. How? By offering a subscription-based business model. Netflix used numerous innovations—like mailing movies directly to the customer—to save on operational costs. In addition, the company continued to innovate, or try new things, by expanding into online streaming. Blockbuster, in contrast, was slow to adapt its business model. Long story short, today Netflix is the most profitable movie rental company in the United States.

4 When constructing a business model, a business should give itself room to grow. If, for example, Blockbuster had been innovative, Netflix might not have succeeded. As it grows, a business should compare results with its business model to see if it is fulfilling its value proposition. Otherwise, it may become the next Blockbuster.

1. According to the passage, what should a business model consider? Choose all correct answers.

   a. sources of revenue
   b. customer interaction
   c. impact on value proposition
   d. website development

2. The expression "set in stone" is another way to say _____ .

   a. cannot be changed
   b. is hard
   c. have difficulty
   d. made to be changed

3. According to the author, what is NOT a quality of a business model?

   a. It should be evaluated.
   b. It should be competitive.
   c. It should be changeable.
   d. It should be innovative.

4. The author mentions Netflix and Blockbuster to _____ .

    a. compare two companies that had successful business models

    b. contrast two companies that had different business models

    c. give a definition of a business model

    d. persuade the reader to use Netflix

5. What was NOT mentioned as one of Netflix's innovations?

    a. It mails movies to the customers.

    b. It is a subscription-based model.

    c. It got into the online streaming market.

    d. It advertises on the Internet.

6. The author suggests that Blockbuster _____ .

    a. actually had a superior product

    b. should have hired new managers

    c. needed to keep its business model the same

    d. would still be competitive today if it had quickly changed its model

C. Reread the passage. Then check your answers to Parts A and B.

D. Scan the passage for supporting-detail signals and circle them. Highlight information in the passage that supports the main ideas: examples, statistics, quotations, definitions. Then answer the questions.

1. In Paragraph 1, the author states: "A business model should not be confused with a business strategy. The *model* explains how the business works, while the *strategy* outlines the business's approach to a competitive market." Which sentence supports that idea?

    a. The main document of any business is the business model.

    b. So what makes a business model different from an ordinary plan?

    c. Think of a business model as something that helps you fulfill the value proposition you offer customers.

    d. For instance, if you opened a café near a university, the details of buying and selling coffee drinks and baked goods would be your business model.

2. In Paragraph 2, the author explains that a business model should be evaluated in terms of available data. What kind of supporting details are given?

    a. statistics

    b. examples

    c. facts

    d. definitions

3. What do the supporting details in Paragraph 3 give?

    a. a definition of a business model

    b. an example of a successful company that innovated

    c. suggestions for being a successful company

    d. statistics about successful strategies

4. What language does the author use in Paragraph 4 to signal a supporting detail?

    a. When

    b. for example

    c. if

    d. Otherwise

EXERCISE 6

Think of a time when you used supporting details to explain an idea. What kind of details did you use: examples, reasons, anecdotes, statistics, or quotations?

VOCABULARY CHECK

A. Review the vocabulary items in the Vocabulary Preview. Write their definitions and add examples. Use a dictionary if necessary.

B. Complete each sentence using the correct vocabulary item from the box. Use the correct form.

achieve	adapt	advantage	construct	evaluate	operate

1. The travel agency is located in San Francisco, but it is .... by a business in Singapore.

2. Attracting a loyal customer base is a goal we hope to ....

3. The owners asked all employees to .... the company, giving each category a score from 1 to 10.

4. One .... of having a hair salon in your home is you don't have to pay a booth fee.

5. After the bakery owners heard customers complaining that the pastries were dry, they .... their recipe to have more butter.

6. We .... our business model to be more detailed.

🔊 Go to MyEnglishLab to complete vocabulary and skill practices, and to join in collaborative activities.

INTEGRATED SKILLS
PARAPHRASING

> **WHY IT'S USEFUL** By paraphrasing, you can better support your ideas and opinions. It also helps you better understand the original information.

As a student, you will have to read and report back on things you have read. **Paraphrasing**, or putting an author's ideas into your own words, is an important skill. It allows you to refer to others' ideas without having to recite all of the information. Rather, you can shorten the idea to its essentials, using your own words.

How to Paraphrase

- Read the whole article or listen to the whole talk (such as a Ted Talk), keeping in mind your purpose.
- When you identify important information, review it two or three times in order to fully understand the author's idea.
- Without looking back at the original, put the main ideas into your own words.
- Change the sentence structure and order of ideas.
- Change the vocabulary. BUT: Keep technical words that have no replacement.
- Do not add new information.
- Make sure you have given credit to the author or source with the necessary citations.

> **TIP**
>
> Find out the citation style required and follow it. Popular academic styles include: APA (*Publication Manual of American Psychological Association*), MLA (*Modern Language Association Style Manual*) and Chicago (*Chicago Manual of Style*).

Consider the following examples:

> **Original sentence:** Kickstarter, whose mission is to help raise money for creative projects, is one of the most popular crowd-funding websites.

> **Paraphrase 1:** Kickstarter, which helps raise funds for creative ideas, is a very popular crowd-funding website.

Paraphrase 1 is not good—it keeps the same sentence structure and uses synonyms to change some of the words.

Paraphrase 2: One way that businesses can get financing is through crowd-funding.

Paraphrase 2 is not good because it forgets to include Kickstarter, which is what the original sentence is describing.

Paraphrase 3: A well-known crowd-funding website is Kickstarter, started in 2009, in which businesses can try to get financing for their new ideas.

Paraphrase 3 is not good because it introduces information not mentioned in the original sentence.

Paraphrase 4: A well-known crowd-funding platform is Kickstarter, whose mission is to try to help new ideas get financed.

Paraphrase 4 is the best because it keeps the same idea but uses new sentence structure and words.

VOCABULARY PREVIEW

Read the vocabulary items in the box. Circle the ones you know. Put a question mark next to the ones you don't know.

finance (v)	convince	thrown out	major (adj)	hire	clever

EXERCISE 7

A. *Crowd-funding* is raising money for a project before it exists. Have you ever helped crowd-fund something?

B. Read a quote from a business expert. Which is the best paraphrase? Explain why the other sentences are not acceptable.

Expert: "One creative kind of business financing that has become successful recently is *crowd-funding.*"

Paraphrases

☐ One innovative way to raise money for a business that is now successful is crowd-funding.

☐ The expert believes one creative way to finance a business is crowd-funding.

☐ The expert believes that crowd-funding is the best way to raise money for a new business.

☐ According to the expert, crowd-funding has recently become a successful means of raising money to start a business.

C. Listen to a podcast episode called "21ˢᵗ-Century Financing: Crowd-Funding." Then paraphrase the excerpts. Use your own words, but keep the main idea.

Glossary

Backer: someone who gives support—money, for example

Investing: giving money or time to something

Go viral: become popular on the Internet

Word of mouth: news passed from person to person

Loyal fan base: a group of people who believe in a product

Campaign: a series of actions intended to achieve a particular result

1. A business will promote its items online, trying to convince as many people as possible to "back," or financially support, its product. These "backers" are often rewarded with discounts and free items.

....

....

2. With crowd-funding, a business can try to market the product *before* investing time and money in its creation.

....

....

3. For famous directors and designers who are tired of working under the rules of a studio, crowd-funding offers them a chance to do things their way—if they find enough people willing to support them.

....

....

TIP

To practice paraphrasing: Read a short passage until you understand it. Then cover it and try to paraphrase the main idea.

4. The best thing that crowd-funding does for the economy is that it allows the market to take chances on new, untested ideas.

....

....

5. Kickstarter usually takes less than 10 percent of the total money raised, meaning that it constantly collects revenue from campaigns, large and small.

....

....

D. Work with a partner. Compare paraphrases in Part C. Discuss any differences. Discuss these questions.

1. Was paraphrasing easy or difficult for you to do? Explain.

2. Paraphrasing is one way to use an author's ideas to help support your own opinion. What are some other ways you use an author's idea in a paper?

E. Listen again. Then answer the questions.

1. What are the benefits of crowd-funding for a small business or entrepreneur?

....

2. What is the benefit of crowd-funding for larger businesses and what does the speaker mean by "test the waters"?

....

3. How has Kickstarter's success been beneficial for its own business growth?

....

4. How does Kickstarter make money?

....

5. Kickstarter is described as a low-risk, high-growth business. What is that?

....

VOCABULARY CHECK

A. Review the vocabulary items in the Vocabulary Preview. Write their definitions and add examples. Use a dictionary if necessary.

B. Complete each sentence using the correct vocabulary item from the box. Use the correct form.

clever	convince	finance	hire	major	throw out

1. The main goal of innovators who crowd-fund is to .... potential investors that their product is needed.

2. Many .... ideas are found on crowd-funding websites. But there are a lot of bad ideas, too.

3. If a new idea on a crowd-funding site proves to be popular, then the entrepreneur might need to .... people to actually develop and produce the product.

4. Most entrepreneurs need to .... their new product or service before they can actually produce it.

5. In coming up with new products, an inventor might design a product, but .... it .... if preliminary feedback is negative.

6. As the president of the company, she was a .... figure in the company's organization.

🔘 Go to MyEnglishLab to complete a skill practice and to join in collaborative activities.

LANGUAGE SKILL

USING SYNONYMS AND EQUIVALENT EXPRESSIONS

WHY IT'S USEFUL By using synonyms correctly, you can express your ideas more clearly and in more interesting ways.

🔘 Go to MyEnglishLab for the Language Skill presentation and practice.

VOCABULARY STRATEGY
BUILDING WORD FAMILIES

WHY IT'S USEFUL By understanding word families, you can increase your vocabulary and improve your overall comprehension of a text.

A **word family** is a group of words with a shared root. Students often learn to spell by learning common spelling patterns, or word families. For instance, the root *port* has many "family members," including *import, important,* and *portable*.

Word families are built by adding prefixes or suffixes to roots, which turns them into different parts of speech with different meanings. For instance, *employ: employer, employee; employed; unemployed, employment, unemployment*.

Prefix	Meaning	Example
in-	not	**in**credible
un-	not	**un**like
multi-	many	**multi**national
post-	after	**post**graduate

Suffix	Part of Speech	Example
-able	adjective	afford**able**
-ful		success**ful**
-ly	adverb	frequent**ly**
-er		market**er**
-ion	noun	construct**ion**
-ment		achieve**ment**

EXERCISE 8

A. Choose the best word from the word families to complete each sentence. Use the correct form.

invest	investor	investment

1. The start-up needed someone to .... some money in it. The entrepreneur hoped a few people would make a considerable ....

create	creator	creative	creatively	creation

2. Many .... who use crowd-funding platforms hope to find people to finance their unique .... They promote their products with .... videos they have .... especially for crowd-funding purposes.

afford	affordable	affordability

3. Many small businesses will relocate to smaller cities where rents are more .... Renting office space in major cities is too expensive for them to .... with their budget.

| construct | constructing | construction | finance | finances | financial |

4. When .... a business model, businesses must consider their ....
Without an appropriate budget, the company will quickly run into ....
difficulties.

| evaluate | evaluator | evaluation | compete | competitor |

5. Businesses must .... their business model periodically; not doing so can
result in them losing out to a(n) ....

| survive | survival | adapt | adaptability | adaptable |

6. In order to .... in today's world, businesses must be .... —in
other words, quick to change depending on the market. If not, their ....
as a company will be unlikely.

B. Complete the word family chart.

	Noun	Verb	Adjective	Adverb
1.		invest		
2.	creation / creator			
3.		afford		
4.	finances			
5.		evaluate		
6.	competition /			
7.	survivor /			
8.	/	adapt		

C. Choose six of the words from Part B and write original sentences. As you write, think about the word families of the other words in your sentences. Is your vocabulary expanding?

1. ....

2. ....

3. ....

4. ....

5. ....

6. ....

⬆ Go to MyEnglishLab to complete a skill practice.

APPLY YOUR SKILLS

WHY IT'S USEFUL By applying the skills you have learned in this unit, you can gain a better understanding of crowd-funding and how to create a successful crowd-funding campaign.

BEFORE YOU READ

A. Discuss these questions with one or more students.

1. Think of something you enjoyed when you were younger—a toy, a TV show, a type of food—that isn't available today. What would you be willing to do to bring it back?

2. Have you seen a "viral" video? What made it a sensation?

3. Have you ever received an incentive, for example, a discount if you sign up for the store's credit card. Do incentives work?

B. You will read an article about a TV show called *Mystery Science Theater 3000*. As you read, think about these questions.

1. For how long was the original *Mystery Science Theater 3000* shown on TV?

2. Why was *Mystery Science Theater 3000*'s crowd-funding campaign successful?

3. How is a business model connected to a television show?

C. Review the Unit Skills Summary. As you read the article, apply the skills you learned in this unit.

UNIT SKILLS SUMMARY

WORK WITH MAIN IDEAS AND DETAILS BY USING THESE SKILLS:

Identify main ideas

• Understand the focus of the text or what it will explain.

Identify supporting details

• Look for information that supports the main idea.

Paraphrase

• Explain the writer's idea but in your own words.

Use synonyms and equivalent expressions

• Know how to use a dictionary to distinguish the meaning of similar words.

Build word families

• Recognize how prefixes and suffixes can change a word's meaning or part of speech.

READ

A. Read the article and notice the main ideas and supporting details. Take notes in a hierarchy diagram like the one on page 38.

The Secret to a Successful Crowd-Funding Campaign

1 What is required to make a successful crowd-funding campaign? Many people are familiar with the idea of "going viral" and think this is the key to crowd-funding success. But getting attention is only one part of it. Successful crowd-funding campaigns must offer a good value proposition and use a well-planned business model. In short, a crowd-funding business venture—while having a few unique characteristics—must be a solid business venture. An example is the surprising success of a Kickstarter campaign centered around a strange, long-canceled television show.

A scene from *Mystery Science Theater 3000* (Season 12, Episode 1, aired April 14, 2017)

2 In 1988 Joel Hodgson wrote, produced, and directed the first episode of *Mystery Science Theater 3000* (MST3K), which aired on a public broadcast television station in Minnesota, USA. The show—a mix of science fiction, comedy, and film critique—combined puppets and a low budget with Hodgson's own unique sense of humor. The show gained a small but loyal fan following and eventually moved from public access to cable television. It was canceled in 1999, a few years after Hodgson had left the show. More than a decade later, Hodgson began a Kickstarter-based crowd-funding campaign in the hopes of returning the show to production.

3 This brings us to the first key to having a successful crowd-funding campaign: *know your market.* Old episodes of MST3K continued to be profitable as DVDs and on video-streaming sites. And former cast members had had success on other shows. So Hodgson and his associates thought that the market would support a continuation of the show.

4 Next, Hodgson focused on *reaching out and connecting with potential supporters.* He had the advantage of a built-in fan following. After putting a video on Kickstarter, the campaign met its first goal of $2 million within a week. Over $5.5 million was collected by the end of the campaign. This is an example of how smaller companies and unknown entrepreneurs must gain attention through social networking and clever marketing. The "pitch video" for a crowd-funding campaign must show supporters why *this* product is worth their time. The value proposition needs to be clear and convincing. Anything an entrepreneur can do to improve the value proposition at this stage—from proving trustworthiness to offering extra features—is a plus. Businesses can improve both their value proposition and their chance of being funded by offering "backer rewards," the extra material given to supporters. A basic contribution gets a backer the product. A more generous contribution , could mean mugs, T-shirts, or other extras. Hodgson offered high-contribution backers the chance to help write an episode. Personalizing the rewards helps a campaign connect with loyal backers.

5   It's important to remember that a crowd-funded business is still a business. Many seemingly successful crowd-funding campaigns run into trouble because despite a great idea, the business plan is poorly thought-out. In the earliest days of crowd-funding, inexperienced, independent creators sometimes *lost* money, even on very popular projects, simply because they didn't know how to budget for the time and labor required to send a lot of backer rewards. The value proposition offered to backers must be supported by a good business model. This is one reason why film and game production studios have been successful on Kickstarter: They already had strong business models in place. As for Hodgson, he began the project with a few actors, writers, and support staff. Later, he worked out a distribution deal with Netflix that would allow him to better reach new viewers. As one of the top media Kickstarter campaigns ever funded, Hodgson's project connected not only with the show's fans, but also with new investors. This proves that a good crowd-funding campaign is good business.

CULTURE NOTE

In the United States, "public" broadcasting stations are television and radio stations whose funding depends on donations from businesses and individuals, and sometime small grants from the federal or state government. Most of these public stations are nonprofit organizations as opposed to commercially owned television and radio stations whose mission is to make a profit.

Glossary

Venture: a new business activity that involves taking risks

Pitch: an attempt to sell something

Distribution: the act of supplying goods to stores, companies, etc.

B. Compare notes with a partner. Did you identify the same main ideas and major details? Were your minor details the same or different? Explain.

C. Reread the questions in Before You Read, Part B. With your partner, use your notes and opinions to answer the questions.

Go to MyEnglishLab to read more closely, answer the critical thinking questions, and complete a summarizing activity.

THINKING CRITICALLY

Use information from the reading to answer these questions.

1. How is crowd-funding beneficial to not only the creators of a project but also the larger community? Explain.

2. Does crowd-funding present any disadvantages for a business that attempts a crowd-funding campaign?

THINKING VISUALLY

Use information from the reading and the visual to answer the following questions.

CROWD-FUNDING: FUNDS RAISED, 2012

WORLDWIDE TOTAL
$2.7 billion

EUROPE
$945 million

NORTH AMERICA
$1.6 billion

ASIA
$33 million

AFRICA
$0.065 million

SOUTH AMERICA
$0.8 million

OCEANIA
$76 million

1. Study the visual. Think about what you know about how crowd-funding works. How do you explain the variation in amounts shown? Since 2012 the totals have risen worldwide. Do you think the international growth in crowd-funding will have any effect on US crowd-funding projects?

   ....

   ....

2. Create a different kind of visual—for example, a bar graph—showing these annual global totals (in billions) for the following years: 2013: $6.1; 2014 $16.2; 2015 $34.4. Then research and add figures for 2016, 2017, and 2018. Based on trends that you have noticed, add a secondary feature: percentage based on category. Use the categories from the box. Be prepared to explain your figures and categories.

philanthropy and civic projects	real estate	science
journalism	music	(your idea)

THINKING ABOUT LANGUAGE

A. Read these excerpts from "The Secret to a Successful Crowd-Funding Campaign." Complete each using the correct form of the boldfaced word. Then write other forms you know. Include the part of speech. Use a dictionary if necessary.

1. What is required to make a _successful (adj)_ crowd-funding campaign? (**success**) (n)

   Other forms: _succeed (v)_

2. An example is the .... success of a Kickstarter campaign centered around a strange, long-canceled television show. (**surprise**) (n)

   Other forms: ....

3. Old episodes of MST3K continued to be .... as DVDs and on video-streaming sites. (**profit**) (n)

   Other forms: ....

4. In the earliest days of crowd-funding, ..., ... creators sometimes *lost* money ... (**experience**) (n) (**depend**) (v)

   Other forms: ....

   Other forms: ....

5. Later, he worked out a .... deal with Netflix that would allow him to better reach new viewers. (**distribute**) (v)

   Other forms: ....

B. **Brainstorm a list of synonyms for each of the words you completed the sentences with in Part A. If necessary, use a dictionary or thesaurus. Test them out in the sentences in Part A. Which ones work? Which ones don't? Why?**

> For help with using synonyms and equivalent expressions, go to MyEnglishLab, Business and Design, Part 1, Language Skill.

⬥ Go to MyEnglishLab to watch Juli Sherry's concluding video and to complete a self-assessment.

Patterns in nature can lead to advances in human medicine

ZOOLOGY

Multiple Sources

UNIT PROFILE

In this unit, you will consider the lives of elephants. You will learn about differences between African and Asian elephants, male and female elephants, and wild and captive ones. In the final reading of the unit, you will study the effects of poaching on elephant behavior and development.

Look at the reading "The Long-Term Effects of Poaching" on page 81. Skim the reading. What from your experience comes to mind? Have you read about or seen anything in the news about this topic?

OUTCOMES

- Make associations
- Synthesize information
- Write quotations to support ideas
- Express contrast and concession
- Improve receptive and productive vocabulary

For more about **ZOOLOGY**, see ❷ ❸. See also Ⓦ and ⓄⒸ **ZOOLOGY** ❶ ❷ ❸.

GETTING STARTED

🔵 Go to MyEnglishLab to watch Professor O'Connell-Rodwell's introductory video and to complete a self-assessment.

Discuss these questions with a partner or group.

1. Why are animals important to the world? What kinds of relationships do people have with animals?

2. Certain animals are endangered—at risk of becoming extinct (gone forever). What should be done to protect these animals? Do you think it's important to help endangered animals? Explain.

3. In her introduction, Professor O'Connell-Rodwell says that there are differences between elephants, depending on where they live. What are some examples of environmental differences? How can these affect an animal or species?

SKILL 1

MAKING ASSOCIATIONS

WHY IT'S USEFUL By making associations, you can get a better understanding of the topic. When you apply your experience and prior knowledge to a reading, the meaning becomes clearer and deeper.

As we read—in our first language or in another language—we think about what we already know about the topic. We also remember experiences that relate to the topic. Together these are called prior knowledge. For instance, if a text is about a country you have traveled in, your prior knowledge "fills in the blanks" with information such as the kinds of food you ate there, the people you met, the language, and the politics. Making these kinds of **associations** creates a deeper reading experience.

Consider the chart:

Kind of Association	Explanation
Personal connections (text to self)	These are personal associations that you make while reading. For example, after previewing a passage about elephants, you may think, "This passage reminds me of the elephant safari I went on in Thailand."
Connections with other texts (text to text)	While reading an article, you may recall another article on a similar topic, or a book that the same author has written. For instance, after reading about Asian elephants, you might say, "This reading reminds me of another book I read, but that one discussed the African species, which seems to be slightly different from the Asian species."
Connections with things in the world (text to world)	Social media and traditional media (TV, newspapers, radio) help inform your world knowledge. When you make text-to-world connections, you apply that knowledge to your reading experience. For example, after reading about African elephants, you might think, "This reminds me of a Facebook post I read by the founder of Save the Elephants about the effects of poaching."

When thinking about associations, you can put your thoughts on paper, in the form of words and images:

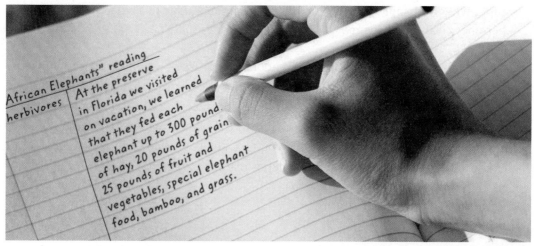

"African Elephants" reading
herbivores   At the preserve
in Florida we visited
on vacation, we learned
that they fed each
elephant up to 300 pounds
of hay, 20 pounds of grain,
25 pounds of fruit and
vegetables, special elephant
food, bamboo, and grass.

VOCABULARY PREVIEW

Read the vocabulary items in the box. Circle the ones you know. Put a question mark next to the ones you don't know.

form (n)	common	ideal	are fond of
roots	explore	threatened	

EXERCISE 1

A. What words do you associate with elephants? In this mind map, write words that come to mind.

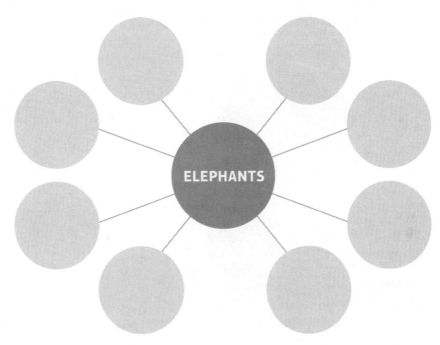

B. Before you read something, do you think about what you already know about the topic? As you read, do you make connections between the information in the reading and what you already know? How can these practices be helpful?

EXERCISE 2

A. Consider these questions.

1. What do you know about elephants?

2. Look at the map on the next page. Which continent is shown? What do you know about this continent? What information about elephants can you infer from the map? Explain.

3. From the title of the article and what you know from the map and photo, what do you think the article is about? Check (✓) your idea.

☐ how African elephants are captured for zoos

☐ a comparison between African and Asian elephants

☐ African elephants and where they are found

B. Read the article. After each paragraph, read the prompt(s). Then annotate the passage with your associations.

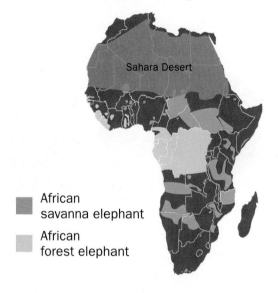

Current Natural Habitats of African Elephants

Sahara Desert

■ African savanna elephant

■ African forest elephant

1　Few animals capture the imagination like the enormous form of the African elephant. There are actually two species of African elephant, though this fact has been made official only in recent years.

Things you know about elephants:
gray, large, have a trunk, tusks

Things you know about African countries:

2　The African savanna elephant, or *Loxodonta africana*, is the larger and more common of the two. Females are around 3 meters tall, with males growing up to a full meter taller. The African elephant has large ears, which are ideal for cooling, and a low-set head. When fully grown, males—or bulls—are a lot larger than females.

Things you have seen online about elephants:

A time when you were hot and what you did to cool off:

3　Elephants are herbivorous. They eat all kinds of plants. African elephants are especially fond of leafy trees. They often dig up roots—sometimes even complete, fully grown trees—using their long, heavy tusks. Nearly every male African elephant possesses tusks. Most female African elephants also have tusks, though certain families can have an unusually high percentage of tuskless females.

Other herbivores:

Objects made from tusks (ivory):

4 African savanna elephants live all over the wide, open areas of sub-Saharan Africa. The animals live in a matriarchal social structure— small female-led families that look after children—while male elephants leave in their teens to explore on their own. This age of leaving home is relatively young, as a healthy elephant can live to be over 70 years old.

A story you read about African wildlife:

Other animals that live to be old:

5 Sadly, elephants are a threatened species. Their numbers decreased throughout the 20ᵗʰ century, and today there are only about half a million left. This has led the International Union for the Conservation of Nature, or IUCN, to put them in the category of "vulnerable"—only one category before "endangered."

News about poachers:

Other endangered or vulnerable animals:

Glossary

Species: a group of plants or animals of the same kind

Savanna: a large flat area of land covered in grass in a warm part of the world

Tusks: two long teeth on either side of an elephant's trunk

Conservation: the protection of natural things such as animals, plants, forests

Endangered: at risk of being killed off forever

CULTURE NOTE

The term *sub-Saharan Africa* is used to describe the countries in Africa that are south of the Sahara Desert. Of the 54 countries in Africa, 42 mainland countries are classified as sub-Saharan. In addition, there are 6 sub-Saharan island nations.

C. Reread the article. Then answer the questions.

1. How many species of African elephants exist? Which one is more common?

   ....

2. If an animal is herbivorous, what does it eat?

   ....

3. Given that elephants are herbivorous, what can you infer is NOT part of their diet?

   ....

4. Elephants live in matriarchal families. What does *matriarchal* mean?

   ....

5. The writer notes that most African elephants have tusks, which they use to dig up food. How would you describe tusks?

   ....

   ....

6. The writer mentions that savanna elephants live in open spaces in sub-Saharan Africa. From what you might know about the Sahara Desert, why do you think they don't live in the northern part of Africa?

   ....

   ....

7. The writer says that elephants are a threatened species. What do you think threatens their existence?

   ....

8. Which paragraph expresses the writer's opinion about the number of African elephants? How does the writer feel?

   ....

D. With a partner, discuss your annotations and answers in Parts B and C. Then discuss these questions.

1. Did the steps in Exercise 1 help you understand the article? Explain.

2. What kinds of associations (text to self, text to text, text to world) did you make while reading? Explain.

VOCABULARY CHECK

A. Review the vocabulary items in the Vocabulary Preview. Write their definitions and add examples. Use a dictionary if necessary.

B. Read each sentence. Then match the underlined vocabulary item with the correct definition. With a partner, explain what the vocabulary item means.

.... 1. The <u>form</u> of the African elephant ear, which looks similar to the continent of Africa, is different from that of the Asian elephant.

.... 2. The circus company known as Ringling Bros. and Barnum & Bailey discontinued using elephants in May 2016. Fortunately, elephants as entertainment is becoming less and less <u>common</u>.

.... 3. The <u>ideal</u> environment for the savanna elephant is wide open spaces with plenty of food and a water supply.

.... 4. In addition to enjoying roots and branches, African elephants <u>are fond of</u> the leaves of the Acacia tree.

.... 5. The <u>roots</u> of trees stretch far underground and are important for supplying the tree with water.

.... 6. Organized safari trips allow tourists to <u>explore</u> Africa and enjoy its wildlife, from the comfort of a vehicle.

.... 7. Other African animals that are <u>threatened</u> by global warming and urbanization include the black rhinoceros, the mountain gorilla, the chimpanzee, and the northern white rhinoceros.

a. in a bad situation; in danger

b. shape

c. often seen or occurring

d. the part of a plant or tree that grows under the ground and gets water from the soil

e. to like something or someone very much

f. the best that something can possibly be

g. to travel around an area in order to find out what it is like

⬤ Go to MyEnglishLab to complete vocabulary and skill practices, and to join in collaborative activities.

SKILL 2

SYNTHESIZING INFORMATION

WHY IT'S USEFUL By synthesizing information from different sources, you can understand more than one side of a topic.

Synthesizing is the practice of reaching conclusions based on information from two or more sources. When you synthesize information, you consider what you read in Text A along with what you learned from Text B—and then consider how this combination of information has changed what you previously thought.

When doing research about a topic, you will read multiple sources. Some of the sources will confirm what you have already read. Other sources will provide new information. And yet other sources will contradict—disagree with—all of the other information. By synthesizing the ideas from all the sources, you can get a much deeper understanding of the topic.

To synthesize, ask yourself these questions as you read:

- What is my opinion about this topic?

- Why am I reading this?

- What is the most important information?

- How is the new information similar to or different from the other information I've read?

- How have my thoughts changed about this topic since I started reading the text?

- What is memorable about this information?

- If a friend asks me about this topic, what will I say?

Graphic organizers, like the mind map you completed on page 57, can help you synthesize your ideas. Read the two passages on the next page. One is about circus elephants and the other is about the elephant researcher Cynthia Moss and an elephant named Echo. Notice the annotations a student made to the passages. Then notice how the student used a graphic organizer (on p. 64) to organize information from the passages.

Source 1

The Elephants of Ringling Bros. and Barnum & Bailey Circus

Ringling Bros. and Barnum & Bailey Circus's connection with elephants stretches back to the late 1800s, most notably with Jumbo, the giant <u>African</u> elephant that P.T. Barnum brought to the United States and showed to sell-out crowds at Madison Square Garden in 1882. Back then, people flocked to the circus to catch a glimpse of the world, to see sights they had only read about, and to be entertained. However, many argue that in today's world, people don't have this same need. Besides, elephants in captivity are often abused by inexperienced handlers. Because of protests by animal rights activists, Ringling Bros. and Barnum & Bailey Circus had its <u>last elephant show on May 1, 2016</u>. The elephants took their final bow in Rhode Island before heading to a conservation center in Florida for retirement.

Source 2

Echo the Elephant

One important African elephant matriarch, named Echo by researcher Dr. Cynthia Moss, led a family unit for over 30 years in the Amboseli National Park in Kenya. Scientists learned many things about elephant matriarchs by observing Echo. Echo was good at her job—she demonstrated an <u>amazing ability to remember water sources in dry, harsh conditions</u>. In her time as matriarch, Echo did it all, from <u>fending off territorial elephant families</u> to <u>caring for her family's children</u>. One of her calves was born unable to stand and barely able to move. Echo's family stayed with the calf until, after a few dangerous days, he found the strength to stand. Her intelligence and awareness helped demonstrate just how advanced an elephant's brain can be.

Before Reading What I know / think about the topic	• Asian elephants are typically used in circuses, as they are easily trained. • Some circuses have stopped using elephants because of the criticism from animal rights activists. • I have seen circus elephants perform and although they were majestic animals, I always felt sorry for them. • Many elephants are found in parts of Africa and this is a good place to study elephants in the wild.
During Reading How my thinking has changed	• I hadn't thought about why elephants were so popular in the late 1800s, but now I understand why they were. • I'm surprised to learn that Jumbo was an African elephant. I had thought Asian elephants were easier to train. • I'm also amazed that animal rights activists were powerful enough to get a circus as large as Ringling Bros. and Barnum & Bailey to stop using elephants. The protests must have gone on for years and probably were held near the circuses. • Reading about Echo reminds me of animal intelligence and that humans are not the only animals that possess great intelligence.
After Reading I now think this (my synthesis)	The readings about Jumbo (the captive elephant) and Echo (the wild one) show how the popular view of elephants has changed over the years. Once seen as unintelligent animals that should be used for entertainment (in circuses, zoos), elephants are now recognized for their enormous intelligence. Because of this, people are starting to demand more humane treatment of these amazing animals.

VOCABULARY PREVIEW

Read the vocabulary items in the box. Circle the ones you know. Put a question mark next to the ones you don't know.

draws on	resources	split (v)	reliable
disagreements	targeted		

EXERCISE 3

A. You will read a new passage and reread another. The topic of the first is how elephants organize themselves within a matriarchal structure—in other words, how females lead elephant families. The second focuses on the elephant matriarch Echo. Before you read, think about the topic and note in the top row of the chart what you already know about elephant matriarchs and Echo.

Before Reading What I know / think about the topic	
During Reading How my thinking has changed	
After Reading I now think this (my synthesis)	

B. Think about the information you noted. At this point, do you think you know a lot about the topic? What questions do you hope the readings will explain? Discuss with a partner.

EXERCISE 4

A. The passages on the next two pages explain the family structure of elephants. What words do you associate with this topic? Add to the mind map.

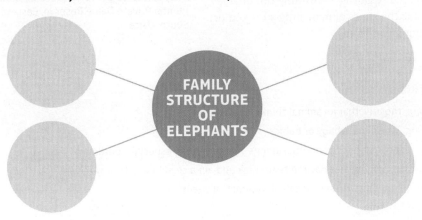

FAMILY STRUCTURE OF ELEPHANTS

B. Now read the two passages. As you read, fill in the "During Reading" row of the chart on the previous page. Then answer the questions that follow the passages.

Large and in Charge

1 A family of elephants is led by a matriarch. This older female draws on her experience and knowledge to help her family survive. Elephants are known for having amazing memories. This is especially true of matriarchs. The matriarch knows the food and water resources throughout a territory, remembers the behaviors and characteristics of hundreds of other elephants, and takes care of the needs of her family, including keeping them safe from danger. Elephant family groups usually include a matriarch, her sisters, and their offspring. Male elephants stay with the family while they are young but leave the family sometime in their teens.

2 Elephant families are described as a "fission-fusion" society—elephants can move from one branch of the family to another, under certain conditions. Large families will often split into smaller family units, especially when resources are few and they need to cover more ground. Sometimes this can all occur in a single day, as families leave to forage and come back together around watering holes at night. Generally, though, the matriarch keeps close ties to her closest relatives. On the other hand, few elephants would risk leaving a reliable matriarch. Matriarchs aren't *completely* in control, however; while other elephants will generally follow her choices and movements, disagreements can happen. Matriarchs heavily influence, but they don't command.

3 [1]Survival instincts seem to decrease in favorable conditions; Asian elephants, with more reliable access to food and water, tend to have looser social groups. [2]For African elephants, though, a strong matriarch is essential. [3]Being a matriarch isn't easy. [4]Matriarchs are big and are often targeted by poachers for their remarkable tusks. [5]A family that loses its matriarch in a violent way often falls apart; some replacement matriarchs have even been observed "quitting"—running off, unable to take the stress of managing a broken or traumatized family.

A female matriarch leads her herd, including baby calves, to a favorite watering hole in Pumba Private Game Reserve, Eastern Cape, South Africa

Glossary

Territory: the area that an animal thinks is its own

Offspring: an animal's baby or babies

Forage: to search for food or other things you may need, especially outdoors

Survival instinct: the natural ability to think and act a certain way to stay alive

Poacher: someone who kills or catches animals illegally

Echo the Elephant

One important African elephant matriarch, named Echo by researcher Dr. Cynthia Moss, led a family unit for over 30 years in the Amboseli National Park in Kenya. Scientists learned many things about elephant matriarchs by observing Echo. Echo was good at her job—she demonstrated an amazing ability to remember water sources in dry, harsh conditions. In her time as

Echo, being viewed by members of the Amboseli Trust For Elephants

matriarch, Echo did it all, from fending off territorial elephant families to caring for her family's children. One of her calves was born unable to stand and barely able to move. Echo's family stayed with the calf until, after a few dangerous days, he found the strength to stand. Her intelligence and awareness helped demonstrate just how advanced an elephant's brain can be.

CULTURE NOTE

Elephants are not the only animals to live in a matriarchal family structure. Honeybees, ants, killer whales, lions, and bonobos (a type of great ape) also live in families led by females. There are also some human societies where females rule. The Mosuo, in southwest China, is one of the largest matrilineal societies—property is passed down to females and marriage doesn't exist. Another matriarchal structure is the Bribri in Costa Rica—women inherit land, children enter the mother's clan, and grandmothers are regarded highly as they pass down traditions from one generation to the next.

Passage 1

1. What is NOT mentioned as a responsibility of an elephant matriarch?

   a. to remember the location of food and water supplies
   b. to care for her family
   c. to teach other family members correct behavior
   d. to protect the family from harm

2. Which is implied by Paragraph 2?

   a. Resources, like food and water, are easily found by elephants.
   b. A matriarch controls every move of her elephant family.
   c. Elephant families always stay together.
   d. Elephants not led by a reliable matriarch live at greater risk.

3. In Paragraph 2, the word *command* is closest in meaning to _____ .

   a. give orders
   b. understand
   c. be in power
   d. persuade

4. In Paragraph 3, Sentence 2, it can be inferred that matriarchs are _____ .

   a. more valuable than males
   b. valuable to their families
   c. easily protected
   d. often killed

5. Which suggests why Asian elephant families are not as rigid?

   a. Paragraph 3, Sentence 1
   b. Paragraph 3, Sentence 3
   c. Paragraph 3, Sentence 4
   d. Paragraph 3, Sentence 5

Passage 2

6. The passage about Echo _____ .

   a. shows the importance of an elephant matriarch
   b. persuades readers that elephants should not be killed
   c. explains how scientists study captive elephants
   d. demonstrates how elephants react to danger

C. **Reread the passages and check your answers in Parts A and B.**

D. **Look back at the chart on page 65. Think about your knowledge before you read and what you learned during the readings to help synthesize your ideas. Complete the "After Reading" row with a synthesis of the two sources.**

EXERCISE 5

Discuss your reading experience with one or more students.

1. When synthesizing, it's useful to look first at how your sources are similar and different. When you compare your information in the "Before" row to the information in the "During" row, what changes occurred? Did one or both courses contribute to this change? In other words, what are the similarities in the passages? What are some of the differences? How can this help shape your new view on the subject?

2. Synthesizing is a skill you use every day. When you listen to the news and then compare it to similar information you read online, you are synthesizing. Think of a time when you compared two sources on the same topic. Was it something you did for class or something you did for fun? What was the experience like?

VOCABULARY CHECK

A. Review the vocabulary items in the Vocabulary Preview. Write their definitions and add examples. Use a dictionary if necessary.

B. Read each sentence. Circle the word or phrase that is the best synonym for the underlined vocabulary item.

1. If students draw on reading skills when reading difficult material, they can better understand the material.

   attract   illustrate   use

2. When traveling where water resources are scarce, like the Sahara Desert, it's important to always have enough water.

   help   sources   restaurants

3. In some matriarchal families, like the Aka community of central Africa, family members split responsibilities evenly between men and women.

   divide   tear   manage

4. Echo, the matriarch of an elephant family in Kenya's Amboseli National Park, was a reliable research subject and was studied for over 40 years by the same researcher, Dr. Cynthia Moss.

   dependable   gentle   strong

5. Disagreements are common in all families, as not everyone will agree all the time on every topic.

   dissatisfaction   arguments   conversations

6. Unfortunately, many wild animals are targeted by hunters who want to have a trophy for their wall and bragging rights with their friends.

   attacked   pointed   affected

◑ Go to MyEnglishLab to complete vocabulary and skill practices, and to join in collaborative activities.

INTEGRATED SKILLS
WRITING QUOTATIONS TO SUPPORT IDEAS

WHY IT'S USEFUL By using quotations, you can add support to your ideas and make your writing more engaging.

As a student, you are often asked to write research papers. You might want to take language directly from one of your sources. In this case, you use **quotations**. Here are three ways to use quotations:

1. A **direct quotation** contains the exact words a person said or wrote. These are put inside quotation marks. A signal phrase introducing the speaker of the quotation or author of the text usually comes before or after the quotation. In academic papers, direct quotations should be limited—most information should be paraphrased (see below). When used, a direct quotation should be connected to your topic and strengthen your argument. For example:

   > In her 2016 autobiography, elephant researcher Darci Chang says, "In 2010, Zoe, a young elephant I was studying, gave birth. Being on that journey with her made me a believer in the need to protect these animals."

2. An **indirect quotation** is when you report what someone said or wrote, without using his or her exact words. No quotation marks are necessary, but credit must be given to the source. Indirect quotations help to support your ideas. Here are two variations of indirect quotation:

Reported speech is very close to direct quotation, the main differences being that there are no quotation marks and there is a change in tense: You must backshift the verb tense, and it may be necessary to change the pronoun. For example:

> According to elephant researcher Darci Chang in her 2016 autobiography, Zoe, a young elephant that Chang had been studying, gave birth. Being on that journey with Zoe made Chang a believer in the need to protect elephants.

A **paraphrase** is looser than reported speech. You capture the speaker's main ideas, but in your own words. For example:

> Researcher Darci Chang studied a young elephant throughout the two-year gestation period, until the elephant gave birth in 2010. In her autobiography, Chang writes that the experience convinced her that it was important to protect the species.

SEQUENCE OF TENSES

Direct Speech		Indirect Speech
Simple present	→	Simple past
Present continuous	→	Past continuous
Present perfect	→	Past perfect
Simple past	→	Past perfect

3. A **hybrid quotation** (mixed quotation) is when you include directly quoted material with an indirect quotation. This is a good way to use important source language but present it in your own words. For example:

> For researcher Darci Chang, who spent time with an elephant named Zoe, the experience was transformative. In her 2016 autobiography, Chang writes that it made her "a believer" in the need to protect elephants.

TIPS

- Whenever quoting a source, give credit to that source. If you don't, it's considered plagiarism.
- Use a variety of quotations—direct, indirect, and hybrid. It makes your writing more interesting and can strengthen your argument.
- In science writing, indirect quotations are preferred, whereas in literature classes, direct quotations are more common as you typically have to directly cite passages of text.
- Direct quotations that are four lines or longer are often formatted differently—inset within the text—and quotation marks are not needed.

VOCABULARY PREVIEW

Read the vocabulary items in the box. Circle the ones you know. Put a question mark next to the ones you don't know.

at home	personality	aimed	doubled	cruel
point out	perform	public	harm (n)	

EXERCISE 6

A. Do you think it's OK to have animals in circuses and in zoos? Why or why not? Discuss with a partner.

B. Read the article. Then read and identify the quotation types that follow.

Living in Captivity

1 Zoos and circuses have come a long way. A hundred years ago, it was common to find elephants exhibited by zoos in empty, concrete-floored spaces—or in large cages. Circus elephants did no better. If they stayed alive and didn't kill anyone, they were given the most basic of care.

2 Today, zookeepers try to make elephants feel at home. But how much does it help? Animal rights activists and elephant experts question the ethics of any use of elephants as entertainment. Wild elephants travel an enormous and varied amount of land, socializing with hundreds of other elephants in their lifetime. Can an exhibit or circus compare? At the very least, how are such groups working to keep elephants safe and healthy?

3 Socially, elephant families are loose. Individuals will join and leave different family units depending on personality. An elephant that has a disagreement with one family, for example, may find her way to a relative that is more agreeable. In a zoo, elephants are often kept with each other, sometimes with no thought about gender, age, or personality. This situation has improved in recent years, but even the best zoos find it difficult to give elephants the sort of social life they need. Dr. Rob Atkinson of the RSPCA (Royal Society for the Prevention of Cruelty to Animals) says, "Elephant handlers try to dominate elephants by psychological means, physical restriction, and punishment, a system known as traditional free contact. … While elephants are still kept in zoos, the RSPCA wants their management to be based on reward, not punishment, and for keepers to be protected from death and injury."

4 Physically, zoos are uncomfortable for elephants. Constantly walking over the same small area of land affects an elephant's feet because the ground is packed down to hard earth. Because there is little space to walk, elephants in zoos often show so-called repetitive stress actions like swaying. These disorders are common in captive elephants. Dr. Joyce Poole, an admired elephant researcher who followed the elephant population of Amboseli National Park in Kenya for 34 years, said, "Wild elephants do not develop foot problems; they are not seen swaying rhythmically back and forth." Her research has found zero incidents of such behavior in over 34,000 sightings of groups containing up to 550 elephants.

5 Zookeepers try to work around these problems through programs aimed at making living spaces more comfortable. Mark Reed, executive director of the Sedgwick County Zoo in Wichita, Kansas, explained, "These days, moats and glass have replaced cages; there are education departments and conservation initiatives."

Toys, interesting-smelling plants, and water sources all help keep a living area interesting. Reed argues that full-time veterinarians and better diets have doubled and in some cases tripled animals' lifespans in captivity. Although these improvements certainly help, captivity is still an unnatural state for an elephant. Captive elephants, on average, have a much shorter lifespan than wild elephants—even when accounting for death by poachers and predators.

6 If zoos are unnatural for an elephant, a circus environment is truly cruel. Activists are quick to point out that almost all acts done by elephants are based on fear of pain. There is simply no way, they say, to make elephants perform without threatening them with pain. Humane Society CEO Wayne Pacelle, describing a circus elephant's training, said, "They're sometimes hit with bullhooks," an iron tool used to hit an elephant's sensitive areas. In addition, Pacelle said, "They're often on chains for 20 to 22 hours a day. And they're really sent on boxcars on railroads to 100, 115 cities a year ... That's no life for an elephant. These are highly intelligent, sociable animals." Atkinson of the RSPCA agrees: "Asking these majestic animals to behave in unnatural ways in the name of entertainment is a disgrace."

7 The public seems to agree with these experts. Many large circuses are closing their elephant shows, moving their elephants to wildlife sanctuaries, and focusing on other forms of entertainment that hopefully cause less harm.

Glossary

Captivity: the state of being kept as a prisoner or in a small space

Exhibit: (v) to put something in a public place so that people can see it; (n) a public display

Cage: (n) a structure made of wires or bars

Veterinarian: someone who is trained to give medical care and treatment to animals

Lifespan: the amount of time that someone or something will live

Chain: (n) a series of metal rings connected together

CULTURE NOTE

The RSPCA and the Humane Society of the United States are not-for-profit organizations committed to animal welfare. The RSPCA is headquartered in the United Kingdom and has animal protection missions around the world. Its goal is to stop the suffering of animals and encourage kindness toward them. The Humane Society targets issues including factory farming of animals, animal fighting, fur trade, and puppy mills.

1. Dr. Rob Atkinson of the RSPCA (Royal Society for the Prevention of Cruelty to Animals) says that elephant handlers try to control elephants psychologically, physically, and by punishing them.

   a. direct   b. indirect   c. hybrid

2. Dr. Joyce Poole, an elephant researcher, says that unlike captive elephants, elephants in the wild are not seen "swaying rhythmically back and forth."

   a. direct   b. indirect   c. hybrid

3. Mark Reed, executive director of the Sedgwick County Zoo in Wichita, Kansas, explained, "These days, moats and glass have replaced cages; there are education departments and conservation initiatives."

   a. direct   b. indirect   c. hybrid

4. Reed also said that full-time vets and better diets had doubled and in some cases tripled animals' lifespans in captivity.

   a. direct   b. indirect   c. hybrid

5. Wayne Pacelle, CEO of the Humane Society, described circus training that included physical abuse. "They're sometimes hit with bullhooks," he said, explaining that the iron tool is used to hit an elephant's sensitive areas.

   a. direct   b. indirect   c. hybrid

6. In addition, Pacelle said, "They're often on chains for 20 to 22 hours a day. And they're really sent on boxcars on railroads to 100, 115 cities a year … That's no life for an elephant. These are highly intelligent, sociable animals."

   a. direct   b. indirect   c. hybrid

C. Reread the article. Then answer the questions.

1. According to the article, what are some of the problems faced by elephants in zoos?

   ....

   ....

2. Why does the author include Mark Reed's quotations in the article?

   ....

   ....

3. What purpose is served by including Dr. Joyce Poole's and Wayne Pacelle's quotations?

   ....

   ....

4. What do some zoos do to try to keep elephants safe?

....

....

5. What elephant training method is criticized in the article?

....

....

6. What is the author's opinion of keeping elephants in captivity? What textual evidence supports this?

....

....

D. Discuss these questions with a partner.

1. In this article, is there a balance of quotations with other information? Explain.

2. What are some of the reporting verbs used to introduce the quotations? Do any of these verbs express the attitudes or feelings of the speaker?

3. Have you ever used quotations in your writing? In an academic setting, what can happen if you forget to give credit or don't include quotation marks with a direct quotation?

E. Write a two-paragraph reaction to the article "Living in Captivity." Follow these steps:

1. In the first paragraph: Summarize the article. Quote some part of it—either directly or indirectly, or a combination (hybrid).

2. In the second paragraph: Respond to the article, including the quoted material, by relating it to your life, connecting it to something you know about, or agreeing or disagreeing with it. Try to use some of the words from the box.

3. Compare reaction paragraphs with a partner. Explain why you used the quotations you did.

cage	veterinarian	lifespan	captivity	exhibit
chain	at home	personality	aim	double
point out	cruel	perform	public	harm

VOCABULARY CHECK

A. Review the vocabulary items in the Vocabulary Preview. Write their definitions and add examples. Use a dictionary if necessary.

B. Complete each sentence using the correct vocabulary item from the box. Use the correct form.

aim	at home	cruel	double	harm
perform	personality	point out	public	

1. Although animals sometimes appear to be .... in their zoo enclosures, more often than not, they are not comfortable and would be better off in the wild.

2. Zookeepers are sometimes seriously hurt or even killed by elephants or other captive animals, which is a reminder that these animals are wild—not pets and can do ....

3. Like humans, elephants have different .... Some are friendly, some are quiet, some are curious, and so on.

4. Zoo owners are quick to .... that elephants who live in captivity never need to worry about finding adequate food or water, as these resources are always readily available.

5. There is some good news in the animal world. The number of amur leopards—the world's rarest cat—.......................... between 2007 and 2015, increasing from 30 to nearly 60.

6. For animals to .... is unnatural. They don't naturally do "tricks."

7. You can blame circus owners and zookeepers. But the ....—the people who pay money to see these animals performing or in cages—is also part of the problem.

8. Traditionally .... at children and people who wanted to see wild animals in person, circuses hid their mistreatment of the animals from the public.

9. People who are .... to animals—hurting them, confining them, or not giving them care—are more likely to hurt humans, as well.

🕤 Go to MyEnglishLab to complete a skill practice and to join in collaborative activities.

LANGUAGE SKILL
EXPRESSING CONTRAST AND CONCESSION

WHY IT'S USEFUL By using language that expresses contrast and language that expresses concession, you can more clearly show the logic of an idea.

⊙ Go to MyEnglishLab for the Language Skill presentation and practice.

VOCABULARY STRATEGY
IMPROVING RECEPTIVE AND PRODUCTIVE VOCABULARY

WHY IT'S USEFUL By learning strategies for increasing receptive vocabulary and productive vocabulary, you can become more fluent and better able to communicate your ideas.

Receptive vocabulary knowledge refers to your ability to understand a word when you see or hear it. In other words, you *receive* the information and decode the meaning of the word.

Productive vocabulary knowledge refers to your ability to use a word when you write or speak; that is, you use the word in speaking or writing to *produce* your idea.

Generally, we learn words receptively. Then, through writing or speaking practice, we can use them productively. It is common for language students to have a much larger receptive vocabulary than productive vocabulary.

Strategies to Increase Receptive Vocabulary
- Notice new words. Then figure out their meaning by
  - thinking about the context: What is the general meaning?
  - searching the context for definitions, synonyms, antonyms, and examples.
  - checking your dictionary.
- Study word lists (e.g., Academic Word List) or your own vocabulary word lists.
- Learn definitions of new words, notice word families, and study collocations.

Strategies to Increase Productive Vocabulary Knowledge
- Write sentences, paraphrases, and summaries using the new vocabulary.
- Use the new vocabulary in speaking: Speak to yourself—or better, with others.
- Tell a story, either in writing or by speaking, and use the new word(s).
- Associate each word with something from your life.
- Use physical actions to learn; for example, to learn *trudge*: Walk slowly with heavy steps as you learn the word.
- Teach the vocabulary to another student or friend.

EXERCISE 7

A. Complete the words. Look for context clues to help you. Use a dictionary, if needed.

1. The elephants' **enor**............. tusks make the animals a target for poachers.

2. The African savanna elephant and the African forest elephant are not the same **spe**............. , but they have many similarities.

3. Some animal rights activists are **opt**............. about the future of the Asian elephant, while others are extremely pessimistic and fear for its survival.

4. When faced by a predator, a bull elephant may **chal**............. it by charging, or running at, the threat.

5. The researcher has studied elephants for over 30 years, and her work has always been considered very **rel**............. ; it has never been proven wrong.

6. Keeping a wild animal in **cap**............. is cruel.

B. Answer each question with a vocabulary item. The first letter of each word is provided. Use context clues to help you. Then use the word in an example sentence.

1. In what types of structures are animals contained?

   Vocabulary item: c............. Sentence: ....

   ....

2. What is the title of the person who trains athletes?

   Vocabulary item: t............. Sentence: ....

   ....

3. Farmers who grow crops or raise livestock, such as cattle, are in what type of business?

   Vocabulary item: a............. Sentence: ....

   ....

4. What do some animal trainers and zoo workers put around the legs of large animals?

   Vocabulary item: c............. Sentence: ....

   ....

5. What is the part of a plant that attaches the plant to the ground and brings food and water to it?

Vocabulary item: r................................ Sentence: ....

....

6. In New York City, the Empire State Building, the Statue of Liberty, and Times Square are examples of what?

Vocabulary item: t............. a............. Sentence: ....

....

C. Write a fictional or nonfictional story about an animal. Try to use most of these words.

disagreement	engaging	explore	be fond of	harm (n)
influence (n)	point out	resource	slightly	

🔊 Go to MyEnglishLab to complete a skill practice.

APPLY YOUR SKILLS

WHY IT'S USEFUL By applying the skills you have learned in this unit, you will have a better understanding of this challenging reading about the effects of poaching on elephant families.

BEFORE YOU READ

A. Discuss these questions with one or more students.

1. What do you know about animal poaching? What animals are targeted by poachers and why?

2. What effects may poaching have on animals?

3. What should be the punishment for poachers?

B. You will read an article about the effects of poaching on elephant families. As you read, think about these questions.

1. What are some of the problems that elephant populations have today?

2. How do elephants react when their matriarch is violently killed?

3. How have some elephants adapted to the problems of poaching?

C. Review the Unit Skills Summary. As you read the article, apply the skills you learned in this unit.

UNIT SKILLS SUMMARY

MANAGE MULTIPLE SOURCES BY USING THESE SKILLS:

Make associations

- Make connections between the text and your background knowledge of the topic.

Synthesize information

- Combine information from various sources to come up with a new understanding of the text.

Write quotations to support ideas

- Recognize and use other speakers' words to express information.

Express contrast and concession

- Use contrastive and concessive expressions to indicate slight differences in meaning.

Improve receptive and productive vocabulary

- Use strategies to expand both your passive and active use of vocabulary.

READ

A. Read the article on the next page. Annotate and take notes. After each paragraph, record your associations in the chart.

Text to Self (What does this remind me of in my life? What are my feelings as I read this? What have I learned?)	
Text to Text (This article reminds me of another article because …)	
Text to World (This article reminds me of a movie / documentary / TV show / conversation / social media video or image …)	

Glossary

Urbanization: the movement of people to and the construction of buildings in the countryside

Migratory route: the pathways that animals use to move from one area to another

Climate change: important changes that have happened to weather patterns during periods of Earth's history, leading to higher- or lower-than-average temperatures, amounts of rain, and so on

Grieve: to feel extremely sad, especially because someone you love has died

Vulnerable: easy to harm, hurt, or attack

Predation: the act of hunting

Trauma: a state of extreme shock that is caused by a very bad or frightening experience

Dominant: strongest, most important, or most noticeable

Ecological: relating to the way that plants, animals, and people are connected to each other and to their environment

Evolve: to develop and change over time

The Long-Term Effects of Poaching

1 The past 50 years have been a difficult time for elephants. Researchers suggest that almost 90 percent of the world's elephant population has been killed in recent decades. The problems that elephants have are many. Increased urbanization cuts off migratory routes. Climate change affects the availability of water. And poachers are an ever-present threat. Elephants adjust to these threats as best as they can; in many ways, it is the creature's problem with poachers that demands the most immediate change. Poachers often target older elephants for their tusks; thus, poachers often take "leaders" away from their elephant families. Without a matriarch, leaderless herds often develop unhealthy behaviors. Scientists need to understand these stress reactions to better help elephants survive difficult conditions.

2 An elephant matriarch leads a family of around a dozen elephants. These matriarchs, older and larger females, are very important to a family's survival. Iain Douglas-Hamilton, an elephant researcher and founder of Save the Elephants, believes that the matriarchs' memory is invaluable. In a 2013 interview with the blog site *A Voice for Elephants*, Douglas-Hamilton explains that elephants' sharp memories allow them to know "when and where to move, or where to avoid," which is especially important for a herd's survival. Because older elephants have larger, more developed tusks, they are a favorite target of poachers. The initial shock of losing a matriarch can leave an elephant family barely able to survive. The family will have a difficult time dealing with unusual situations. Elephants grieve quite deeply, and a grieving family can suffer emotionally for a long time. This grief has led to violent acts of revenge in which grieving elephants attempt to attack poachers. Sadly, these situations usually end poorly for the elephants.

Effects on Behavior

3 When poachers kill all of the adult elephants in a region, the result is young elephants left alone, orphaned. As Douglas-Hamilton explains, "We know that the orphans have much lower prospects of survival because they're more vulnerable to predation, being lost, and taking the wrong decisions."

(Continued)

In other words, these orphans are much more likely to be targeted by lions or hyenas or just not know where to go. Surviving orphans may join up with other families, but this is not an easy change. There is no promise that they will be treated well by a strange family. Such elephants often show signs of emotional trauma, staying emotionally distant for years.

4 Sometimes, orphans are forced to form families consisting of orphan elephants. These families lack the "generational wisdom"—the years of knowledge—of their elders. Orphan families often struggle with a lack of leadership. The matriarch of these families, often unusually young, has a high amount of stress that she is probably unprepared for. While some elephants will rise to the occasion, researchers have seen many young orphan-matriarchs who are unable to deal with the stress. Research accounts describe orphan matriarchs that "quit" their new family, running off and separating just to avoid the stress of unprepared leadership.

Confiscated elephant tusks

Effects on Development

5 Some African elephants are, through genetics, benefitting from a new survival strategy. Due to poachers repeatedly targeting elephants that have large tusks, an increasing number of female elephants are growing up to be tuskless. This characteristic often occurs when a few tuskless elephants are the only survivors of a major poaching event—tuskless elephants are simply the only ones that survive to reproduce. With no other elephants around, these tuskless elephants have free access to large amount of food. Furthermore, elephants in this situation often have calves more often than normal, thus increasing the number of tuskless elephants.

6 Some think tuskless elephants may become the dominant form of elephant in certain ecological areas. Tuskless elephants might be a lot safer from poachers, but there are disadvantages. Tusks evolved to help elephants dig for food and defend themselves. Tuskless elephants are less likely to be killed but more likely to have trouble with finding food and protecting their young. It's unusual to see such a big change in a species in such a short period of time. Time will tell what kind of effect these changes will have on the elephant population.

CULTURE NOTE

Articles or documentaries about poaching often focus on the effects that it has on elephants without exploring the underlying reasons why poaching is so common. In many of the areas where animals are poached, unemployment and poverty rates are high. Poaching, or serving as guides to poachers, is a source of money.

B. Compare notes with a partner. Did you have the same connections to the text?

C. Reread the questions in Before You Read, Part B. With your partner, use your notes and opinions to answer the questions.

◐ Go to MyEnglishLab to read more closely, answer the critical thinking questions, and complete a summarizing activity.

THINKING CRITICALLY

Use information from the reading to answer these questions.

1. The reading explores the effects of poaching on elephant behavior and physical development. Based on this information, predict what will happen to the elephant population.

   ....

   ....

2. What can be done on an individual, local, and / or national level to stop the poaching of elephants and the sale of ivory tusks?

   ....

   ....

THINKING VISUALLY

Use information from this map to answer the questions on the next page.

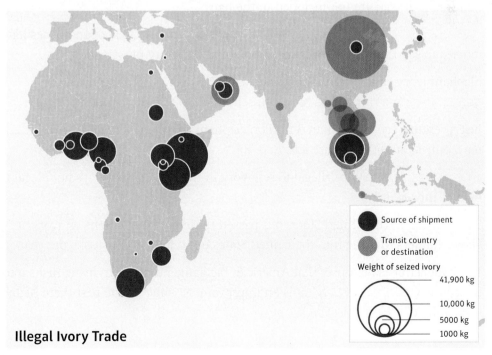

Source of shipment

Transit country or destination

Weight of seized ivory

41,900 kg

10,000 kg

5000 kg

1000 kg

Illegal Ivory Trade

1. Look at the map on the previous page showing the trade of illegal ivory. Where does the ivory mostly come from? Where is it going? Cross reference the map with a world atlas and add country names. Is there anything surprising? What can you infer about the trade of ivory? Explain.

   ....

   ....

2. Scan this unit for statistics (numbers that tell a story) about elephants to create a new graphic. What does it show?

THINKING ABOUT LANGUAGE

A. Complete the sentences. Use the words from the box to make expressions of contrast or concession. More than one correct answer may be possible.

> For help with expressing contrast and concession, go to MyEnglishLab, Zoology, Part 1, Language Skill.

although	despite	whereas	though
however	but	while	on the other hand

1. .... the sale of new ivory is strictly prohibited in the United States, this country still provides a large market for its illegal trade.

2. In 2016, the Obama administration passed a law forbidding the sale of most ivory items; .... , antique ivory items that can be proven to be more than a hundred years old are not included in the ban.

3. .... being allowed to sell antique ivory, many US auction houses have refused to sell those items because of potential difficulty proving their age.

4. Elephant ivory can be sold for as much as $1,500 per pound in Asia, ... a rhinoceros horn can sell for up to $25,000 a pound.

5. Just a century ago, more than 3 million elephants roamed Africa; .... now, only about 500,000 are left.

6. .... it may be illegal to sell ivory in the United States, it's not illegal to own or inherit it.

7. .... the United States has passed these new regulations on ivory, it allows hunters to bring into the United States up to four trophy tusks per year.

8. Elephant activists are upset that American big game hunters can bring tusks into the country. .... , it is an improvement, since in the past there hadn't been a limit.

B. Write a statement about each set of topics, using an expression of contrast. Then write a statement of concession. Try to use new vocabulary in your statements to help turn your receptive vocabulary into productive vocabulary.

1. Asian elephants vs. African elephants

....

....

2. female elephants vs. male elephants

....

....

3. matriarch elephants vs. younger elephants

....

....

4. captive elephants vs. wild elephants

....

....

5. poaching elephants vs. protecting elephants

....

....

6. selling ivory vs. buying ivory

....

....

↻ Go to MyEnglishLab to watch Professor O'Connell-Rodwell's concluding video and to complete a self-assessment.

The past is full of new discoveries

HISTORY

Reading Fluency

UNIT PROFILE

In this unit, you will learn about two "accidental" archaeological discoveries and their importance in providing information about societies of the past. Specifically, you will read about the discoveries of the ruins at Pompeii and the Rosetta Stone. In the final reading of the unit, you will consider the issue of ownership.

Look at the reading "Who Owns the Rosetta Stone?" on page 111. Skim the reading. How much time would you need to read it and fully understand it?

OUTCOMES

• Increase smoothness and pace to build fluency
• Develop accuracy
• Read aloud to build fluency and comprehension
• Identify thought groups
• Recognize collocations

For more about **HISTORY**, see ❷❸. See also ⌊W⌋ and ⌊OC⌋ **HISTORY** ❶❷❸.

GETTING STARTED

◐ Go to MyEnglishLab to watch Dr. Hunt's introductory video and to complete a self-assessment.

Discuss these questions with a partner or group.

1. Archaeology is the study of ancient societies by examining what remains of buildings, graves, tools, and so on. What do you think about when you hear the word *archaeology*?

2. Why is it important to find, preserve, and study relics (objects from a past time)?

3. In his introduction, Dr. Hunt mentions two important archaeological discoveries. What are they? How do you think they have helped advance our understanding of history?

SKILL 1

INCREASING SMOOTHNESS AND PACE TO BUILD FLUENCY

WHY IT'S USEFUL By increasing smoothness and pace, you can become a more efficient reader—saving you time—and improve your English comprehension.

Fluency is composed of two parts: the ability to read smoothly and at a steady pace—that is, without hesitating or stopping—and the ability to fully understand what you read. In higher education, students are expected to read extensively on a wide range of topics. In order to complete the work and get the most out of reading, it's essential that you develop the ability to read quickly and understand. Although it takes time to develop, reading smoothly and at a steady pace will help you become more fluent.

Techniques for Reading Faster

- **Read every day**. The more you read, the more vocabulary you will know, and the easier it will become to read quickly.

- **Read silently**. Do not read aloud or move your lips when reading. If you read aloud, your brain is thinking about two things: pronunciation and comprehension.

- **Do not translate** into your first language—you will be thinking in your first language and not in English.

- **Read in chunks**. Don't read each word individually and think about every word's meaning. Reading in chunks helps you read more smoothly. Consider the following examples and which is easier to read:

Pompeii	is	one	of	the	only	archaeological	sites	from	the	Roman	era

that	shows	us	how	ordinary	people	lived.

Pompeii is	one of the only	archaeological sites	from the Roman era	that shows us

how ordinary people lived.

- **Skip over unknown words**. It's not necessary to understand every word in order to comprehend a text.

- **Guess meaning from context**. Don't slow your reading by looking up an unknown word online or in a dictionary. Instead, look at the surrounding information. Sometimes logic will tell you the meaning. Consider this example. Assume the bolded word is an unknown word:

> Rocks fell from the sky, causing people to tie pillows to their heads for **protection**.

Using logic, ask yourself, "What are the pillows on their heads for? Protection." You can also use word parts to try to understand meaning. For example, what part of the following bolded word do you recognize?

> Pompeii is an archaeological site—one that has been continuously **excavated** since its rediscovery in 1748.

The prefix *ex-* is in many words you already know—*exit, excuse, exam*. It means "out" or "without." So, given the subject area—archaeology—you might guess that *excavate* means "to take out."

- **Time yourself**. Time yourself reading a passage once. Then read it again but force yourself to do it a little faster. Then read it again and go even faster. Repetition has been shown to improve fluency.

VOCABULARY PREVIEW
Read the vocabulary items in the box. Circle the ones you know. Put a question mark next to the ones you don't know.

port	goods	trade (v)	soil (n)
wealthy	escaping	citizens	disaster

EXERCISE 1

A. Review the techniques for reading faster. Then read this excerpt, the introductory paragraph to "Understanding Pompeii." Write your start and finish times. Calculate your reading time.

Start Time: .... Finish Time: .... Reading Time: ....

> Pompeii was a city of the Roman Empire and a thriving port on the southwest coast of the Italian peninsula. Ships brought goods from as far as India and the Arabian Peninsula to trade in Pompeii. The land had rich, fertile soil, and local people grew many different crops. Wealthy Romans treated Pompeii and the neighboring city of Herculaneum like resort towns. Yet tragedy struck the city in 79 CE when the nearby Mount Vesuvius—a volcano—erupted.

Review the techniques again. Then reread the paragraph and write your start and finish times. Calculate your reading time. Did it change?

Start Time: .... Finish Time: .... Reading Time: ....

B. How long did it take to read the paragraph the first time? Did you read it faster the second time? If you read it a third time, do you think you would read it even faster? What did you do when you came across a word you didn't know? In general, do you consider yourself a slow, average, or fast reader in English?

EXERCISE 2

A. Based on the introductory paragraph, what do you think the article will be about? Check (✓) your idea.

☐ a brief history of the city of Pompeii

☐ an explanation of who discovered Pompeii

☐ an introduction to Italian architecture

TIP

When reading fluently, don't stop to look up words you don't know—guess the meaning from the context or skip over them. Why? Because when you read at a steady pace, your overall comprehension is better. Constantly turning to a dictionary will slow your reading down, will prevent you from reading in chunks, and can distract you from the main idea of the text.

B. Write your start and finish times as you read the whole article. Calculate your reading time.

Start Time: ....   Finish Time: ....   Reading Time: ....

Understanding Pompeii

1 Pompeii was a city of the Roman Empire and a thriving port on the southwest coast of the Italian peninsula. Ships brought goods from as far as India and the Arabian Peninsula to trade in Pompeii. The land had rich, fertile soil, and local people grew many different crops. Wealthy Romans treated Pompeii and the neighboring city of Herculaneum like resort towns. Yet tragedy struck the city in 79 CE when the nearby Mount Vesuvius—a volcano—erupted.

2 Clouds of smoke and ash erupted from the mountain, soon settling in the surrounding area. Pliny the Younger, who would later become famous as a Roman author, watched the eruption from far to the west. He described the smoke, ash, and spread of darkness throughout the surrounding area: "We had scarcely sat down to rest when darkness fell, not the dark of a moonless or cloudy night, but as if the lamp had been put out in a closed room." Back in Pompeii, darkness was the least of the city's problems. Rocks fell from the sky, causing people to tie pillows to their heads for protection. Many fled, but thousands died before escaping—buried in burning ash or suffocating in deadly volcanic fumes. In the end, the entire city was buried in the ashes of Vesuvius.

3 While the eruption was a tragedy for Roman citizens, the disaster was of enormous benefit to historians. The volcanic ash that ended Pompeii also preserved it—a once living city frozen in a single moment. Centuries later, archaeologists have learned more about Roman life, culture, and art from Pompeii than from any other ancient archaeological site.

4 Pompeii is one of the only archaeological sites from the Roman era that shows us how ordinary people lived. Other great works of architecture and Latin literature mainly show us the life of Rome's wealthy, educated men. In Pompeii, we see how the rest of the empire lived: We learn about poor citizens, slaves, women, and even pets from artwork, graffiti, literature, architecture, and the bodies of the dead themselves. Through this one disaster, we are able to see what life was really like in the ancient world. Today, Pompeii is an archaeological site—one that has been continuously excavated since its rediscovery in 1748. Each generation's archaeologists have used the latest research tools available to document and preserve the ruins of Pompeii. The disaster itself may have been a tragedy, but it is a tragedy that helped give us a valuable window onto the past.

Glossary

Suffocate: to die because there is not enough air

Excavate: to dig up the ground in order to find something that was buried there in an earlier time

CULTURE NOTE

The Roman Empire can be traced back to 27 BCE when Julius Caesar's nephew, Octavian, became Augustus, the first emperor of the Roman Empire. At its height in 117 CE, the Roman Empire encompassed much of modern-day western Europe and some countries of the Middle East. However, its vast size was partly responsible for its demise, as it was difficult for Rome to control the entire area. Romulus Augustulus, the last emperor of the full Roman Empire, was defeated in 476 CE, which marked the end of the Roman Empire.

C. **Without looking back at the article, read the statements. Circle *T* (True) or *F* (False). Correct the false statements. Skip any items you don't feel like you can answer.**

T / F 1. During the Roman Empire, Pompeii was a favorite vacation place for city dwellers.

T / F 2. Because of its inland location, Pompeii was not ideal as a trading center.

T / F 3. Pliny the Younger, who witnessed the eruption, explained that Pompeii turned dark because it had been a moonless night.

T / F 4. It can be inferred from the article that most of the city's residents died from the volcanic eruption.

T / F 5. The volcanic ash caused the residents' death because it made it difficult for them to breathe.

T / F 6. From studying the ruins of Pompeii, people have learned much about life during the Roman Empire.

T / F 7. During the Roman Empire, there was a richness in culture and equality among citizens.

T / F 8. The author believes that although it was a tragedy, the eruption of Mount Vesuvius was key to our understanding of early Roman life.

D. **Reread the article and write your start and finish times. Calculate your reading time. Then go back to Part C and complete any unanswered items. Check your answers in Parts A and C.**

Start Time: .... Finish Time: .... Reading Time: ....

EXERCISE 3

Discuss these questions with a partner.

1. Did your reading time improve when you read the article a second time? Was it easy to understand the main ideas without knowing all the words? Explain.

2. Does your reading speed depend on the type of reading material? Explain.

VOCABULARY CHECK

A. Review the vocabulary items in the Vocabulary Preview. Write their definitions and add examples. Use a dictionary if necessary.

B. Read each sentence. Then write the correct definition of the underlined vocabulary item. Use the definitions from the box.

> to leave a place or dangerous situation
> bought or sold goods or services
> places where ships arrive and leave from
> the earth in which plants grow
> an event—such as a storm—that causes harm or suffering
> people who live in a particular town, state, or country
> things that are bought and sold
> rich

1. In 2014, a <u>disaster</u> struck Japan when Mount Ontake erupted, resulting in 61 deaths.

   Definition: ....

2. A volcanic eruption does not care about class. Both poor and <u>wealthy</u> residents will be affected if they live near a volcano.

   Definition: ....

3. Because of advanced technologies and a better understanding of volcanoes, many researchers can predict when an eruption will occur, which allows people to <u>escape</u> well before the event.

   Definition: ....

4. Many of Italy's southern <u>ports</u> are filled with ships carrying migrants who have fled their countries looking for safety.

   Definition: ....

5. Migrants, who are not <u>citizens</u> of the countries where they arrive, often face discrimination and hardship as they adjust to life in a new country.

   Definition: ....

6. Some migrants offer their services in exchange for <u>goods</u>; for instance, someone who can sew might fix an item of clothing in return for something to eat.

   Definition: ....

7. Farmers prefer to grow crops in <u>soil</u> that is rich in nutrients because it will help their plants to grow quickly.

   Definition: ....

8. In Pompeii, vintners and farmers <u>traded</u>, exchanging wine and agricultural products.

   Definition: ....

⊙ Go to MyEnglishLab to complete vocabulary and skill practices, and to join in collaborative activities.

SKILL 2

DEVELOPING ACCURACY

WHY IT'S USEFUL By increasing accuracy, you can more fully comprehend and engage with the material you are reading.

Accuracy is one component of fluency. Someone who speaks with a high level of accuracy will do so without errors in grammar or pronunciation. In reading, an accurate reader will read at a steady pace without misreading or misinterpreting words. When working on accuracy, the focus is on form and meaning, not speed.

Tips for Being an Accurate Reader:

- Skim the information before you read. Notice the title, headings, and photos. Think about what information you might find in the text. Then read, and while reading, think about the information you are reading.

- Select texts at the appropriate level. Texts that are too challenging will be too difficult to decode and will affect comprehension.

- Notice the grammar.

- Mark keywords that help convey the main idea of the passage. Look for context clues to help you understand challenging vocabulary and note any additional words you want to look up.
- Ask for clarification if something is confusing.

A reader who has developed his or her accuracy skills should be able to read something once and then be able to apply his or her knowledge immediately. Study the following example and student responses, which show the difference between accuracy and inaccuracy in reading.

> Thousands of years ago, Alexander the Great's Macedonian Empire conquered Egypt. Alexander appointed a new king, forming the Ptolemaic Dynasty. Ptolemy I, and his many **descendants**, did not speak or read Egyptian—but Greek.

Student A's understanding:

> **The Macedonian Empire** conquered Egypt. Because Ptolemy I and his **family** were Macedonian, they spoke Greek.

Student B's understanding:

> **Alexander the Greek** conquered Egypt. He then made his **followers** speak Greek.

Student A's understanding of the passage is accurate. Student B's understanding is inaccurate because she misidentifies Alexander the Great and incorrectly defines the word *descendants*.

VOCABULARY PREVIEW

Read the vocabulary items in the box. Circle the ones you know. Put a question mark next to the ones you don't know.

| ruled | stones (n) | royal | notice (v) | odd | confirmed |

EXERCISE 4

A. Review the steps for being an accurate reader. Then read this excerpt from the upcoming article "Understanding the Rosetta Stone." Answer the questions on the next page without looking back at the excerpt.

> Thousands of years ago, Alexander the Great's Macedonian Empire conquered Egypt. Alexander appointed a new king, forming the Ptolemaic Dynasty. Ptolemy I, and his many descendants, did not speak or read Egyptian—but Greek. Still, they ruled Egypt for years, often through royal decrees and proclamation. These decrees were sometimes carved onto steles, long tall stones, and placed in public areas. Kings, priests, and other officials regularly made decrees in this way. They often used hieroglyphs—a system of writing using pictures as letters that had been used in Egypt since ancient times.

1. What country did Alexander the Great's empire conquer?

   ....

2. What was the name of the new king of Egypt that was appointed: Alexander, Macedonia, or Ptolemy I?

   ....

3. What was the first language of the new king and dynasty?

   ....

4. How did royalty communicate new rules and statements to its empire?

   ....

5. What were hieroglyphs?

   ....

B. Place the events from the excerpt in order, along the timeline.

> The Ptolemaic Dynasty is formed.
> Ptolemy I rules Egypt.
> The Macedonian Empire conquers Egypt.
> Ptolemy I's descendants rule Egypt.
> Alexander the Great appoints a new king.

TIP

Timelines are a great way to order information. Even without knowing exact dates, you can order events and better understand the relationships between them.

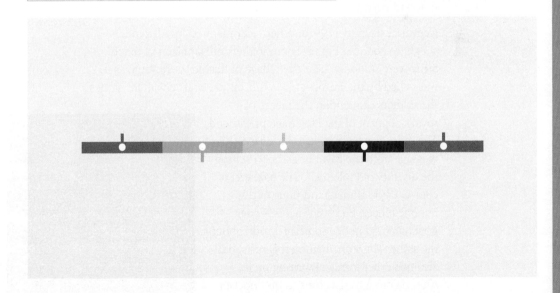

C. Reread the excerpt to check your answers. Did you answer the questions correctly? If yes, your accuracy is great. If you had some errors, what can you do to improve your accuracy?

EXERCISE 5

A. The following article explains the significance of the Rosetta Stone's discovery. What do you think about when you hear the expression *the Rosetta Stone*? From what you have read in the first paragraph on page 94, and from looking at the photo below, what do you think will appear in the article?

B. Read the article carefully, remembering to think about what you are reading. Notice the annotations in the first paragraph. Underline important names and dates. Circle keywords and write definitions in the margins.

> **Glossary**
>
> Carve: to cut into something with a knife or sharp tool

Understanding the Rosetta Stone

1 Thousands of years ago, Alexander the Great's Macedonian Empire conquered Egypt. Alexander appointed a new king, forming the Ptolemaic Dynasty. Ptolemy I, and his many descendants, did not speak or read Egyptian—but Greek. Still, they ruled Egypt for years, often through royal decrees and proclamation. These decrees were sometimes carved onto *steles*, long tall stones, and placed in public areas. Kings, priests, and other officials regularly made decrees in this way. They often used hieroglyphs—a system of writing using pictures as letters that had been used in Egypt since ancient times.

[handwritten margin notes: What year exactly? Look up. — to defeat — to control — to cut into rock or wood — Are these like cave paintings in Lascaux Caves?]

2 Centuries later, in 1799, another ruler inspired by Alexander sought to conquer Egypt. Some soldiers of Napoleon's French army were stationed near the village of Rashid, or Rosetta, as it was called by the Europeans. While taking apart a wall for stones, the soldiers came upon the pieces of a royal statement of the Ptolemaic priesthood. The stele, or what was left of it, was a message from the royal priesthood stating the divinity of Ptolemy V. The soldiers, of course, could understand none of this— but one officer, Pierre-François Xavier Bouchard, *did* notice something odd about the stone. The stone had hieroglyphs, but also two other forms of writing on it. After he brought the stone to his superior officers, the stone soon became famous as a treasured relic. At the war's end, when France was defeated, Britain took possession of the Rosetta Stone.

3 What made the stone's proclamation special was the writing—it was written in multiple languages. No one in Europe in 1799 had any idea how to read hieroglyphs—but the other two alphabets were a different matter. Demotic, the second alphabet, turned out to be a written form of old Egyptian; it was similar to Coptic, which was another dialect of old Egyptian that survived in some religious services. The bottom alphabet, ancient Greek, was well known to scholars of the day. Because the Ptolemaic kings spoke Greek, royal decrees would include Egyptian *and* Greek. The Demotic was soon translated—it was obvious that the Demotic and Greek texts said the same thing. Researchers realized that, with luck, the hieroglyphs might be decipherable as well.

4 The hieroglyphs *were* eventually deciphered by a Frenchman named Jean-Francois Champollion. For the first time in thousands of years, people could read and understand what ancient hieroglyphs actually said. The research also confirmed that both the hieroglyphs and Demotic were written forms of old Egyptian as a spoken language. Hieroglyphs were not, as some thought, pictographs—rather, they were an alphabetical system. This allowed modern researchers to finally read ancient Egyptian texts, inscriptions, and signs; without the Rosetta Stone, we may never have figured out how to read ancient Egyptian.

C. Choose the correct answers.

1. The Rosetta Stone's discovery was most important because it allowed _____ .

 a. the British to have an important treasure
 b. researchers to understand ancient Egyptian hieroglyphs
 c. the ancient Egyptians to communicate with its citizens
 d. three different languages to communicate an idea

2. The article suggests that the Rosetta Stone _____ .

 a. was discovered intentionally
 b. was in good condition when it was discovered
 c. was discovered unintentionally
 d. was translated quickly

3. In Paragraph 2, it can be inferred from the phrase "Another leader [Napoleon] inspired by Alexander sought to conquer Egypt" that _____ .

   a. Napoleon was a great leader
   b. Napoleon had been a Greek scholar
   c. Napoleon liked the Egyptian climate
   d. Napoleon wanted to expand his power

4. The last sentence of Paragraph 2 says, "At the war's end, when France was defeated, Britain took possession of the Rosetta Stone." What does this imply?

   a. Napoleon was seen as a hero by the French.
   b. France took control of Egypt.
   c. The British army had been fighting the French.
   d. The British stole the Rosetta Stone.

5. In Paragraph 4, the clause "The hieroglyphs *were* eventually deciphered" suggests that _____ .

   a. they were easier to understand than the Demotic text
   b. it took many years, after the Rosetta Stone's discovery, to understand the hieroglyphs
   c. it was easy to translate the hieroglyphs on the Rosetta Stone
   d. hieroglyphs were the preferred language of the Egyptian rulers

6. Having both Demotic and Greek text on the Rosetta Stone was most beneficial in that researchers _____ .

   a. could understand that both said the same thing, so they could predict that the text in hieroglyphs probably said the same
   b. could understand Demotic and then could figure out the Greek text
   c. couldn't understand what had been written on the stele
   d. could take credit for rediscovering the Rosetta Stone

D. Reread the article. Then check your answers in Part C.

EXERCISE 6

Discuss your reading experience with one or more students.

1. Did you answer all the questions correctly in Exercise 5, Part C? How do you rate your accuracy level when reading in English? Do you think you need to read more slowly to be a more accurate reader? If you answered everything correctly, do you think you could read a little faster with the same level of accuracy?

2. To increase your reading accuracy, it's important to understand a reading's vocabulary. What are some useful strategies for figuring out a word's meaning? List three and discuss.

   - ....
   - ....
   - ....

VOCABULARY CHECK

A. Review the vocabulary items in the Vocabulary Preview. Write their definitions and add examples. Use a dictionary if necessary.

B. Complete each sentence using the correct vocabulary item from the box. Use the correct form.

confirm	notice	odd	stone	royal	rule

1. Queens and kings will generally .... until their death unless they step down or are overthrown.

2. Fences can be made out of a variety of materials: wood, wire, and even ....

3. A(n) .... family may include a queen, king, princes, and princesses.

4. Archaeologists must be patient and careful when digging so that they .... any artifacts that might be hidden.

5. When learning a new language, everything seems .... because it's different from your first language. But with practice, it will become familiar.

6. After registering for classes, students can .... their registration by going online and checking their schedules.

🔘 **Go to MyEnglishLab to complete vocabulary and skill practices, and to join in collaborative activities.**

INTEGRATED SKILLS

READING ALOUD TO BUILD FLUENCY AND COMPREHENSION

WHY IT'S USEFUL By reading aloud, you can develop fluency, improve comprehension, and strengthen critical reading skills.

In some academic classrooms, students may be asked to read aloud or listen to a professor reading aloud. Both situations can be helpful in developing fluency and strengthening comprehension.

Reading Aloud: Passive

Listening to a professor read aloud provides a wonderful model of a fluent reader. You can notice where the professor places stress on a word or how intonation is used in a sentence. You can hear where the professor pauses between groups of words (thought groups) and how this gives listeners time to digest the information. Some professors might also model reading strategies—pausing while reading to comment on the content, to define a word or concept, or to relate it to something previously read or discussed.

Reading Aloud: Active

As a student, reading aloud can help you improve your fluency by improving your accuracy—especially if someone monitors your reading and provides feedback. Repeated readings of the same passage will also help you read more quickly and smoothly as you become more familiar with the vocabulary and the arrangement of the words. When reading aloud, the focus is not on being the quickest reader; rather, attention should be placed on reading expressively—stressing words, pausing between others, and varying your intonation. This will make it easier for others to understand you and also make the reading more engaging.

Pronunciation Review

Word stress: In multisyllabic English words, one syllable will receive the main stress (pronounced louder than the others). The bolded syllables are stressed:

Italy   **It**alians   **art**ists   **build**ings   mag**nif**icent

Placing the correct stress on multisyllabic words is important when reading aloud, to help your listeners understand you.

Thought groups: When reading aloud, pause between thought groups. Thought groups usually consist of about two to five words that have a specific meaning. Notice the thought groups here, separated by slashes (/):

For more about thought groups, see MyEnglishLab, History, Part 1, Language Skill.

One of the most / interesting things / discovered in Pompeii / is the city's graffiti.

Intonation: When you speak or read aloud, your voice should rise and fall to express meaning or emotion. For instance, when asking a *yes / no* question, your intonation should rise at the end of the sentence; to show sadness, your voice may fall.

VOCABULARY PREVIEW

Read the vocabulary items in the box. Circle the ones you know. Put a question mark next to the ones you don't know.

graffiti	evidence	separate (v)	acceptable
post (v)	memories	complaint	calculated

EXERCISE 7

A. *Graffiti* is writing or pictures that are drawn illegally on the walls of buildings, trains, and so on. Do you think graffiti is a form of art, a form of communication, or a crime?

Artistic depiction of daily life in Pompeii, from the collection *The Houses and Monuments of Pompeii*, by Fausto and Felice Niccolini. Using the technique of color lithography, the brothers documented the archaeological findings at Pompeii and released their artwork in the form of 400 color plates between 1854 and 1896.

Glossary

Illiterate: unable to read or write

Mockery: when someone laughs at someone or something and tries to make the person seem stupid

Take a toll: to have a bad effect on someone or something over a period of time

🔊 **B. Read along silently as you listen to the first part of a lecture called "The Writing on the Wall." Mark where each bolded word is stressed.**

Sentence 1:

> One of the most **interesting** things discovered in **Pompeii** is the city's graffiti.

Sentence 2:

> The writing on the wall may not seem **valuable**, like **jewelry** or statues, but to academics studying life in the **Roman** Empire, Pompeii's graffiti is a treasure in itself.

Sentence 3:

> This is largely because of who wrote the **graffiti**.

Sentence 4:

> Most writing that has survived from the Roman **Empire** was written by **wealthy**, male, politically **powerful**, and highly **educated** free citizens.

Sentence 5:

> Graffiti was a writing of the people—men and **women**, **children** and adults, free and **enslaved**.

Sentence 6:

> Graffiti written by women in Pompeii is **especially** important; Pompeiian graffiti is one of our **only** sources of text **written** by Roman women, as little else survived.

🔊 **C. Read aloud softly as you listen to the entire lecture. If the speaker places stress on a word differently from what you would expect, make a mark above that word to remind you of how to pronounce it. Also, note any rising or falling intonation that is different from what you would expect.**

1   ¹One of the most interesting things discovered in Pompeii is the city's graffiti. ²The writing on the wall may not seem valuable, like jewelry or statues, but to academics studying life in the Roman Empire, Pompeii's graffiti is a treasure in itself. ³This is largely because of who wrote the graffiti. ⁴Most writing that has survived from the Roman Empire was written by wealthy, male, politically powerful, and highly educated

free citizens. [5]Graffiti was a writing of the people—men and women, children and adults, free and enslaved. [6]Graffiti written by women in Pompeii is especially important; Pompeiian graffiti is one of our only sources of text written by Roman women, as little else survived.

2 Almost all surviving graffiti of the era was found in Pompeii. In fact, before the discovery of graffiti in Pompeii, many historians assumed that most people in the Roman Empire were illiterate. Pompeii's graffiti demonstrated that basic literacy was much more common than originally believed. There is even evidence that graffiti was a form of literary practice; numerous examples appear to show both children and adults practicing their alphabet and writing using graffiti.

3 One thing that separates ancient Pompeiian graffiti from modern examples is that ancient graffiti was socially acceptable. Ancient graffiti actually has more in common with modern social networking. People would, quite literally, share thoughts and feelings on each other's "walls" centuries before Facebook digitized the practice. This wasn't seen as a problem but just another way to use writing to communicate. Citizens posted thoughts, clever jokes, advertisements, and all manner of things. Numerous examples of graffiti even survive inside the homes of the wealthy. These include memories of friends, a mother complaining about her son's romantic life, and even playful mockery. We may not know who Epaphra was, but some "friends" used graffiti to remember Epaphra's poor performance in a tennis game, making Epaphra famous—though maybe not in a way that Epaphra would have liked. Popular sayings like the idea that "Small problems get worse if you ignore them" seem to have been rewritten throughout the city by different people. Pompeiian graffiti even contained examples of meta-humor, or self-aware humor about humor. One popular meta-joke was, "Oh walls, you have held up so much tedious graffiti that I am amazed you have not already collapsed in ruin." This is found in different districts throughout the city.

4 Of course, some restaurant and hotel owners of ancient Pompeii may have felt differently about graffiti. Customer reviews have been found in Pompeii, ranging from praising a delicious meal to complaining about a poor-quality hotel room. For example, someone complaining about the lack of bathroom facilities at an inn decided to write a complaint on the walls to warn other customers. Commercial graffiti was not limited to customer reviews, however. There are many examples of graffiti advertising—for sales, for apartments, and for services. Some forms of graffiti even seem to be business deals where the buying and selling of goods was calculated on the wall.

5 The graffiti of Pompeii was, thankfully, well documented. Painted-on graffiti and graffiti carved only into the surface level of paint proved especially difficult for researchers to preserve. Weather, earthquakes, and the bombing that occurred during World War II have also taken their toll on Pompeii's graffiti. Another difficulty, ironically, has been

(Continued)

modern graffiti—from tourists of recent centuries. It seems that despite the eruption of Vesuvius and centuries of abandonment, even modern visitors find the walls of Pompeii an irresistible means of expression.

CULTURE NOTE

Although graffiti is illegal in most places, it's still a popular way of communicating ideas. It has even evolved into a legitimate art form popularized by artists like Keith Haring, Shepard Fairey, and Banksy. Banksy, whose real identity is unknown, is someone who has combined political and social messages within his art. For his street art, he typically uses stencils to quickly post an image before being noticed by the public. His art is so sought after that one piece has sold for more than $1 million at auction.

D. Practice reading the lecture transcript aloud. Work in groups of five. Each person reads one paragraph. Then read the following statements. Circle *T* (True) or *F* (False). Correct the false statements.

T / F 1. Adult males were the only ones who wrote graffiti in ancient Pompeii.

T / F 2. The writing of Roman women is well documented throughout Roman history.

T / F 3. Pompeiian graffiti is evidence that there was a higher level of literacy in the Roman Empire than previously imagined.

T / F 4. It can be inferred that paper was not readily available for writing practice during ancient Roman times.

T / F 5. Graffiti was practiced only on the exterior (outside walls) of buildings.

T / F 6. Graffiti was used as a means of promotion as well as a way of expressing criticism.

T / F 7. Much of the graffiti in Pompeii has been destroyed due to natural and human-made causes.

T / F 8. The author suggests that citizens of ancient Pompeii enjoyed expressing themselves publicly like people do today.

E. Reread the transcript and check your answers in Part D. With a partner, discuss these questions.

1. Was it difficult to read at the same pace as the speaker?

2. While you were reading aloud, were you able to understand the lecture? Did reading it again help your accuracy when answering the questions?

3. As you were reading, were you surprised at how the speaker stressed any words? If yes, which ones?

4. Do you often read aloud at home—to yourself or to someone else? How do you check that you are pronouncing a word correctly?

5. Do you think rereading something aloud a few times can make you a more fluent reader? Explain.

VOCABULARY CHECK

A. Review the vocabulary items in the Vocabulary Preview. Write their definitions and add examples. Use a dictionary if necessary.

B. Complete each sentence using the correct vocabulary item from the box. Use the correct form.

evidence	complaint	calculate	graffiti
separate	memory	post	acceptable

1. Some cities' buildings are covered in spray-painted .... , while others are clean.

2. In order to advertise the upcoming yard sale, they .... signs around the neighborhood to inform people of its date and location.

3. Before starting an expensive excavation, archaeologists will look for .... that something is buried in that area, either by using remote sensing or by simply walking over an area and digging holes.

4. One thing that .... the discovery of Pompeii from the discovery of King Tut's tomb is that Pompeii was discovered accidentally, while the tomb was discovered intentionally.

5. Removing an artifact to protect it or have it examined are examples of .... behavior at a dig site.

6. Only a few people have a photographic .... , which means they can remember anything they have ever read; however, most people can improve their memory by using reading strategies.

7. Some people write a letter of .... if they are unhappy with the quality of service they have received, whereas others believe that if you have nothing good to say, you should keep quiet.

8. One strategy for improving fluency is to try to read more quickly, which can be done if you time yourself when reading and then .... how long it took you.

⦿ Go to MyEnglishLab to complete a skill practice and to join in collaborative activities.

LANGUAGE SKILL

IDENTIFYING THOUGHT GROUPS

WHY IT'S USEFUL Fluent readers read in chunks of words called "thought groups." Chunking information into thought groups can help you recognize and remember important information.

⊙ Go to MyEnglishLab for the Language Skill presentation and practice.

VOCABULARY STRATEGY

RECOGNIZING COLLOCATIONS

WHY IT'S USEFUL By using a dictionary to learn collocations (words that are commonly used together) in thought groups, you can become more fluent in English.

Fluent readers chunk information into thought groups, and collocations often appear within those thought groups.

> For more about thought groups, go to MyEnglishLab, History, Part 2, Language Skill.

Consider this sentence:

> Pompeii is one of the only archeological sites from the Roman era that shows us how ordinary people lived.

When separated into thought groups, the sentence can look like:

> Pompeii is / one of the only / archaeological sites / from the Roman era / that shows us / how ordinary people lived.

Within the thought groups are collocation(s):

> Pompeii is / <u>one of the only</u> / <u>archaeological sites</u> / from <u>the Roman era</u> / that shows us / how <u>ordinary people</u> lived.

Look at this dictionary entry for *site*. Notice the definitions and the example showing "archaeological site." Other common collocations are also listed.

---

site¹ /saɪt/ ••• S3 W1 AWL *noun* [countable] ◀))

1 the location of an event, often important or historic:
◀)) *an archaeological site*
◀)) *the site of the 1773 massacre*
◀)) *found at the site*

2 the location or planned location of a structure:
◀)) *a good building site*

3 an Internet page: website:
◀)) *visits to this site*
◀)) *posted to the site*

A native speaker would find it strange if someone said or wrote, "Pompeii is one of the only archaeological places / areas / spots … ." instead of using "archaeological sites." Although the meaning would be clear, it wouldn't be as accurate.

Some dictionaries might not provide a list of collocations, but they may provide examples taken from a **corpus**. A corpus is an online collection of how words are used in a variety of media. Both the *Corpus of Contemporary American English* and the *American National Corpus* can be searched to see how words are commonly used.

EXERCISE 8

A. Review the dictionary entries for *turmoil* (below) and *era* (on the next page). Then complete each chart.

---

tur·moil /ˈtɝˌmɔɪl/ ●○○ *noun* [singular, uncountable] ◀))

a state of confusion, excitement, and trouble:

◀)) *His life was **in turmoil**.*

COLLOCATIONS

NOUN

▼ **in turmoil**

◀)) *His life was **in turmoil**.*

▼ **political / economic / religious turmoil**

◀)) *Most of the country is in **political turmoil**.*

Word: *turmoil*	
Definition	
Collocation with an adjective / noun	
Collocation with other part of speech	
Example sentence with *turmoil*	

e·ra /ˈɪrə, ˈɛrə/ ●●○ *noun* [countable] ◀))

1   a period of time that is associated with particular events or qualities, or that begins with a particular date or event:
◀)) *the post-Cold-War era*

era of
◀)) *We live in an **era of** instant communication.*

2   EARTH SCIENCE **one of the three long periods of time that the history of the Earth is divided into, starting 550 million years ago:**
◀)) *the dinosaurs of **the Mesozoic Era***

Word: *era*	
Definition	
Collocation with an adjective / noun	
Collocation with other part of speech	
Example sentence with *era*	

B. Read the passage, which contains some incomplete collocations. Circle the underlined word that best completes each collocation. Use a dictionary if necessary.

Once the Rosetta Stone was discovered, researchers **throughout the** (1) <u>Earth</u> / <u>world</u> / <u>globe</u> / <u>planet</u> knew that it was an opportunity to decode the meaning of ancient Egyptian hieroglyphs. The only problem was that those researchers didn't know **how to** (2) <u>crack</u> / <u>understand</u> / <u>split</u> / <u>solve</u> **the code**. They were limited because they misunderstood how hieroglyphic writing worked. Scholars of the day thought that hieroglyphs were pictograms, writing where pictures **take the** (3) <u>location</u> / <u>place</u> / <u>point</u> / <u>area</u> of words. This misunderstanding was so strong that even insightful linguistic researchers (4) <u>jogged</u> / <u>walked</u> / <u>ran</u> / <u>had</u> **into trouble** because of it. The British doctor Thomas Young, who (5) <u>had</u> / <u>made</u> / <u>was</u> / <u>went</u> **an interest in** antiquities, is an excellent example of this. Young noticed that certain sets of hieroglyphs were always carved inside of "cartouches," or decorative frames. Young **figured** (6) <u>in</u> / <u>out</u> / <u>by</u> / <u>on</u> that these were likely the names of royalty, "Ptolemy" and "Cleopatra," on the Rosetta Stone. This was a great discovery—but Young assumed that it wasn't much help. Young thought that the names were only written that way since they were not Egyptian—but Greek. Without realizing just how close he came to solving the meaning of hieroglyphs, Young stopped this path of study.

C. Choose three of the collocations from Part B and make sentences about yourself or something you have read. Tell them to a partner.

🚫 Go to MyEnglishLab to complete a skill practice.

APPLY YOUR SKILLS

WHY IT'S USEFUL By applying the skills you have learned in this unit, you will have a better understanding of this challenging reading about who "owns" archaeological relics.

BEFORE YOU READ

A. Discuss these questions with one or more students.

1. If an archaeologist finds an ancient treasure on someone else's land, who should it belong to—the archaeologist who found it or the person whose land it was found on? Explain.

2. Many priceless objects are kept in museums to be viewed and enjoyed by the public. If a country is experiencing civil unrest or war, what should be done to protect those priceless objects? Explain.

3. In English, there is a popular expression about finding something: "Finders keepers, losers weepers." How would you explain this, and does your first language have a similar expression?

B. You will read an article about the ownership of found relics. As you read, think about these questions.

1. What are some arguments in favor of the UK returning the Rosetta Stone to Egypt?

2. What are some arguments in favor of the UK retaining ownership of the Rosetta Stone?

3. How do ancient archaeological relics end up on the black market?

C. Review the Unit Skills Summary on the next page. As you read the article, apply the skills you learned in this unit.

UNIT SKILLS SUMMARY

BECOME A MORE FLUENT READER BY USING THESE SKILLS:

Increase smoothness and pace to build fluency

• Skip over unknown words, guess meaning from context, and reread texts to become a quicker and smoother reader.

Develop accuracy

• Read texts appropriate to your level and pay close attention to lexical and grammatical clues that will help you understand the text.

Read aloud to build fluency and comprehension

• Pay attention to word stress and read in chunks when reading aloud to better communicate your ideas.

Identify thought groups

• Group prepositional phrases, noun phrases, and verb phrases into thought groups to easily identify important information, and to make your reading more fluent.

Recognize collocations

• Recognize collocations in thought groups and use a dictionary or corpus to find other common collocations.

READ

A. Read the article on the next page. Annotate and take notes. Try to read smoothly, at a good pace, and accurately.

Glossary

Dynasty: a family of rulers

Country of origin: where something comes from

Petition: (v) to make a legal request

Pedigree: background

Colonialism: the system by which a powerful country rules another less powerful country

Conquest: victory over people

Delegitimize: to make something unacceptable

Prominent: important

Meddle: to get involved in someone else's business

Trinket: a small prize or pretty object

Who Owns the Rosetta Stone?

1   Who "owns" ancient Egyptian artifacts? The culture of the pharaohs is long dead; there is no politician left affiliated with the dynasties of Ramses or Tutankhamun. Do artifacts belong to the nation that discovered them, or to the nation now occupying the soil of that long-lost kingdom? Many nations, like Italy and Greece, believe that historically significant artifacts should be returned to their country of origin. Both Italy and Greece have found success in retrieving relics of their past. In recent decades, the government of Egypt has been petitioning the United Kingdom to return the Rosetta Stone—a famous piece of ancient Egyptian history that allowed 19th-century scholars to decode the meaning of hieroglyphs. Despite threats from Egypt to limit archaeological access, the British Museum is unlikely to give up the Rosetta Stone anytime soon. What is the UK's case for keeping the stone?

The Rosetta Stone, in a case at the British Museum in London

The Case for Keeping the Stone

2   The UK's main objections to returning the Rosetta Stone revolve around protection, infrastructure, and access. Many artifacts are thought to be safer in highly advanced, highly secured areas of ultra-modern museums. British academics feel that Egypt simply doesn't have the infrastructure needed to properly protect and preserve an artifact as important as the Rosetta Stone; after all, many equally important archaeological sites and valuable artifacts located in Egypt are currently falling apart due to a lack of funding and support. Why should the British Museum turn over the stone when conditions are not ideal? Plus, if the goal of a museum is to present history to the world, the British Museum is a statistically superior choice. Millions more people go to the British Museum than the Egyptian Museum every year. Moving the stone, they say, would deprive many of the chance to see it.

A Murky World of Uncertain Pedigree

3   Many artifacts removed from their country of origin were not freely given; artifacts were frequently taken through colonialism, conquest, or theft. Today, hundreds of museum pieces are the product of thieves taking advantage of situations in the past. Theft remains a common occurrence on even famous and well-attended archaeological digs—to say nothing of grave-robbing and treasure-hunting. These criminals aren't just rogue professors working off the clock; some of these looters can be downright dangerous. Right now, terrorist groups such as ISIS (the Islamic State of Iraq and Syria) are funded partially through the sale of stolen and looted artifacts on the black market. Anything that reduces the demand for illegitimate antiquities improves not just the world of antiquities but the world itself.

(Continued)

4   The Italian government has led a campaign to return stolen Pompeiian artwork. This campaign has been hugely successful—not only has Italy recovered hundreds of national treasures, but the funds acquired from tourism and publicity have been used to support historic preservation programs. Global campaigns to return stolen treasures help delegitimize illegal sales and can discourage the trade in illegally obtained relics.

The Case for Returning the Stone

5   The Rosetta Stone is a lasting symbol of Egyptian culture; having the stone "in exile" in the land of Egypt's former colonial conqueror is a sore spot for Egyptian historians. Egyptian experts have been trying to retrieve the stone due to its prominent place in Egyptology. Our entire understanding of Egyptian hieroglyphs is due to the Rosetta Stone. Italy and Greece have benefitted from the publicity and prestige brought by the return of stolen artifacts; Egyptian scholars insist that Egypt deserves the same privilege and benefits. The same scholars shrug off British criticism regarding the upkeep of historic sites—after all, Egypt has been independent of colonial meddling for only a short time. It takes a great deal of effort to build up archaeological infrastructure, and many believe Egypt has a rightful claim to the stone.

6   Ancient Egypt's wealth of history has been hit especially hard by looters and thieves. People everywhere are fascinated by ancient Egyptian artifacts, but this fascination has a dark side—there is a high demand for stolen goods on the black market. By keeping a famous relic that was acquired through war and conquest, the British Museum could be viewed as legitimizing the most questionable archaeological practice. Returning the Rosetta Stone would be a powerfully symbolic act; doing so would demonstrate both the importance of international cooperation and the need for respect. To end the trade in stolen artifacts, collectors must see relics not as trinkets for the wealthy but as cultural treasures tied to their nation of origin—and best preserved for the good of *all*.

CULTURE NOTE

The antiquities trade, or the sale of archaeological and ancient relics, has been going on for centuries. Although the trade of some antiquities is allowed under strict guidelines, the market for illegally obtained antiquities is still going strong despite the United Nations Educational, Scientific and Cultural Organization's (UNESCO) 1970 Convention. This convention forbade the selling or transferring of cultural property and allows countries to recover stolen antiquities from other member countries, including the US and the UK. In recent years, civil wars in many countries have made archaeological sites and museums especially vulnerable to looting, and some estimates indicate that millions, if not billions, of dollars are being made on the black market from the antiquities trade.

B. Compare notes with a partner. Talk about your reading experience: Were you able to read smoothly and at a good pace?

C. Reread the questions in Before You Read, Part B. With your partner, use your notes and opinions to answer the questions.

◑ Go to MyEnglishLab to read more closely, answer the critical thinking questions, and complete a summarizing activity.

> **TIP**
>
> Reread the passage "Who Owns the Rosetta Stone?" and write your start and finish times. Calculate your reading time. Compare it to your first time—did your time change?
>
> Start Time: ....
>
> Finish Time: ....
>
> Reading Time: ....
>
> Are you happy with how fast you are reading? What do you think you could do to improve your speed or your accuracy?

THINKING CRITICALLY

Use information from the reading to answer these questions.

1. In the passage, you read arguments for keeping the Rosetta Stone in the UK and for returning it to Egypt. In your opinion, which argument is stronger for who should "own" the Rosetta Stone? Explain.

   ....

   ....

2. Do you think museums should return ancient relics that were taken from other countries during times of conquest or occupation? Explain.

   ....

   ....

THINKING VISUALLY

Use the information from the following chart and the map (on the next page) to answer these questions.

1. Read the rankings of the most historically important sites in the world. Do you agree? Add two more sites and then write your own rankings. Now mark the map to indicate the locations. Do you see any trends?

Your Ranking	What: Ranking / Historic Site		Where: Place Found	When: Year Discovered
	1	Olduvai Gorge	Tanzania	
	2	The Behistun Rock	Iran	
	3	The Rosetta Stone	Egypt	
	4	Peking Man	China	
	5	The Lascaux Cave	France	

(Continued)

Your Ranking	What: Ranking / Historic Site		Where: Place Found	When: Year Discovered
	6	The Ruins of Pompeii	Italy	
	7	Tutankhamun's Tomb	Egypt	
	8	The Royal Library of Ashurbanipal	Iraq	
	9	The Dead Sea Scrolls	The West Bank	
	10	Qin Shi Huang's Terracotta Army	China	
	11	Machu Picchu	Peru	
	12	Moai Figures	Easter Island, Chile	

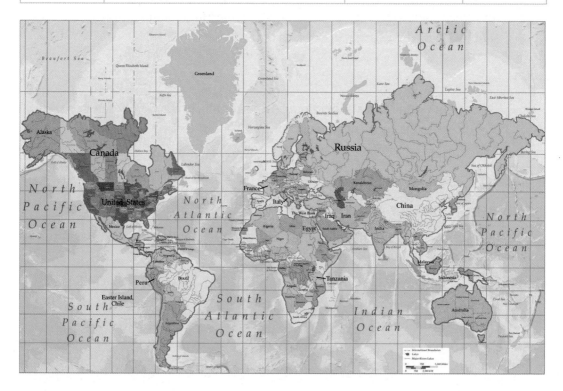

2. Do light research to find out the year each site was discovered. Add those dates to the chart. What conclusions can be drawn from the dates? Express your idea in the form of a graphic (pie chart, diagram, etc.).

THINKING ABOUT LANGUAGE

A. Read these excerpts from "Who Owns the Rosetta Stone?" Use slashes (/) to separate each excerpt into thought groups.

For help with identifying thought groups, go to MyEnglishLab, History, Part 1, Language Skill.

1. The culture of the pharaohs is long dead.

2. Despite threats from Egypt to limit archaeological access, the British Museum is unlikely to give up the Rosetta Stone anytime soon.

3. Why should the British Museum turn over the stone when conditions are not ideal?

4. Plus, if the goal of a museum is to present history to the world, the British Museum is a statistically superior choice.

5. Many artifacts removed from their country of origin were not freely given.

6. After all, Egypt has been independent of colonial meddling for only a short time.

B. Underline each collocation in the excerpts in Part A. Then choose three and write example sentences.

1. ....

....

2. ....

....

3. ....

....

Go to MyEnglishLab to watch Dr. Hunt's concluding video and to complete a self-assessment.

Our everyday experiences are based on how we interact with nature

CHEMICAL ENGINEERING

Cohesion

UNIT PROFILE

In this unit, you will learn the difference between weight and mass, and be introduced to the vocabulary of physics. You will also learn about a different kind of avalanche. In the final reading of the unit, you will consider how the world looked years ago and why it has changed.

Look at the reading "How Land Moves" on page 139.
Read the first two sentences of Paragraph 2. What cause-and-effect relationship can you find?

OUTCOMES

• Identify cause and effect
• Examine examples
• Summarize
• Work with pro-forms
• Utilize the Frayer model

For more about **CHEMICAL ENGINEERING**, see ❷ ❸.
See also W and OC **CHEMICAL ENGINEERING** ❶ ❷ ❸.

GETTING STARTED

 Go to MyEnglishLab to watch Professor Spakowitz's introductory video and to complete a self-assessment.

Discuss these questions with a partner or group.

1. Think of the language you use to talk about measurement. For example, how do you talk about someone's weight? Or how fast something goes? Are these terms universal, or do they depend on the culture and context?

2. Have you or anyone you know ever seen an avalanche, a mudslide, or a volcano explosion? Where was it, what caused it, and what effect did it have?

3. In his introduction, Professor Spakowitz introduces the idea of prediction. How can knowing how one physical problem behaves be informative to scientists?

SKILL 1

IDENTIFYING CAUSE AND EFFECT

WHY IT'S USEFUL By identifying cause and effect, you can better understand the relationship between events and ideas.

Cause-and-effect signals help you recognize that two events are related. They explain how one action made another happen. An **effect** is the result of an action. The action or circumstance that led to that result is the **cause**. Science articles and textbooks are full of discussions about cause and effect.

For example, study this example:

effect   cause
An avalanche occurs when a large amount of unstable snow is disturbed.

Here are a few words and phrases that can signal cause and effect:

	Transition	Verb	Noun
Cause	because (of) _____ due to _____ if _____ on account of _____ when _____	_____ creates is brought about by _____ is caused by _____ _____ leads to occurs when _____ _____ produces _____ results in	_____ is the **cause** _____ is the **reason** _____ is the **source**
Effect	accordingly, _____ as a result, _____ consequently, _____ for _____ for this reason, _____ hence, _____ in order to _____ so _____ the reason for _____	brings about _____ _____ is caused by _____ occurs when	the **consequence** is _____ the **effect** is _____ the **outcome** is _____ the **result** is _____

TIP

Often only one half of a cause-effect relationship is known. Effect: We may know the effect but not the cause. Consider this example: the growing number of earthquakes in parts of the US. People knew the ground under their feet was shaking, but they didn't know the cause. (Experts now say the cause is fracking—the process of injecting liquid into the ground to extract oil or gas.) Consider a different example: Cause: A drug trial has started. The participants are taking the drug—we know that action has happened—but we don't know the effects. Understanding *causality* is important.

VOCABULARY PREVIEW

Read the vocabulary items in the box. Circle the ones you know.
Put a question mark next to the ones you don't know.

makes sense	everyday	measure (v)	multiply
results in	therefore	lower (adj)	universe

EXERCISE 1

A. Look at the image on the next page, which shows an astronaut's weight on the moon versus on Earth. What effect does being on the moon have on the astronaut's weight? Complete the sentences using the words from the box.

| higher | lower (adj) | causes | reason | consequently |

1. Being on the moon .... the astronaut's weight to be ....

2. The gravity on Earth is stronger than on the moon. .... , the astronaut's weight is .... on Earth.

3. The .... for the change in weight is the amount of gravity on each object.

B. From the image, what can you say about how weight is affected in space? How does being in space affect mass? Identify the cause and effect in each sentence in Part A. Which words signal those actions?

EXERCISE 2

A. Based on the image in the article (on the next page), how would you explain the difference between weight and mass?

> ### Glossary
> Physicist: a scientist who has special knowledge and training in physics
>
> Gravity: the force that pulls objects to the ground

B. Read the article. Then read the statements that follow. Circle T (True) or F (False). Correct the false statements.

The Difference Between Mass and Weight

1 What is the best way to lose weight? Ask a doctor, and she will tell you to exercise more. Ask a friend, and he will tell you to eat less. But ask a physicist, and she might say something much different: Go to the moon. That's a strange answer, but it makes more sense if you see the difference between mass and weight like a scientist.

2 In everyday conversations, people use the words *mass* and *weight* to describe the same thing: the size of something. But in physics, *mass* and *weight* have different meanings. *Mass* is the amount of material in an object. If you exercise and become thinner, then you are losing mass. Scientists measure mass in kilograms (kg). *Weight*, however, is a bit different. Weight is the mass of an object multiplied by gravity's pull, or *acceleration*.

This is how weight is measured: weight = mass x acceleration (gravity)

Or: $N = m \times a$

(Continued)

3 The N is for *newton*—the unit for measuring weight. Acceleration is measured in meters per second squared (m/s²), which on Earth is 9.8m/s². So, if the mass of an object on Earth is 100 kilograms, then its weight is 100 kg × 9.8 m/s², which is 980 N.

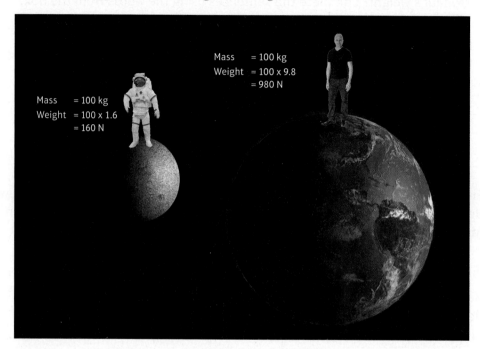

Mass = 100 kg
Weight = 100 x 9.8
= 980 N

Mass = 100 kg
Weight = 100 x 1.6
= 160 N

4 So why do you lose weight by going to the moon? The reason is that the moon is a lot smaller than Earth. This size difference results in a much weaker gravitational pull: 1.6 m/s². If you take that same 100-kilogram object and measure its weight on the moon, then it will be 160 N. That is about one-sixth of that object's "Earth weight." But the mass has not changed; it is still 100 kilograms. Do you want to lose more weight? Go into space. In space, there is almost no gravity. Therefore, when you measure your weight in space (100 kg × 0 m/s²), it will be 0.

5 Going to all of these different places will not help you lose mass, however. In order to lose mass, you will need to eat healthier and exercise. And as a result of your mass loss, your weight will be lower everywhere, too: on the moon, on Earth, or on any other planet in the universe.

TIP

Can you guess who the newton (N) is named after? The famous 17th-century English mathematician Sir Isaac Newton, of course. In fact, many features of science are named after the person who discovered, invented, or inspired them. The newton was named after Newton in recognition of his second law of motion. Other examples include the measure of temperature (C or Celsius), named after the Swedish scientist Anders Celsius, and the measure of power (W or watt), after the Scottish scientist James Watt. If the name of something is capitalized, or sounds like a name, there's a good chance that there's a story behind it. By doing a little research you can not only learn the story but also have better luck remembering the term and its meaning.

T / F   1. In physics, mass and weight are the same thing.

T / F   2. Mass is the amount of material in an object.

T / F   3. Scientists measure weight in pounds (lbs).

T / F   4. In physics, *acceleration* is another word for *gravity*.

T / F   5. A person's mass is the same on Earth and the moon.

T / F   6. A person's weight is the same on Earth and the moon.

T / F   7. The gravitational pull of the moon is weaker than the gravitational pull of Earth.

T / F   8. If an astronaut were floating in space, and not standing on an object, his or her weight would be 0.

C. Reread the passage. Then check your answers in Parts A and B.

D. Read the excerpts. Underline the words that signal a cause-and-effect relationship. Then label the cause and the effect.

1. Paragraph 2

cause	effect
If you exercise and become thinner,	then you are losing mass.

2. Paragraph 3

... (i)f the mass of an object on Earth is 100 kilograms, then its weight is 100 kg × 9.8 m/s², which is 980 N.

3. Paragraph 4

This size difference results in a much weaker gravitational pull: 1.6 m/s².

4. Paragraph 4

Go into space. ... Therefore, when you measure your weight in space (100 kg × 0 m/s²), it will be 0.

5. Paragraph 5

> In order to lose mass, you will need to eat healthier and exercise.

6. Paragraph 5

> And as a result of your mass loss, your weight will be lower everywhere, too: on the moon, on Earth, or on any other planet in the universe.

EXERCISE 3

Discuss these questions with a partner.

1. Did identifying cause-and-effect words help you understand the relationship between gravity and the weight of an object?

2. How could cause-and-effect signals be used in the following situations?
   - a doctor talking to a patient about an illness
   - a teacher giving a lesson about global warming
   - an employer speaking to an employee about being late

VOCABULARY CHECK

A. Review the vocabulary items in the Vocabulary Preview. Write their definitions and add examples. Use a dictionary if necessary.

B. Read each sentence. Then write the correct definition of the underlined vocabulary item. Use the definitions from the box.

to find the size, length, or amount of something	all of space, including all the stars and planets
ordinary, usual, or happening routinely	to make something happen
smaller than the usual or compared amount	to do a calculation in which you add a number to itself a particular number of times
so, as a result	
to be the logical thing to do	

1. In 2016, as Hurricane Matthew hit Haiti, instruments <u>measured</u> winds at up to 135 mph (217 kph).

   Definition: ....

2. Because space exploration with humans aboard is so expensive and dangerous, it <u>makes sense</u> to send up unstaffed spacecraft.

   Definition: ....

3. Engineers have found technical problems with the spacecraft. <u>Therefore</u>, the launch has been delayed.

Definition: ....

4. To convert your weight from kilograms to pounds, <u>multiply</u> kilograms by 2.2. For example, 100 kilograms × 2.2 = 220 pounds.

Definition: ....

5. If we discovered other intelligent life somewhere in the <u>universe</u>—for example, on Mars or Venus or even another galaxy—how would we communicate with them?

Definition: ....

6. Because the cost of the lab equipment was <u>lower</u> than expected, the university was able to hire an additional professor.

Definition: ....

7. The <u>everyday</u> use of an automobile, say to work and back, releases 4.7 metric tons of carbon dioxide every year, which contributes to the problem of global warming.

Definition: ....

8. Because of warmer temperatures, ice caps are melting, which is <u>resulting in</u> a rise of sea levels.

Definition: ....

🔊 Go to MyEnglishLab to complete vocabulary and skill practices, and to join in collaborative activities.

SKILL 2
EXAMINING EXAMPLES

WHY IT'S USEFUL By recognizing examples and the words that signal them, you can better understand the support behind a writer's ideas.

Academic writing is filled with complex ideas and language. **Examples** help readers understand those concepts. Writers use them to persuade, explain, show, and support an idea, especially when the idea is difficult or abstract. In turn, readers are then able to think of additional examples of their own, which further clarifies the writer's point.

Study this sentence:

> … There are instances where time seems to go slower; **for example**, when people are doing things that they consider boring, time seems to stand still.

In the example, the second half of the sentence supports the first by giving an example of an occasion in which time seems to go slower: when doing something boring.

To identify examples, look for the following signal words:

Words That Signal an Example

an example of	for instance,	like	to clarify
consider	include	specifically	to demonstrate
e.g.,	in particular	such as	to exemplify
for example,	in this case	take the case of	to illustrate

These signals are used to show **cohesion**, or a relationship, between two ideas. Therefore, at least two ideas are needed in a sentence with an example. In the following example, the phrase *such as* links the idea of *awards* with specific examples of *medals* that Usain Bolt has won.

> **TIP**
>
> You may also hear the words in the list referred to as *signal words* or *cohesive devices.*

> Usain Bolt, the Jamaican sprinter, has won <u>numerous awards</u>, **such as** <u>the gold medal in the 100-meter sprint at the 2008, 2012, and 2016 Olympics</u>.

VOCABULARY PREVIEW

Read the vocabulary items in the box. Circle the ones you know. Put a question mark next to the ones you don't know.

amazing	description	average (adj)	quantity
direction	consider	for instance	

EXERCISE 4

A. Complete each statement with a signal word or phrase from the box. More than one answer may be possible. Add punctuation as needed.

also	as a result	because	first
for example	for instance	in addition	such as

1. In the Olympics, there are many different types of sporting events—............................ track and field, gymnastics, and swimming.

2. It is possible to measure the speed of many different objects: .... a train that is moving, a person that is running, or an airplane that is flying.

3. The young swimmer has won many events, ... the 100-meter backstroke, the 200-meter breaststroke, and the 50-meter butterfly.

B. Think about the words that you used to indicate an example. How often do you use those words in your everyday life? Is there one word or expression that you notice using more often than the others? If so, which one do you use most often? In what kinds of readings do you encounter examples?

EXERCISE 5

A. The following article is about using the vocabulary of physics to describe Usain Bolt's speed. From the image, what you already know about Usain Bolt, and what you might know about physics, what kinds of examples might the writer use to explain the vocabulary of physics?

B. Read the article. Then answer the questions that follow.

> **Glossary**
>
> Vector: a quantity that has a direction as well as a size, usually represented by an arrow

How to Talk About Usain Bolt in the Vocabulary of Physics

1 When you hear the name *Usain Bolt*, one thing comes to mind: speed. The Jamaican-born runner became known as the fastest person on Earth in 2009 after he ran 100 meters in 9.58 seconds. How do you describe such an amazing race? A reporter might write something like this: *Bolt stood at the starting line, waiting for the race to begin. As he heard the starting gun, he ran forward, reaching his top speed just before he crossed the finish line.* But in the language of physics, the description would be different.

Usain Bolt, center

(Continued)

2 A physicist's vocabulary includes the words *scalar, vector, velocity*, and *acceleration*, and they all could be used to describe a race. The first is *scalar*: A scalar is the size, or magnitude, of something. For example, speed is a scalar—it describes how fast something moves; an airplane's average speed of 250 meters per second (m/s) is a scalar quantity.

3 *Vectors* are different. They have a magnitude and direction. An example of a vector is *velocity*—the speed that something moves in a specific direction. Again consider Usain Bolt's race. His fastest speed was 12.2 m/s—a scalar quantity. And his highest velocity—a vector quantity—was 12.2 m/s *toward the finish line*. It is possible for Bolt to run with a different velocity, but at the same speed. For instance, Bolt could run *away from* the finish line. In this case, his top speed is still 12.2 m/s, but his velocity is −12.2 m/s. Here, the speed is the same, but the velocity changes because the direction is different.

4 Another example of a vector that physicists use is *acceleration*. Acceleration is the change in velocity per second, or m/s^2. Take the case of Bolt's race again: As he waited to start, both his speed and velocity were 0. From the time that he started to the time that he hit his top speed, his velocity changed from 0 to 12.2 m/s. His top acceleration during this time was an amazing $9.5 \ m/s^2$.

5 So this is how to describe Bolt's race using physics vocabulary: *Bolt was at the starting line with a speed scalar of 0 m/s. He began moving with an acceleration vector of +9.5 m/s^2. As he finished, his velocity vector was +12.2 m/s.* This may not be how a typical sports reporter writes about a race, but it works for a physicist.

1. Which is an example of a scalar?
   a. speed
   b. velocity
   c. acceleration
   d. vector

2. Which is NOT an example of a vector?
   a. a person running a race
   b. an airplane traveling from New York to London
   c. a person driving to work
   d. a taxi that has stopped to pick up a passenger

3. Which would have the highest rate of acceleration?
   a. a person waiting at the starting line of a race
   b. a bicycle chained to a bike rack
   c. a horse walking steadily at 5 miles per hour
   d. a car going from 0 to 60 miles per hour in a minute

4. Vectors have _____ .
   a. magnitude and speed
   b. magnitude and direction
   c. direction and time
   d. mass and weight

5. The expression "take the case" is another way to say _____ .
   a. bring the suitcase
   b. for example
   c. as a result
   d. in addition

6. Usain Bolt's fastest speed was 12.2 m/s. This means that he was running _____ .
   a. 12.2 miles per second
   b. 12.2 meters per scalar
   c. 12.2 miles per scalar
   d. 12.2 meters per second

C. Reread the passage and check your answers in Parts A and B.

D. Scan the passage and underline all signal words that indicate an example. Then choose three of them and write original sentences. Remember to use two ideas in each sentence. The first idea will set up the situation, and the second will use a signal word to add an example.

1. *A reporter might write something like this: "Bolt stood at the starting line, waiting for the race to begin."*

2. ....

3. ....

4. ....

EXERCISE 6

Discuss your reading experience with one or more students.

1. What examples did the writer use to explain a scalar and then a vector? Did the examples help your understanding of scalars and vectors?

2. When learning another language, learners will often ask for examples in order to better understand an idea. For instance, when studying grammar, a learner might ask for an example of how the past perfect is used. Think of situations in which you find getting or giving examples helpful.

VOCABULARY CHECK

A. Review the vocabulary items in the Vocabulary Preview. Write their definitions and add examples. Use a dictionary if necessary.

B. Read each sentence. Circle the word or phrase that is the best synonym for the underlined vocabulary item.

1. The movie *Hidden Figures* shows the <u>amazing</u> contribution that Katherine Johnson, Dorothy Vaughan, and Mary Jackson made to the American space program. What they did was really impressive.

   wonderful   untrue   good   false

2. After reading the <u>description</u> of the accident, including specifics about the road conditions, the insurance company decided to pay for all of the damages.

   opinion   details   summary   diagram

3. The <u>average</u> person walks at a pace of 3.1 miles per hour. But, of course, some people walk faster and some walk slower.

   typical   near the middle   not very good   regular

4. There was a concerning <u>quantity</u> of lead in the tap water, about 15 parts per billion. So bottled water was recommended for consumption.

   number   value   size   amount

5. The satellite traveled away from Earth, in the <u>direction</u> of Mars, to take photographs and collect scientific data.

   way   road   map   instruction

6. Parents must <u>consider</u> the effects that cell phones will have on their children's lives before allowing them to have their own phone.

   believe   feel   think about   enjoy

7. There are many jobs available to people who have a degree in physics—<u>for instance</u>, research scientist, high school teacher, applications engineer, and data analyst.

   momentarily   for example   quickly   therefore

◐ Go to MyEnglishLab to complete vocabulary and skill practices, and to join in collaborative activities.

INTEGRATED SKILLS

SUMMARIZING

WHY IT'S USEFUL By writing a summary, you can better understand the information. You can also use it as a study tool as you review for a test, or share it with classmates in your study group.

As a student, you will read from a variety of resources. You will need to **summarize** some of that material. When you summarize, you report the writer's main ideas in a shortened form.

How to Summarize

- Skim the text. Look at the title, any images, and the introduction. What is the topic?

- Read the article, identifying with annotations the main idea and most important details.

- Using your annotations, paraphrase the information, being sure to credit the source.

- Never include your own opinion or add information that wasn't included in the original report.

- Keep in mind that a summary should be about one-third the length of the original text.

Writing Tips

- Cut out redundant words. Example: Instead of *twelve noon*, use *noon*.

- Don't use wordy expressions and verbs. Examples: Instead of *due to the fact that*, use *because*; instead of *is aware of*, use *know*.

- Try to avoid expletive constructions. Examples: *there is / are, it is*.

VOCABULARY PREVIEW

Read the vocabulary items in the box. Circle the ones you know. Put a question mark next to the ones you don't know.

sites	extremely	mud	melting (adj)	even (adv)	occurs

EXERCISE 7

A. Have you seen an avalanche? What kinds of natural hazards exist where you live?

B. Read the first paragraph of the following reading. Which statement best summarizes the main idea?

☐ The Alps are a popular tourist destination.

☐ The Alps are a dangerous place to vacation.

☐ Avalanches have killed many people in Switzerland and Austria.

☐ It's important to understand the origins and movements of avalanches.

C. Now read the whole passage. As you read, make annotations about the main ideas. This will be helpful when summarizing.

Glossary

Current: (n) the flow of something in a specific direction

Avalanches, Sediment, and Gravity

1 Many believe that the Alps are the most beautiful mountains in all of Europe. They are home to nearly 14 million people, and they welcome over 100 million tourists to their amazing sites each year. During the winter months, ski resorts fill up with skiers and snowboarders looking to enjoy the snow-filled mountains. But the mountains are also known for something else: avalanches. Avalanches are large amounts of snow that crash down the sides of mountains. They can be extremely dangerous, especially in places where there are a lot of tourists, like the Alps. And they can happen any time. For instance, during the 1950–1951 winter, there were more than 600 avalanches

in the Swiss and Austrian portions of the Alps, which destroyed hundreds of buildings and killed over 200 people. So it is important to understand avalanches, particularly their causes and how they move.

2 It is probably pretty clear that gravity is the main reason why avalanches happen. In avalanches, gravity causes snow and sediment—material such as sand, mud, and pebbles that is moved from one place to another—to fall. How sediment moves is called *sediment gravity flow*. Gravity is always pulling objects downwards. So when snow is sitting on the side of a mountain, gravity is trying to pull it down. As the amount of snow increases, the effect of gravity increases as well. This, along with things like melting snow, rapid changes in temperatures, and even human weight, may cause an avalanche.

3 Inside an avalanche's flow, all sorts of things happen. The snow at the bottom moves along the ground, taking other types of sediment—trees, rocks, mud— with it. This forms something called a *turbidity current*. Essentially, the snow travels in a fluid mixed with air and rocks, but the air also causes some of the snow to move faster or more easily above the main flow on the ground. It is fairly easy to know where the avalanche will go because it follows the laws of gravity; the avalanche is heavier than the air that it travels through, so it falls to the lowest point that it can. By knowing this, scientists can help local governments and citizens plan for avalanches.

4 Interestingly, snow is not the only thing to fall in an avalanche. In deserts, another type of sediment gravity flow occurs. Sand avalanches happen on large "mountains" of sand, called sand dunes. These sorts of avalanches are the result of gravity, but they move somewhat differently. Their movement is described as *grain flow*. Grains—very small pieces of sand—begin to fall, usually as a result of wind. The sand in grain flows moves within itself; it does not become part of the air like snow in avalanches. In grain flows, the smaller grains move to the bottom of the flow, and the larger grains stay on top. Over time this causes the smaller pieces to become parts of rocks because of the weight of the larger grains above them.

5 Whether sand or snow, understanding the processes of sediment gravity flow can give useful information about the world. Scientists can then use that information to learn more about rocks in the desert, or perhaps more importantly, it can help to keep people safe in the mountains.

D. Review your annotations and complete the following summary organizer. Then compare organizers with a partner. Discuss any differences and the questions below.

SUMMARY ORGANIZER	
Paragraph	Main Idea
1	
2	
3	
4	
5	

1. Did you include the same ideas for each paragraph? After comparing answers, would you include any different information or change anything?

2. Did you include any of your personal opinions or add any new information? Is this a good practice in summary writing?

3. Summarizing can be done orally or in writing. Give a 1-minute summary of what you have read, using your notes and summary organizer.

E. Answer the following questions. Then discuss answers with a partner. Did summarizing help you answer the questions?

1. Give an example of the effects of avalanches.

....

2. What is the main cause of avalanches?

....

3. Explain how sediment gravity flow is connected to avalanches.

....

4. How is what happens during a grain flow different from what happens during an avalanche?

....

5. How can studying sediment gravity flows be useful to everyday people?

....

VOCABULARY CHECK

A. Review the vocabulary items in the Vocabulary Preview. Write their definitions and add examples. Use a dictionary if necessary.

B. Complete each sentence using the correct vocabulary item from the box. Use the correct form.

even	extremely	melting	mud	occur	site

1. With a total of just 15 inches of snow for the season, many ski resorts closed early because of a(n) .... dry winter.

2. It was sunny outside, and the dripping sound we heard was caused by .... snow.

3. While tire chains are helpful in snowy and icy conditions, they do little to assist a vehicle stuck in ....

4. Each time an avalanche .... , ski patrol, including rescue dogs, are dispatched to the area.

5. The avalanche was gigantic. .... long-time avalanche scientists were surprised by the size.

6. In my view, two of the most beautiful natural .... in the US are the Grand Canyon in Arizona and Niagara Falls on the border between New York and Ontario, Canada.

⬆ Go to MyEnglishLab to complete a skill practice and to join in collaborative activities.

LANGUAGE SKILL

WORKING WITH PRO-FORMS

WHY IT'S USEFUL By recognizing pro-forms, you can better follow the relationship between ideas. This will help you understand the main ideas and details of the materials you read.

◑ Go to MyEnglishLab for the Language Skill presentation and practice.

VOCABULARY STRATEGY

UTILIZING THE FRAYER MODEL

WHY IT'S USEFUL By using the Frayer model to learn vocabulary words, you can make them more meaningful, and therefore, more memorable.

The **Frayer model** is a graphic organizer. It builds vocabulary by helping learns to connect background knowledge with new concepts. Developed in 1969 by Dorothy Frayer and her colleagues at the University of Wisconsin, the model allows users to analyze words and develop their vocabulary.

In the model, the vocabulary item is in the middle, with the categories *definition*, *facts / characteristics*, *examples* (which can include pictures), and *non-examples* (which are related ideas or words) on either side. Users can fill in the organizer with information from assigned readings, their own experience, or additional research.

DEFINITION:	FACTS / CHARACTERISTICS:
large amount of snow that moves down the side of a mountain	▪ is cold ▪ may be deadly ▪ is heavy ▪ is caused by gravity ▪ can be started by an earthquake

AVALANCHE

EXAMPLES:	NON-EXAMPLES:
▪ avalanches in Austrian / Swiss Alps (1950–1951) ▪ Huascaran Avalanche, Peru (1970)	▪ blizzard ▪ snowstorm ▪ snowflakes

EXERCISE 8

A. Read the passage and then use the information, and other information you may know, to complete the Frayer models for *mud* and *mudslide*.

The pull of gravity can cause avalanches in snowy conditions and may result in mudslides on land. A mudslide is when a lot of wet earth (or mud) suddenly moves down the side of a hill. A large amount of rain or the melting of a lot of snow on a mountaintop can erode, or gradually destroy, the hill. This may trigger the mudslide. The mudslide may move quickly or slowly, but it usually picks up speed and grows in size as it collects more debris, such as rocks, trees, and even cars. Mudslides can have devastating effects and can ruin property or even cause death. In China in 2010, heavy rainfalls caused a mudslide that washed away some of the town of Zhouqu and killed more than 1,000 people.

DEFINITION:	FACTS / CHARACTERISTICS:
wet	▪ caused when water mixes with .... ▪ is sticky ▪ ....

MUD

EXAMPLES:	NON-EXAMPLES:
▪ After it rains, the ground is muddy. ▪ Sometimes kids like to play in mud puddles.	▪ dirt ▪ snow ▪ ....

DEFINITION:	FACTS / CHARACTERISTICS:
when a lot of wet earth suddenly	▪ caused by the pull of .... ▪ may be started by .... ▪ may move slowly or .... ▪ may contain rocks, ..., ... ▪ can ruin .... ▪ may cause ....

MUDSLIDE

EXAMPLES:	NON-EXAMPLES:
▪ Zhouqu, China ▪ year: .... ▪ deaths:	▪ avalanche ▪ .... ▪ ....

B. Read this excerpt from "How to Talk About Usain Bolt in the Vocabulary of Physics." Then complete the Frayer model for the word *scalar*.

> A physicist's vocabulary includes the words *scalar, vector, velocity,* and *acceleration,* and they all could be used to describe a race. The first is *scalar:* A scalar is the size, or magnitude, of something. For example, speed is a scalar—it describes how fast something moves; an airplane's average speed of 250 meters per second (m/s) is a scalar quantity.

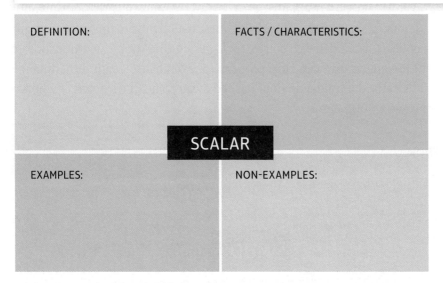

DEFINITION:

FACTS / CHARACTERISTICS:

SCALAR

EXAMPLES:

NON-EXAMPLES:

C. Now read this excerpt and create your own Frayer model for the word *vector*.

> Vectors are different. They have a magnitude and direction. An example of a vector is velocity—the speed that something moves in a specific direction. Again consider Usain Bolt's race. His fastest speed was 12.2 m/s—a scalar quantity. And his highest velocity—a vector quantity—was 12.2 m/s *toward the finish line.* It is possible for Bolt to run with a different velocity, but at the same speed. For instance, Bolt could run *away from* the finish line. In this case, his top speed is still 12.2 m/s, but his velocity is −12.2 m/s. Here, the speed is the same, but the velocity changes because the direction is different.

D. Consider these questions.

1. Compare answers in Parts B and C with a partner. Do you have any similarities? Did you include any information not in the text? If yes, was it something you already knew or learned from research?

2. How does thinking about the facts / characteristics, examples, and non-examples help you understand the word more than just knowing the definition?

❶ Go to MyEnglishLab to complete a skill practice.

APPLY YOUR SKILLS

WHY IT'S USEFUL By applying the skills you have learned in this unit, you can gain a better understanding of this challenging reading about how land moves.

BEFORE YOU READ

A. Discuss these questions with one or more students.

1. People disagree on the number of continents. What number were you taught, and why do you think there are differences in the numbers?

2. Alfred Wegener was a weather scientist who later developed a theory about the movement of land. What might cause this kind of change in interest?

3. Gravity explains landslides (when rocks slide from a high point to a low point). Think of two other examples of gravity at work.

B. You will read an article about how land moves. As you read, think about these questions.

1. What was Pangaea?

2. What was Wegener's theory of continental drift? What evidence did he have?

3. What was the process that caused continents to move?

C. Review the Unit Skills Summary. As you read the article, apply the skills you learned in this unit.

UNIT SKILLS SUMMARY

IDENTIFY COHESION BY USING THESE SKILLS:

Identify cause and effect

• Look for signal words (*because, so, as a result*) that introduce actions and reactions.

Examine examples

• Look for signal words that introduce demonstrations of complex ideas.

Summarize

• Report on the writer's main ideas while being careful not to add information.

Work with pro-forms

• Look for and use pro-forms, such as pronouns, to see and add cohesion in a text.

Utilize the Frayer model

• Learn words by noting a definition, facts, examples, and non-examples.

READ

A. Read the article on the next page. Annotate as you read and take notes in the mind map.

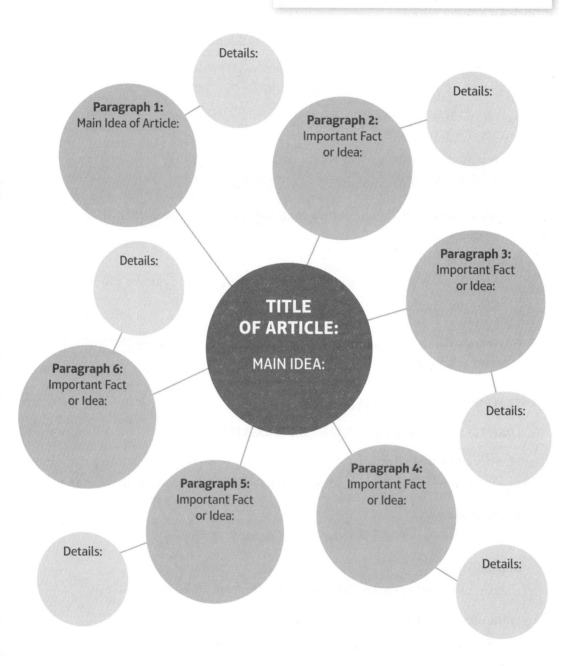

Details:

Paragraph 1: Main Idea of Article:

Details:

Paragraph 2: Important Fact or Idea:

Details:

Paragraph 3: Important Fact or Idea:

Details:

Paragraph 6: Important Fact or Idea:

TITLE OF ARTICLE:

MAIN IDEA:

Details:

Paragraph 5: Important Fact or Idea:

Paragraph 4: Important Fact or Idea:

Details:

Details:

How Land Moves

1 Everyone has taken a look at a world map and thought that the continents—North America, South America, Africa, Eurasia, Australia, and Antarctica—look like pieces of a puzzle. In fact, that was the thought that led to the idea of *continental drift*—the moving of the continents over Earth's surface—which was originated by Alfred Wegener over a century ago. Years later, this became the basis for *plate tectonics*, the scientific study of how the continents move in Earth's lithosphere.

2 Wegener was a meteorologist, a person who studies the weather. So he spent a lot of time looking at maps. One day, he noticed that the continents looked like they could fit together. Specifically, he thought that the continents were once connected to each other in a large landmass, which he called *Pangaea*. Over time he developed this idea into the theory of continental drift.

3 To support his idea, Wegener needed to find evidence—physical "reasons" to show that a theory is correct; the idea that the continents "fit" together on a map was certainly not enough. So he found evidence from other things that connected the continents. One such example came from the rocks in mountains. Studying geological research, he found that mountain ranges on different continents were created at the same time. For instance, he found that the mountain rock in Scotland was very similar to that in the eastern United States. They also fit in the right places when he put the continents together on a map. The same thing happened with fossils from extinct animals. Research showed that fossils of an animal from millions of years ago could be found both in West Africa and in eastern South America. Since the animal did not have wings, it certainly did not fly between the two continents. This still was not enough evidence, however. So, lastly, he looked at research on changes in Earth's climate and the movement of glaciers, the huge masses of ice found in mountains, the Arctic, and Antarctica. Over Earth's history, glaciers have grown much

BEFORE

AFTER

bigger, moving on top of the ground as they do so. This causes damage (called striations) to the rocks and ground. Wegener discovered that striations made by glaciers were found in tropical rainforests around the world. This, he thought, would surely be enough evidence to show that his continental drift theory was correct.

(Continued)

4 Science, however, does not always work so easily. When Wegener first wrote about the theory in 1915, very few people agreed with it. In fact, most scientists thought that his idea was crazy. One main problem, they said, was that continents do not move. Also, scientists could not see how continental plates—the thick rock that holds continents—were able to move through much denser ocean plates at the bottom of oceans. Because Wegener did not describe how the continents moved, his ideas were not taken seriously.

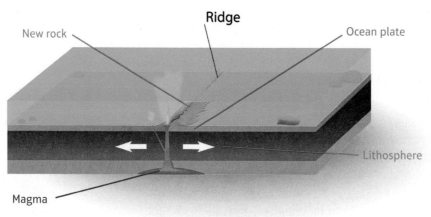

New rock

Ridge

Ocean plate

Lithosphere

Magma

Figure 1 Mid-oceanic divergent plate boundary

5 Not until years later did scientists start to accept the theory of continental drift. There were two important reasons for this. The first came when scientists discovered that the rock of ocean plates was growing. From research deep in the middle of the oceans, they found that new rock was always being made in the middle of the ocean floors. The new rock pushed the ocean plates, causing them to grow. This showed that plates are not fixed—they change. (See Figure 1.) Second, scientists were able to see that continental plates do, in fact, move. But only a little. For instance, the North American and Eurasian plates move away from each other at a rate of a few centimeters per year. But if some plates move as a result of others growing, why isn't Earth growing, too? This is because the rock of one plate gets pushed under the rock of another plate when they hit each other. All of this eventually became part of plate tectonics. And because of *plate tectonics*, scientists are pretty certain that Wegener was right about Pangaea; all of the continents were once part of a single landmass. Now the question is, what caused Pangaea to break apart in the first place?

6 The leading theory says that gravity caused Pangaea to break apart. In a process known as *gravitational spreading*, gravity worked on the thick, tall landmass, pulling the high land lower. As the land moved downward, large parts broke off and became their own landmasses: the continents. This took millions of years to happen, but it is the most likely cause of continental drift. If only Wegener were still alive to see the evidence that led to a much deeper understanding of his brilliant idea.

CULTURE NOTE

Another type of drift is now occurring in some ice shelves in Antarctica. Ice shelves are floating sheets of ice attached to land that are formed from glacier or ice sheet flows. If the water is cold enough, that ice doesn't melt but instead floats on the ocean. Larsen C is an ice shelf that comprises 48,000 kilometers of northwestern Antarctica. However, due to warmer water and air temperatures, Larsen C is disintegrating. In fact, the Antarctica Peninsula has warmed 2.5°C since 1950. Because of this warmer temperature and water, the surface of the ice shelf melts and drips down cracks. Over time, that melting expands those cracks. In fact, a section of Larsen C broke off in the summer of 2017, creating a 5,800-square-kilometer iceberg. It was one of the largest chunks to break off in recent years, but is expected to break into smaller pieces.

B. Compare notes with a partner. Did you identify similar causes and effects?

C. Reread the questions in Before You Read, Part B. With your partner, use your notes and opinions to answer the questions.

◐ Go to MyEnglishLab to read more closely, answer the critical thinking questions, and complete a summarizing activity.

THINKING CRITICALLY

Use information from the reading to address the following questions.

1. Was the scientific community in Alfred Wegener's time correct not to accept Wegener's theory? Explain.

2. If land is constantly being formed in the middle of the ocean, and plates are constantly moving, should people today be concerned about the gradual movement of the continents? Explain.

THINKING VISUALLY

Use information from the reading to address the following questions.

1. Look at the images on page 139. They show support for the idea of a Pangaea. Think about the regions you are familiar with. Does this idea of Pangaea add to or change your understanding of geography? Do additional research to find visuals showing Wegener's theory about the overlap of flora and fauna.

2. Now create your own map of the world, 1 million years from now. Show how you imagine gravitational spreading and continental drift will affect geography. What else might happen to your Earth of the future? Include those details. Present your map to the class.

THINKING ABOUT LANGUAGE

A. Read these excerpts from "How Land Moves." Notice the pro-form, in bold. Then draw an arrow to its referent.

For help with pro-forms, go to MyEnglishLab, Chemical Engineering, Part 1, Language Skill.

1. Wegener was a meteorologist, a person who studies the weather. So, **he** spent a lot of time looking at maps.

2. … (He) thought that the continents were once connected to each other in a large landmass, **which** he called Pangaea.

3. Over Earth's history, glaciers have grown much bigger, moving on top of the ground as **they** do so.

4. Wegener discovered that striations made by glaciers were found in tropical rainforests around the world. **This**, he thought, would surely be enough evidence to show that his continental drift theory was correct.

5. This is because the rock of one plate gets pushed under the rock of another plate when **they** hit each other.

6. If only Wegener were still alive to see the evidence that led to a much deeper understanding of **his** brilliant idea.

B. Choose a question from the following list. Then draft a summary where you explain the answer, being careful not to give your opinion of the topic. Use pro-forms to connect ideas in your summary and avoid repeating referents.

- How are weight and mass different?
- What is the theory of special relativity?
- How does gravity affect candles?
- What was the evidence for Wegener's theory of continental drift?

🔊 Go to MyEnglishLab to watch Professor Spakowitz's concluding video and to complete a self-assessment.

Critical Thinking Skills

Part 2 moves from skill building to application of the skills that require critical thinking. Practice activities tied to specific learning outcomes in each unit require a deeper level of understanding of the academic content.

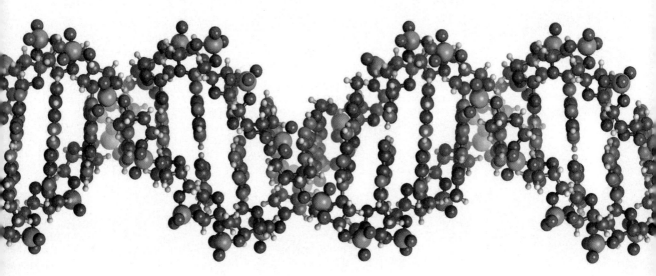

How advances in biosciences raise legal, social, and ethical concerns

Facts and Opinions

UNIT PROFILE

In this unit, you will learn how some athletes use performance drugs to try to get ahead and how scientists use genes in therapies to fight disease. You will also hear a short lecture about the use of animals in genetic engineering. In the final reading of the unit, you will consider whether fooling with Mother Nature is a good idea or not.

Look at the first sentence of the reading "Reversing the Aging Process" on page 166. Does it contain a fact or opinion? What about the first sentence of the second paragraph? How do you know?

OUTCOMES

• Identify facts
• Identify opinions
• Fact-check
• Examine language for subjectivity
• Guess meaning from context

For more about **BIOETHICS**, see **1** **3**. See also W and OC **BIOETHICS** **1** **2** **3**.

GETTING STARTED

⬆ Go to MyEnglishLab to watch Professor Greely's introductory video and to complete a self-assessment.

Discuss these questions with a partner or group.

1. Genetically modified (GM) foods are foods that have been changed by science—to taste better or be stronger against disease. They are examples of *genetic engineering*. What do you know about genetically engineering animals and humans? What would be some benefits? Some problems?

2. Medicine has changed over time. For example, people used to put leeches (blood-sucking worms) on their bodies to clean their blood. Today we use drugs like penicillin and other antibiotics to fight illness. A new medical treatment called *gene therapy* can replace and repair genes. Should people be able to have gene therapy—and other new therapies—before the practice is 100 percent safe? Or should the government make them wait? Why or why not?

3. In his introduction, Professor Greely talks about a new biological tool called CRISPR. Why are scientists excited about CRISPR technology?

SKILL 1

IDENTIFYING FACTS

WHY IT'S USEFUL By understanding what is a fact and what it isn't, you can better analyze and understand a text.

Objective statements (**facts**) are statements about a topic that can be proven and do not change from person to person. They are used to inform (describe or analyze) a topic.

Writing can have different purposes: to inform, persuade, or entertain, for example. If the purpose of a text is to inform, it probably contains facts and its tone is typically more formal and objective. Most academic textbooks, for example, use this tone.

The opposite of objective language is **subjective** language—language that expresses the writer's opinion (*should, ought, I believe*) and contains descriptive words (*the best, the most, the worst*). You'll learn more about **opinions** in Skill 2.

Examples of Facts

- names of people and places
- dates and times
- statistics
- scientific knowledge—for example: *Human beings have 23 chromosomes.* Scientific knowledge is factual information based on analysis, documentation, or other scientifically accepted forms of proof.
- common knowledge—for example: *The sun rises in the east and sets in the west.* Common knowledge is something everyone knows to be true, often by experience. Common knowledge is also information known to a cultural or national group, or shared by members of a certain field.

Study these statements:

Lance Armstrong, the cyclist, was born on September 18, 1971, in Texas.

Experts estimate that up to 5.1 million Americans suffer from Alzheimer's disease.

Red blood cells carry oxygen to the body.

These statements are all facts because they can be verified by multiple reliable sources, or proven through research. They cannot be argued.

VOCABULARY PREVIEW
Read the vocabulary items in the box. Circle the ones you know. Put a question mark next to the ones you don't know.

athletes	essential	competitors	banned
available	encouraging	risks (n)	

TIP
Add this vocabulary and any other useful items from the passage to your vocabulary flashcards, journal, or study list.

Lance Armstrong cycling in the first stage of the Giro d'Italia in Venice, Italy, in 2009

EXERCISE 1

A. Read this excerpt from the upcoming article "Performance-Enhancing Drugs." Notice the underlined information. Circle the kinds of facts found in the information. Then rewrite the information as simple factual statements.

(1) <u>Discovered by scientists in the late 1950s, EPO</u> is a naturally-occurring hormone— a chemical made by the body—that helps create red blood cells, the part of the blood that carries oxygen. (2) <u>Because oxygen is essential to athletic performance,</u> having more red blood cells can make athletes stronger when exercising, giving them an advantage over other competitors. (3) <u>But having too much EPO in the body can cause blood clots and lead to a stroke, which is often deadly</u>. That is why blood-doping using added EPO (both natural and engineered) is banned by almost all athletic organizations.

1. a) name   b) date   c) statistic   d) scientific knowledge   e) common knowledge

....

2. a) name   b) date   c) statistic   d) scientific knowledge   e) common knowledge

....

3. a) name   b) date   c) statistic   d) scientific knowledge   e) common knowledge

....

a) name   b) date   c) statistic   d) scientific knowledge   e) common knowledge

....

a) name   b) date   c) statistic   d) scientific knowledge   e) common knowledge

....

B. Think about your reading experience. What facts did you learn about EPO? What is the purpose of the excerpt: to inform, persuade, or entertain? What is the tone? Discuss with a partner.

EXERCISE 2

A. Consider these questions.

1. What have you read or heard about performance-enhancing drugs?
2. From the title of the article on the next page and what you know, predict what the author might explain.

B. Now read the article. Then read the statements that follow. Circle *T* (True) or *F* (False). Correct the false statements.

Glossary

Strategy: a plan of actions with a goal in mind

Genetically engineered: changed at the gene level using biotechnology

Blood clot: a mass of thickened blood

Focus: (n) something that receives special attention

TIP

To save time, preview the questions before you read the passage. This will help you identify and annotate information needed to answer the questions.

Performance-Enhancing Drugs

1 [1] Dating back to even before the first Olympic Games in Greece in the 8th century BCE, people have expected top performances from athletes. [2] In response, athletes have aimed to please, using things like diet, workouts, and strategy to improve. [3] Starting in the late 20th century, science gave athletes another way to gain an advantage: genetically engineered, performance-enhancing drugs (PEDs). But not all PEDs are allowed in competition.

Rita Jeptoo of Kenya winning the women's division of the Boston Marathon in 2013

[4] Two of the more high-profile athletes caught using illegal PEDs in recent years include three-time Boston Marathon champion Rita Jeptoo and seven-time Tour de France winner Lance Armstrong. [5] Both were found to have used an illegal drug called erythropoietin, or EPO. [6] Discovered by scientists in the late 1950s, EPO is a naturally-occurring hormone—a chemical made by the body—that helps create red blood cells, the part of the blood that carries oxygen. [7] Because oxygen is essential to athletic performance, having more red blood cells can make athletes stronger when exercising, giving them an advantage over other competitors. [8] But having too much EPO in the body can cause blood clots and lead to a stroke, which is often deadly. [9] That is why blood-doping using added EPO (both natural and engineered) is banned by almost all athletic organizations.

2 Greater understanding of genetics over the past 50 years is why performance enhancers such as EPO are easily produced today. Scientists first identified the gene responsible for producing EPO and then developed a process to genetically engineer the hormone outside of the human body. Originally the goal was to make EPO for people who did not produce enough themselves—people with blood diseases such as anemia, for example. But eventually EPO became more widely available.

The Blood-Doping Process

| A month or two before competition: The first treatment is administered; the athlete may receive two treatments per week. | About three weeks later: Effects of the treatments are beginning to be felt in the form of more energy and endurance, as the red blood cell count increases. | Day of competition: Increased red blood cell count allows more oxygen to be carried from the lungs to the muscles, giving the athlete's muscles more "fuel." |

3 PEDs are not limited to helping physical performance; they are also used to help cognition—the mental process of learning and understanding. One focus of cognitive PEDs has been to reduce the negative effects of Alzheimer's disease—an illness that severely reduces cognitive performance, such as memory. The drugs modafinil and donepezil, for example, have proven beneficial to Alzheimer's patients. They have also been shown to increase cognitive function in healthy individuals, which concerns some people. They worry that, like EPO, these drugs could be misused.

4 PEDs were developed to help people with illnesses live better lives. Only these individuals, under their doctor's supervision, should be allowed to use PEDs. No one wants athletic trainers and academic tutors encouraging athletes and students to use these sorts of drugs, given the serious health risks and the ethical implications.

T / F   1. EPO has been approved as an athletic performance drug.

T / F   2. An athlete who has red blood cells is stronger than other athletes.

T / F   3. Red blood cells are responsible for moving oxygen in the body.

T / F   4. Having too much EPO in the body can be deadly.

T / F   5. All athletic organizations have prohibited the use of EPO.

T / F   6. PEDs can help people who are dealing with memory loss.

T / F   7. Healthy students could benefit from taking cognitive PEDs.

T / F   8. The author believes that anyone should be allowed to use PEDs.

C. Reread the article. Then identify the following kinds of facts in Paragraph 1.
Write the fact and the number of the sentence. Then paraphrase the information,
rewriting it in your own words. More than one correct answer may be possible.

1. A date: _8th century BCE_   Sentence ___1___

    Paraphrase: _The first Olympics were held in the 8th century BCE._

2. A date: _____   Sentence _____

    Paraphrase: _____

3. A name: _____   Sentence _____

    Paraphrase: _____

4. Common knowledge: _____   Sentence _____

    Paraphrase: _____

5. Scientific knowledge: _____   Sentence _____

    Paraphrase: _____

D. Check your answers in Exercise 2, Parts A–C.

EXERCISE 3

Discuss these questions with a partner.

1. Academic textbooks contain objective texts that aim to inform. What are other
sources of primarily objective material?

2. Why do you think it's important to be able to identify objective statements?

VOCABULARY CHECK

A. Review the vocabulary items in the Vocabulary Preview. Write their definitions and add examples. Use a dictionary if necessary.

B. Complete each sentence using the correct vocabulary item from the box. Use the correct form.

athlete	available	ban	competitor	encourage	essential	risk

1. In extreme sports, there are serious health .... , from broken bones to death.

2. Synthetic drugs are widely .... in drugstores everywhere.

3. Doctors always .... patients to complete their antibiotics, advising them that taking the full course protects society as a whole.

4. Like water and sleep, oxygen is .... to life.

5. There is a debate about whether student ....—from college basketball players to members of the university tennis team—should be paid.

6. Historically, the University of Connecticut women's basketball program has produced fierce .... They are nearly impossible to beat.

7. One extreme view is that sports-governing bodies should let athletes use .... substances.

🔵 Go to MyEnglishLab to complete vocabulary and skill practices, and to join in collaborative activities.

SKILL 2

IDENTIFYING OPINIONS

WHY IT'S USEFUL By recognizing subjective language, you can better analyze and understand a text.

Subjective statements express personal beliefs, **opinions**, values, and feelings. They cannot be proven true or false. *Subjective* is the opposite of *objective*. Subjective language is found in editorials, reviews, descriptive writing, and critiques. It is not acceptable in scientific findings or news journalism. While reading, you can recognize subjective statements by the language used.

Study the examples in this chart:

Judgmental Language	Personal Language	Emotive Language
Writers convey how they feel about something by using judgmental language.	When expressing a judgment, writers may use the first person (*I, me, my*).	Writers use superlatives and exaggeration to get an emotional reaction.

Verbs	Adjectives		Superlatives
assume	beautiful	I believe	the best
believe	dangerous	To me	the most amazing
feel	evil	from my perspective	the most difficult
imagine	good	in my experience	the worst
suppose	safe	in my judgment	**Adverbs of Frequency:**
suggest	ugly	In my opinion	**Exaggerations**
think		in my view	always
Modal Verbs	**Adverbs**		never
of Obligation	apparently		**Quantifiers**
have to	maybe		all
ought to	obviously		every(body)
must	perhaps		no(body)
should	unfortunately		

VOCABULARY PREVIEW

Read the vocabulary items in the box. Circle the ones you know. Put a question mark next to the ones you don't know.

technique	strengthen	figured out	affects	damaging	treatments

EXERCISE 4

A. Read the excerpts from "Gene Therapy," a critique of gene therapy. Mark the words that make the statements subjective. Then explain your answers to a partner.

1. Gene therapy is an exciting, experimental technique for treating serious diseases.

2. Despite all of these wonderful benefits, however, gene therapy isn't widely available. But perhaps that's good.

B. Gene therapy is a new way to fight diseases. From the sentences above, how do you think the writer feels about gene therapy? Discuss with a partner.

EXERCISE 5

A. Read the title of the passage. What kinds of diseases might be helped by a treatment called "gene therapy"?

B. Read the passage and underline the subjective language in Paragraphs 3 and 4.

Gene Therapy

1   They say that necessity is the mother of invention, a belief medical scientists know well. Since preventing and stopping disease is an ongoing necessity, one new invention has experts hopeful: gene therapy.

2   Gene therapy is an exciting, experimental technique for treating serious diseases. Unlike the surgeries and drugs of traditional medicine, gene therapy uses genes to treat or protect against disease. For people with genetic diseases such as sickle cell anemia, gene therapy can be used to replace bad genes with healthy ones. For other types of diseases such as cancer, gene therapy might strengthen the immune system to fight cancer cells. It even has the possibility of helping people stop smoking by changing the way the brain responds to nicotine. Despite all of these wonderful benefits, however, gene therapy isn't widely available. But perhaps that's good.

3   There are a number of reasons why. First, it is an experimental method of treatment, which means it is still being researched; scientists have not yet figured out how to make gene therapy safe—that is, risk-free. Two clinical trials in recent decades have had devastating results. In one, a gene-therapy trial in France, a number of people in the trial developed

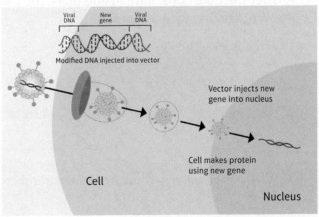

Viral DNA | New gene | Viral DNA

Modified DNA injected into vector

Vector injects new gene into nucleus

Cell makes protein using new gene

Cell

Nucleus

Gene therapy using an adenovirus vector

(Continued)

leukemia, a type of cancer that affects the bones. In another, in the United States, an 18-year-old male died after being given a virus as part of the therapy. In addition, there is also the frightening possibility that genes could affect the wrong types of cells, damaging the healthy ones. Finally, it is believed that gene therapy will be very expensive, and future treatments could cost millions of dollars for patients.

4   While research moves forward, scientists must focus on making gene therapy safe. Anyone with a deadly disease would try anything to get better, but we should not have to risk our lives when receiving treatment that might not be successful. Obviously, medical scientists have to continue working tirelessly on making gene therapy a safe and successful treatment, as nearly everyone in the world may, in one way or another, eventually depend on it.

TIP

One way to get a "snapshot" of the facts and opinions in a reading is to record ideas in a **T-chart**. You can list facts in one column, and opinions in the other.

GENE THERAPY

Facts:	Opinions:

C. **Answer the questions. Reread and mark the paragraphs where you found the answers. Discuss with a partner.**

1. What is gene therapy?

   ....

2. What are some ways that gene therapy can be used to treat diseases?

   ....

3. Why is gene therapy considered an experimental technique for treating disease?

   ....

4. What happened in France at a gene-therapy trial?

....

5. What happened in the US trial?

....

6. According to the author, what should be the focus of gene-therapy research?

....

D. **Read each statement and decide if it is a subjective statement. Write *S* (Subjective) or *O* (Objective). Discuss with a partner.**

.... 1. Gene therapy is the most exciting new development in gene research.

.... 2. Gene therapy has been used in clinical research trials.

.... 3. The cost of gene therapy is too high for anyone and must be lowered.

.... 4. Some people in gene-therapy trials have gotten sick from the therapy.

.... 5. The goal of the research is to make gene therapy more effective.

.... 6. Gene therapy should not be used with humans until it is safe.

EXERCISE 6

Discuss your reading experience with one or more students.

1. Even though the reading is about something factual and scientific—gene therapy—the writer expresses an opinion in many parts of the passage. Based on what you read, how do you think the writer feels about gene therapy? Do you agree with the writer?

2. There are many words that can be used to signal a writer's judgment, for example, adjectives (*safe*), adverbs (*maybe*), verbs (*believe*), modals (*should*), and quantifiers (*all*). Think of three other words or expressions that can signal subjectivity.

• ....

• ....

• ....

VOCABULARY CHECK

A. Review the vocabulary items in the Vocabulary Preview. Write their definitions and add examples. Use a dictionary if necessary.

B. Read each sentence. Circle the word or phrase that is the best synonym for the underlined vocabulary item.

1. The doctor had developed a surgical <u>technique</u> for operating on the heart that involved minimal cutting.

   job   task   method   treatment

2. In order to <u>strengthen</u> their bodies, marathon runners must do a combination of weight training and cardiovascular exercises.

   make stronger   weaken   stress   rest

3. Some drugs <u>damage</u> healthy cells, sometimes causing them to die.

   repair   kill   break   injure

4. Astronomers have spent countless hours trying to <u>figure out</u> if life exists on other planets, but they haven't solved the question yet.

   believe   question   understand   agree

5. Asthma is a disease that <u>affects</u> the lungs, making breathing difficult.

   changes   improves   acts   develops

6. Traditional <u>treatment</u> for cancer ranges from radiation to chemotherapy to surgery.

   research   advice   discussion   therapy

↻ Go to MyEnglishLab to complete vocabulary and skill practices, and to join in collaborative activities.

INTEGRATED SKILLS

FACT-CHECKING

WHY IT'S USEFUL By confirming that information is factual, you can feel more confident in your understanding of the ideas.

As a student, you will consult a variety of sources while doing academic research. These sources will contain many statements of fact. Most of the time, if the sources are reliable, these facts will have been reviewed and confirmed. However, sometimes mistakes occur—information has changed, or a writer has included his or her opinion.

Therefore, it is important to always check the information. A critical mind asks things like "Does this make sense?" "Where does this information come from?" and "How do we know this?"

How to Fact-Check

- Read the entire article or listen to the entire broadcast.
- Look out for subjective language.
- Confirm statistics / numbers, and check names of people and places.
- Ask yourself if the information makes sense. If something doesn't seem correct, check it by doing a little research.
- Evaluate the following:
  - the source (Who is responsible for publishing the information—an individual, a government, an organization, a company? What are the qualifications of the author?)
  - the purpose (Is it to inform? Entertain? Persuade? Exchange information?)
  - the content (Is the information objective or subjective? Is it accurate?)
  - the currency (Is the information up-to-date?)

TIP

What cannot or does not need to be fact-checked?

- Common knowledge: Common knowledge means that everyone knows that it is true—that the information presents a universal truth, for example: *A good night's sleep leaves you feeling rested.*
- Opinions: Opinions are subjective and may express a personal belief, for example: *I believe that genetic engineering is wrong.*
- Predictions: Predictions are subjective and are impossible to verify, as the event has not occurred, for example: *In 50 years, genetic testing will be done in every doctor's office.*

FACT-CHECKING

Resource	Example	For ...
dictionaries	*Merriam-Webster* HowJSay	spellings of names definitions of terms pronunciations
encyclopedias	Wikipedia *Encyclopedia Britannica*	dates of events general descriptions of events
maps and atlases	Google Earth Rand McNally	location of places

(Continued)

FACT-CHECKING		
Resource	Example	For ...
Internet sites	journalistic reporting social media government pages	journalists' stories tweets, posts, blogs images video audio
subscription databases (available in public and university libraries)	LexisNexis Academic Academic Search Premier AccessScience Medline	detailed information
primary sources (available in public and university libraries)	transcripts of interviews or speeches raw scientific data diaries or letters	information you want to interpret yourself
firsthand experience	watch the film yourself download the document and read it yourself visit the historic site yourself	having an unfiltered experience

VOCABULARY PREVIEW

Read the vocabulary items in the box. Circle the ones you know. Put a question mark next to the ones you don't know.

behave	expected (adj)	possibilities	relations	continue	valuable

EXERCISE 7

A. Think of a science-fiction book or movie you are familiar with. What parts, good and bad, do you think could actually happen?

B. Read these excerpts from the upcoming lecture "Genetically Engineering Animals." Underline the information that you would fact-check. Then label that information with *date*, *name*, *place*, or *event*.

> 1. In 1993, the film *Jurassic Park* filled audiences with fear and excitement as dinosaurs ran free, destroying everything around them.

2. For example, in 1999 scientists in Singapore engineered the DNA of a type of small fish so that it could glow with different colors.

3. Geneticist George Church of Harvard University is using a new technology called CRISPR to genetically engineer pigs to have extra parts—human parts—such as ears, lungs, and hearts.

🎧 C. **Now listen to the lecture. Then read each excerpt and decide if it should be fact-checked. If yes (✓), underline the information to be checked. With a partner, talk about the resources you would use to fact-check the information.**

Glossary

Generation: the period of time between the birth of parents and the birth of their children

Species: a group of animals or plants of the same kinds

CRISPR: the abbreviation for *clustered regularly interspaced short palindromic repeats;* parts of DNA being used in gene therapy

Commercial: (adj) for making money

Suffering: pain and stress

☐ 1. Humans have been "genetically engineering" animals for thousands of years. We have made small, cute dogs from their bigger, scarier relations: wolves.

☐ 2. Scientists have already genetically engineered pigs to be born with human ears.

☐ 3. Other researchers think they can create cows and goats that produce milk containing important medicines.

☐ 4. Many scientists … think genetic engineering should be used only to help people or other animals.

CULTURE NOTE

In November of 2015, the Food and Drug Administration (FDA), which is responsible for the safety of the US food supply, approved the first genetically altered animal that could be sold for human consumption. The fish, called AquAdvantage, is an Atlantic salmon that has been given a gene from a fish called the ocean pout. It has also been given a growth hormone from the Chinook salmon. This genetically engineered salmon grows about twice as fast as a regular Atlantic salmon.

🔊 D. Listen again to the lecture. Answer the questions with a partner. Then complete the fact sheet.

1. What did scientists in Singapore create and when?

2. Before CRISPR technology, what was the problem with the human ears that were genetically engineered using pigs?

3. How does geneticist George Church's CRISPR technology hope to address the problems of growing human parts on pigs?

4. What other example does the speaker give of genetic engineering involving animals?

5. What are the concerns about genetically engineering animals?

FACT SHEET Genetically Engineered Animals

• **Genetically engineered fish:**

....
(date) (created by whom) (event)

• **Genetically engineered pigs, pre-CRISPR technology:**

....
(event / problem)

• **Genetically engineered pigs, CRISPR technology:**

....
(name of scientist) (university) (event)

• **Other genetically engineered animals:**

....
(type of animals) (event)

E. Compare fact sheets with a partner and discuss any differences. Then discuss these questions and be prepared to share with the class.

1. Did understanding subjective and objective language help you distinguish fact from opinion? Why or why not?

2. When listening to or reading information, do you fact-check, or do you assume that everything is true? What does it depend on?

3. Fact-checking all information can be time-consuming. What can you do to save time but still get reliable information?

VOCABULARY CHECK

A. Review the vocabulary items in the Vocabulary Preview. Write their definitions and add examples. Use a dictionary if necessary.

B. Read each sentence. Then match the underlined vocabulary item with the correct meaning.

.... 1. The child <u>behaved</u> well, saying *please* and *thank you* whenever he was helped.

.... 2. As <u>expected</u>, the cells died. But the researchers were surprised at how quickly it happened.

.... 3. Living in Morocco meant studying Arabic and the <u>possibility</u> of learning French if there was time.

.... 4. After the beloved scientist died, many of her <u>relations</u> and friends gathered to remember her.

.... 5. The debate about genetically altered animals will <u>continue</u> into the future.

.... 6. Being curious is a <u>valuable</u> personality trait for all scientists to have.

a. opportunity

b. go on

c. predicted

d. important

e. family

f. acted

○ Go to MyEnglishLab to complete a skill practice and to join in collaborative activities.

LANGUAGE SKILL

EXAMINING LANGUAGE FOR SUBJECTIVITY

WHY IT'S USEFUL By understanding how subjective language is formed, you can better create your own opinions.

○ Go to MyEnglishLab for the Language Skill presentation and practice.

VOCABULARY STRATEGY

GUESSING MEANING FROM CONTEXT

WHY IT'S USEFUL By guessing meaning from context, you can increase your reading fluency—making reading assignments more enjoyable.

Academic texts will contain many unknown vocabulary words, but effective readers guess the meaning of the word instead of stopping to look up the definition. Guessing the meaning from context is the ability to infer the meaning using contextual clues.

By looking at the surrounding words, thinking about how the word is formed, and applying your background knowledge of the subject, you can often understand the word without having to use a dictionary.

These clues can help you infer the meaning of a word:

- **definition or synonym after a comma, dash, or colon, or in parentheses**

  Gene therapy is an <u>experimental</u> method of treatment, which means it is **still being researched**.

  EPO is a naturally-occurring <u>hormone</u>—**a chemical made by the body**—that helps create red blood cells, the part of the blood that carries oxygen.

  Many patients' bodies <u>reject</u> (**refuse**) organs from others.

- **examples after the expressions *for example, i.e., such as, for instance***

  One focus of cognitive PEDs has been to reduce the negative effects of Alzheimer's disease—an illness that severely reduces <u>cognitive performance</u>, **such as memory**.

- **antonym and contrast**

  Scientists <u>have not yet figured out</u> how to make gene therapy safe. On the other hand, they **know** what effect conventional drug treatments will have.

- **word forms: getting additional information from prefixes and suffixes**

  multi- (meaning: "many"): <u>Multiple</u> sources said they had seen the athlete using EPO.

  -less (meaning: "without"): Thanks to the <u>tireless</u> efforts of the emergency medical technicians, many lives were saved.

EXERCISE 8

A. Use context to understand the boldfaced words. Follow these steps:

1. What part of the context helped you? Underline it.

2. What kind of context clue is it? Circle the letter (a, b, c, d).

3. Write a simple definition of the boldfaced word.

1. **Genetic engineering**—changing the DNA in an organism's genes—has progressed so quickly in recent years that these dreams are now close to becoming reality.

   a. definition   b. example   c. antonym or contrast   d. word form

   Definition: ....

2. Both Lance Armstrong and Rita Jeptoo were found to have used an **illegal** drug called erythropoietin, or EPO.

a. definition   b. example   c. antonym or contrast   d. word form

Definition: ....

3. Having too much EPO in your body can be **fatal**, for example, causing a deadly stroke.

a. definition   b. example   c. antonym or contrast   d. word form

Definition: ....

4. In the past, treating sickle cell anemia involved replacing a person's bone marrow, a **complicated** treatment. In contrast, with recent advances in molecular biology, treatment now may be a lot simpler.

a. definition   b. example   c. antonym or contrast   d. word form

Definition: ....

5. Many scientists **disapprove** of commercial uses and think genetic engineering should be used only to help people or other animals.

a. definition   b. example   c. antonym or contrast   d. word form

Definition: ....

B. Read each sentence. Then guess and write the meaning of each boldfaced word based on context.

1. Blood-doping—using added EPO (both natural and engineered)—is banned by almost all athletic organizations. In other words, its use has been **forbidden**.

Meaning: ....

2. No one wants athletic trainers and academic tutors encouraging athletes and students to use these sorts of drugs, given the serious health risks, or **dangers**.

Meaning: ....

3. For other types of diseases such as **cancer**, gene therapy might strengthen the immune system to fight cancer cells.

Meaning: ....

4. Humans have been "genetically engineering" animals for thousands of years; we have made small, cute dogs from their bigger, scarier relations—**wolves**.

Meaning: ....

5. The treatments we have today may be **worthless** in the near future, replaced by better, faster, more targeted methods.

   Meaning: ....

6. People who oppose genetic therapies may learn to **accept** them, especially if they know of someone who has benefited from them.

   Meaning: ....

C. Consider these questions.

1. Compare answers with a partner. Do you have similar meanings? What context clues helped you to infer the meaning of the word?

2. How often do you use a dictionary or thesaurus when reading in your first language? How often do you use it when reading in English? When can using a dictionary be useful? How could it be unhelpful?

❶ Go to MyEnglishLab to complete a skill practice.

APPLY YOUR SKILLS

WHY IT'S USEFUL By applying the skills you have learned in this unit, you can gain a better understanding of this challenging reading about aging and reversing the aging process.

BEFORE YOU READ

A. Discuss these questions with one or more students.

1. People spend a lot of time and money trying to be healthy or live longer. What are some actions that people can take to have a healthy and long life? Explain.

2. Gene editing, the ability to change parts of DNA, has become more common with improved technology. Scientists are now working on reversing the aging process, using gene editing. What are the possible pros and cons of this process?

3. If you could make a change to your genome that would let you live longer, would you? Explain.

B. You will read an article about aging and reversing the aging process. As you read, think about these questions.

1. What is longevity and what factors can influence it?

2. How can genetic engineering give people longer lives?

3. What are the possible positive and negative effects of altering genes for longevity?

C. Review the Unit Skills Summary. As you read the article, apply the skills you learned in this unit.

UNIT SKILLS SUMMARY

DISTINGUISH FACTS FROM OPINIONS BY USING THESE SKILLS:

Identify facts

- Look for names, numbers, and common and proven knowledge.

Identify opinions

- Keep an eye out for statements containing judgement, personal, and emotional language.

Fact-check

- Evaluate the accuracy of statements by asking questions such as "Does this make sense?" and "Where does this information come from?" If something doesn't seem right, double-check it by consulting another source.

Examine language for subjectivity

- Form comparative and superlative adjectives, and use modals of advisability, advice, necessity, obligation, and prohibition to express opinions and beliefs.

Guess meaning from context

- Look for clues that help you infer the meaning of the words, such as definitions and synonyms, examples, antonyms, and word forms.

READ

A. Read the article on the next page. Take notes in the T-chart. Annotate the article, marking new vocabulary and noting your opinion.

TOPIC	
Facts:	**Opinions:**

Reversing the Aging Process

1   Robert Marchand recently became the fastest cyclist in his age group by riding his bicycle nearly 23 kilometers in one hour. This may not seem very far when you compare it to the world record of 56 kilometers set just a few years ago. Marchand's record was a bit "easier" to get because, well, he has no competition. Marchand is 105 years old and the only one in his age group. The Frenchman has said his success is because of healthy living—he eats many fruits and vegetables and cycles often. But others see it as a result of something else: his genes.

2   *Longevity*, which means "long life," is something that most people want. We eat healthy foods and exercise because we hope to live longer. And a lot of research shows that healthy living does this. For example, author Dan Buettner writes in *The Blue Zones Solution* about members of a Seventh Day Adventist group in California whose members do not eat meat, drink alcohol, or smoke cigarettes. They been shown to live up to ten years longer than the average person. So, if lifestyle is all that we need for longevity, then there should be a lot of people who live to be centenarians—people who are 100 years old or more. But in fact, only about 1 person in 6,000 becomes a centenarian—less than 0.02 percent. So what is the reason only certain people become centenarians?

3   Some of it has to do with our genes. Research suggests that genes are one of the many reasons for differences in longevity. In studies of centenarians, a few interesting results were found. First, scientists were able to connect longevity to about 150 places in the centenarians' DNA. This means that there is not one gene for longevity—there are *many* genes for long life. But there is something even more interesting: The research showed that about 15 percent of the general population has these longevity genes.

Frenchman Robert Marchand, 105, cycling in Saint-Quentin-en-Yvelines, France, in 2017. At the event, Marchand set a new world record in the new "over-105" category by riding nearly 23 kilometers in 1 hour.

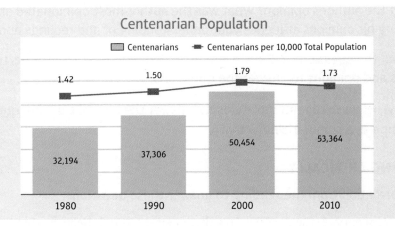

Centenarian Population

Legend: Centenarians | Centenarians per 10,000 Total Population

Year	Centenarians	Centenarians per 10,000 Total Population
1980	32,194	1.42
1990	37,306	1.50
2000	50,454	1.79
2010	53,364	1.73

4   But what about the other 85 percent of people *without* longevity genes? Could genetic engineering give these people longer lives? Geneticist George Church of Harvard University's Harvard Medical School definitely thinks so. One part of aging is caused by the deterioration of a cell's mitochondria (which produces energy for the cell). By using CRISPR, researchers have activated a protein that helps to reverse the aging of mitochondria within the cells. The mitochondria became stronger and it also reverses other age-related problems, such as muscle deterioration. He argues that this is not only good for people but for business as well. Because many countries have aging populations, it would be valuable to have people who could live longer and healthier lives as they could continue working, be economically independent, and be less dependent on government healthcare programs. In turn, they would continue to pay taxes on their earnings, which would help pay for pension and medical benefits for others. This, he says, could solve problems for the economy—by keeping people in their jobs—and could also give centenarian cyclists like Robert Marchand more competition in the future.

5   But some don't think this is a good idea. For one, it is possible that in altering one of the genes for longevity, the brain or heart, for example, might be affected. A second problem with genetic engineering for longevity is this: If we change our genes before having children, then our children's genes would be changed, too, as they receive a copy of chromosomes from each parent. It is impossible to know the effects that this genetic engineering might have on babies. Experiments might be fine for mice in a laboratory, but it is not something we want to try on humans. Certainly, it is better to be careful than to rush into a bad decision.

6   No one really knows what the future of genetic engineering and longevity will look like. For now though, fans hope that Robert Marchand continues to cycle—likely without any competition—and that his record is not broken anytime soon.

CULTURE NOTE

Harvard Medical School, established in 1782, is a graduate school of Harvard University. It is located in Boston, Massachusetts, US. Acceptance is very competitive. In 2016, over 7,000 applied for 165 spots.

B. Compare notes with a partner. Was the passage mostly factual, or was it more about the author's opinion? What was the author most opinionated about? How did reading his opinions influence your understanding of and feelings about the topic?

C. Reread the questions in Before You Read, Exercise B. With your partner, use your notes and opinions to answer the questions.

⬤ Go to MyEnglishLab to read more closely, answer the critical thinking questions, and complete a summarizing activity.

THINKING CRITICALLY

Use information from the reading to answer these questions.

1. In Paragraph 4, the passage says that George Church believes that countries with aging populations would benefit from anti-aging technology. Specifically, it says that Church believes the technology could solve economic problems. What does Church mean by this? Do you agree?

2. Aging is not classified as a disease by the US Food and Drug Administration (FDA), which oversees the approval of new medical interventions. Do you believe it should be and that the work of Church is as important as work being done on genetic diseases? What are some arguments for and against classifying aging as a disease, and what is your opinion?

THINKING VISUALLY

Use information from the reading and the bar graph to answer these questions.

1. Consider the information in the bar graph. What can you say about causes of death?

2. Imagine that it is 2040 and CRISPR technology has gained widespread use. Predict changes in the causes and figures. Add to the graph and discuss with a partner.

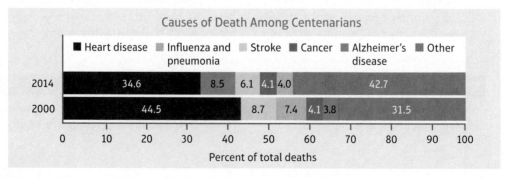

Causes of Death Among Centenarians

■ Heart disease ■ Influenza and pneumonia ■ Stroke ■ Cancer ■ Alzheimer's disease ■ Other

Year	Heart disease	Influenza and pneumonia	Stroke	Cancer	Alzheimer's disease	Other
2014	34.6	8.5	6.1	4.1	4.0	42.7
2000	44.5	8.7	7.4	4.1	3.8	31.5

Percent of total deaths

THINKING ABOUT LANGUAGE

A. Complete the chart with adjectives from "Reversing the Aging Process." Is the adjective positive, neutral, or negative? Then write the other forms.

For help with examining language for subjectivity, go to MyEnglishLab, Bioethics, Part 2, Language Skill.

Adjective	Comparative Form	Superlative Form
fast		
	farther	
		the healthiest
long		
		the most interesting
	better	
	more valuable	
	worse	

B. Return to the reading and follow these steps:

1. Mark each word you don't understand. Then use the context clues to determine the meaning.

2. Write the meaning in the margin.

3. With a partner, compare words and definitions.

4. Use a dictionary to define any words you still don't understand.

🔊 Go to MyEnglishLab to watch Professor Greely's concluding video and to complete a self-assessment.

Design principles help create business innovation

BUSINESS AND DESIGN

Inferences and Predictions

UNIT PROFILE

In this unit, you will read about a popular idea called "corporate social responsibility." You will also hear about a company that is putting the idea into action. In the final reading of the unit, you will learn about the Global Compact and the United Nations Sustainable Development Goals.

Look at the reading "Working Together for a Better World" on page 190. Quickly read the first paragraph. As you read, think about what information will come next. Then try to predict the answer to the question "Who has the ability to make differences around the world?"

OUTCOMES

• Make inferences
• Predict
• Identify parts of a lecture
• Interpret hedging language
• Compile a vocabulary journal

For more about **BUSINESS AND DESIGN**, see ❶ ❸.
See also Ⓦ and ⓄⒸ **BUSINESS AND DESIGN** ❶ ❷ ❸.

GETTING STARTED

○ Go to MyEnglishLab to watch Juli Sherry's introductory video and to complete a self-assessment.

Discuss these questions with a partner or group.

1. What big problems is the world facing today? Which one do you care the most about? Who should fix it? Is there a role for business owners?

2. Imagine two ice cream shops in your town. You learn that one gives some of its profits to a community group that helps the homeless. The other invests its profits in the shop itself, including its employees. Which shop do you buy your next triple fudge sundae from? Why?

3. In her introduction, Juli Sherry says there's a topic that businesses are really interested in nowadays. What is it? How can a mission statement help a company express its social goals?

SKILL 1

MAKING INFERENCES

WHY IT'S USEFUL By making inferences, you can understand information not directly stated in a text. Improving your inferencing skills can also help you to draw conclusions and better comprehend texts.

Inferences are guesses using facts, observations, and logic. When you read something and understand information that is not directly stated, you are inferencing. Inferencing is something only a reader (or listener) can do. A writer (or speaker) can only intend or imply something.

As readers, we bring our own biases, logic, values, and experiences to a reading experience—and we use these as tools to help "fill in the blanks" that writers may leave. Consider this example:

In 1959, Hawaii was admitted to the United States as the 50th state, Fidel Castro came to power, and Disney's *Sleeping Beauty* mesmerized moviegoers. Meanwhile, Ruth Handler was making her own contribution to American culture, creating and selling Barbie®. The impossibly proportioned blond doll, named after Handler's daughter, is deservingly credited with sparking a feminist backlash that would grow along with the toy's wild popularity throughout the decades.

From this example, you can infer these things:

1. Ruth Handler was a toy inventor and entrepreneur.
2. She was a mother.
3. Her daughter's name was Barbie.
4. Barbie, the doll, was loved and hated.
5. The author believes that Barbie is antifeminist.

Techniques for Inferencing

- **Be an active reader.** Ask questions of the text such as "Why is the author mentioning this detail?"

- **Activate background knowledge.** Ask yourself what you already know about the topic. Be aware of what "insights" or information you find yourself adding—or inferring. Ask yourself, "What information in the text supports my inference?"

- **Understand vocabulary.** Words are powerful. Good writers use words purposefully. What can you infer from the language?

- **Look at the whole package: title, text, visuals (photos, graphs).** What story is the writer trying to tell?

VOCABULARY PREVIEW

Read the vocabulary items in the box. Circle the ones you know. Put a question mark next to the ones you don't know.

access (n)	viewed	obtained	refusing	follow	permitted

EXERCISE 1

A. Read the title and look at the image in the article on the next page. From this information, what can you tell about the article?

☐ It will focus on volunteering.

☐ It will explain how to be successful in business.

☐ It will describe how and why businesses help their communities.

TIP

To make inferences, ask yourself questions. When you finish a sentence or a paragraph, ask yourself, "What is the meaning of what I have read?" "Why did the author write this?" "What does this information tell me, or what can I deduce from this information?"

B. Think about your inferencing experience. What questions did you ask yourself when looking at the title and image? What knowledge of your own helped shape your inference?

EXERCISE 2

A. What do you know about businesses that help or give back to their communities? What kinds of help do they provide?

Glossary

Philanthropy: the practice of giving money to people who need it

Supply chain: a system of delivering goods

Sustainably: in a way that does not cause damage to the environment

Ethical: connected to the idea of right and wrong

Labor: (n) related to workers and the workplace

Guarantee: (v) to promise something

B. Read the article. Then read the statements that follow. Circle *T* (True) or *F* (False). Correct the false statements.

Doing Good Is Good for Business

1 Starbucks, the popular coffee chain, can be found in 75 countries with over 25,000 stores, with more to open in the future. With billions of dollars in profit, Starbucks, however, does much more than sell coffee; it has invested in its employees, its neighborhoods, and its world.

Employees from a company volunteering at a soup kitchen

2 Like Starbucks, many businesses today practice what's known as *corporate social responsibility* (CSR). Through CSR, companies recognize that there is more to success than just profit. Businesses, like Starbucks, can make a real difference in solving world problems while at the same time benefiting the business.

3 In a good CSR strategy, businesses often use philanthropy to help solve especially large and difficult problems. Businesses may try to help bring water to hard-to-reach areas and clean up after natural disasters. For instance, in many countries where the coffee they use is grown, Starbucks works actively with community organizations and invests in projects to help communities have access to clean water and to address issues of health.

(Continued)

4 Many businesses practice CSR by working to protect the environment. In the past, environmental protection was viewed as a social cause unrelated to a business; today, environmental protection is a necessary part of business practice. Socially responsible businesses investigate their supply chain: They make certain that materials are obtained sustainably and production is done safely. By refusing to work with suppliers that do not follow environmental protection policy, businesses not only improve their own treatment of the environment but also influence others to do the same. Starbucks, also, has a good environmental CSR and invests heavily in renewable energy and energy conservation, and works with farmers to develop climate-smart practices.

5 Finally, an important form of CSR is ethical labor practice. Businesses should guarantee that workers in their supply chain are treated as well as regular employees. This has led to campaigns to improve working conditions, to end the practice of child labor, and to ensure that everyone involved is treated fairly. For instance, Starbucks's Coffee and Farmer Equity Practices assures that workers are paid fairly, receive all nationally recognized benefits, and are not forced to work more than legally permitted.

6 While individual business leaders have often cared about these issues, it is only recently that so many businesses have put such importance on CSR. Despite some difficulties, progress has been quick. Large businesses like Starbucks that continue to address CSR and work to solve environmental and labor problems will find that it benefits not only them but the world.

T / F   1. Many people around the world buy coffee from Starbucks.

T / F   2. CSR is concerned with how businesses make money.

T / F   3. Helping communities improve their access to water is one example of a CSR project.

T / F   4. When Starbucks gets involved in a community project, it does all the work itself.

T / F   5. Child labor is an example of an unethical labor practice.

T / F   6. Only a few businesses currently have CSR policies.

T / F   7. The author of the article is enthusiastic about CSR.

C. Reread the article. Then check your answers in Parts A and B.

D. Discuss these questions with a partner.

1. The first sentence of the article says that Starbucks will be opening more stores. What inferences can you make from that information?

2. The article says that many businesses are involved in CSR because "there is more to success than just profit." What is the author suggesting that companies care about? In your experience, is that true?

3. In the final paragraph, the author writes that there are still "some difficulties," but doesn't include details. What might those difficulties be? Why do you think the article doesn't explain them?

EXERCISE 3

Discuss these questions with a partner.

1. What information in the article allowed you to infer the answer to Question 1 in Exercise 2, Part B?

2. In what other daily situations might you use inferencing?

VOCABULARY CHECK

A. Review the vocabulary items in the Vocabulary Preview. Write their definitions and add examples. Use a dictionary if necessary.

B. Read each sentence. Circle the word or phrase that is the best synonym for the underlined vocabulary item.

1. Without <u>access</u> to basics like food and water, a community cannot survive.

   a. reach   b. buy

2. I <u>view</u> business philanthropy as something less than pure; I believe money is behind every decision.

   a. consider   b. watch

3. For the eggs in our shop to be labeled "organic," each must be <u>obtained</u> from chickens whose owners follow a long list of federally regulated organic practices.

   a. held   b. received

4. We <u>refused</u> the clerk's offer to exchange the coffee grinder. We wanted a full refund.

   a. accepted   b. didn't accept

5. If we <u>follow</u> the rules, we won't have any problems.

    a. do   b. don't do

6. The rules <u>permit</u> smoking outside only.

    a. allow   b. require a pass for

◑ Go to MyEnglishLab to complete vocabulary and skill practices, and to join in collaborative activities.

SKILL 2
PREDICTING

WHY IT'S USEFUL By predicting, you can process new information more quickly.

Predicting is when you use the facts and ideas in a text, as well as your inferences, to make a guess about what will come next. When reading, good readers think about what action, topic, or words may come next. Consider this example:

> I wanted to open my own business, but needed some extra money to get my business started. I needed a loan, so I went to ....

Did you predict *a bank*? If so, you made a good prediction. Making predictions while reading will help you get ready for, understand, and be interested in the material.

To make predictions, as you start to read, ask yourself these questions:

- What will happen next? Why do I think this will happen?

- What else could happen?

- From what I know about the topic, what could it be about?

VOCABULARY PREVIEW
Read the vocabulary items in the box. Circle the ones you know. Put a question mark next to the ones you don't know.

employees	update (v)	reflect	updated
stated	partners	guide (v)	journey (n)

EXERCISE 4

A. Read each question. Then check (✓) your predictions.

1. When a business owner writes a mission statement, he or she explains to customers and employees the purpose of the business. A mission statement is usually one or two sentences long. Predict: What words would you find in a mission statement?

   ☐ customers

   ☐ to help

   ☐ profit

   ☐ to provide

   ☐ money

   ☐ quality services / products

2. Amazon is a business that sells products through the Internet and delivers them to your home. Predict: What words might be in Amazon's mission statement?

   ☐ brick and mortar (building)

   ☐ customers

   ☐ online

   ☐ expensive

   ☐ finding

3. Toyota is considered one of the most successful automobile companies in the world. In order to stay successful, it needs customers. Predict: What words might appear in Toyota's mission statement?

   ☐ quality services / products

   ☐ customers

   ☐ online

   ☐ unenjoyable

   ☐ expensive

B. Think about your predicting experience. What questions did you find challenging? Which were easy? Was it easier if you knew something about the company being described? Explain.

EXERCISE 5

A. The article below is about the characteristics of a good mission statement. A mission statement briefly describes *why* a business exists. Why might a business—and its customers—want to have a mission statement?

B. Read the excerpt and predict the last word of each sentence.

> The mission of PBS, a network of publicly supported television stations, is "to create content that educates, informs, and inspires." Mission statements are short, descriptive statements that help define a business's goals and (1) ....
> While value propositions explain *what* a business offers a customer and business plans define *how* a business works, a mission statement is all about describing *why* a business (2) .... This keeps employees focused on what matters most, while providing customers with a brief summary of what is (3) ....
> From PBS's mission statement, it's clear that providing quality educational programming inspires its (4) ....

C. Preview the questions that follow the article. Then read the article and answer the questions.

Short But Sweet—Writing Successful Mission Statements

1 The mission of PBS, a network of publicly supported television stations, is "to create content that educates, informs, and inspires." Mission statements are short, descriptive statements that help define a business's goals and purpose. While value propositions explain *what* a business offers a customer and business plans define *how* a business works, a mission statement is all about describing *why* a business exists. This keeps employees focused on what matters most, while providing customers with a brief summary of what is important. From PBS's mission statement, it's clear that providing quality educational programming inspires its business.

2 A mission statement should say what needs the business is trying to address. For inspiration, look at Amazon's ambitious mission statement, which says the company tries "to be the most customer-centric company in the world, where people can find and discover anything they want to buy online." Amazon neatly summarizes what it hopes to offer customers and shows employees what it is working to achieve.

When writing a mission statement, business owners shouldn't make the mistake of trying to write an advertisement. A mission statement is written with a very specific purpose, and it is not to promote the business. What's more, mission statements should be regularly reviewed; if a business has moved focus to different areas, the mission statement should be updated to reflect that!

3 Mission statements should explain the principles that guide the company. Google, for example, says that "Google's mission is to organize the world's information and make it universally accessible and useful." This shows that the company wants to help people by accomplishing something both useful and complicated. The mission statement is simply stated, but it contains all of Google's core values.

4 Some mission statements focus on letting the customers know they are taken care of. For example, Toyota promises "to attract and attain customers with high-valued products and services and the most satisfying ownership experience in America." This assures the customer that owning a Toyota will be rewarding, not only at the beginning but for the duration of the experience.

5 These mission statements all come from large, successful companies. Business owners shouldn't worry if they can't write a perfect mission statement right away! They should take their time and discuss it with their customers and partners. They need to remember to focus on the *purpose* of their business, including how they plan to guide that purpose in the coming years. If they do that, their business statement will be another tool they can use in their journey from a small start-up to a successful business.

Glossary

Customer-centric: paying more attention to the needs of customers than to sales or profit

Core values: the principles that you consider to be most important, and which affect all aspects of what you do

1. What effect can a mission statement have on a business's employees and customers?

   ....

2. What's the difference between a value proposition, a business plan, and a mission statement?

   ....

3. What information should a mission statement include?

   ....

4. From Amazon's mission statement, what can you infer about people who use Amazon?

   ....

5. What is complicated about Google's mission?

....

6. What is the author's reason for mentioning Toyota?

....

D. Reread the article. Then check your answers in Parts B and C.

CULTURE NOTE

PBS is famous for creating the popular television show *Sesame Street*, which has been educating children worldwide since 1969. Its popular fictional characters include Big Bird, Elmo, and Abby Cadabby. PBS relies on viewers' contributions to support its programming.

EXERCISE 6

Discuss your reading experience with one or more students.

1. Did predicting—thinking about information that might come next—help prepare you for the reading? How does having background knowledge about some of the material help you make predictions? Is it easier to make predictions in your first language? Explain.

2. Predicting is not only an important academic reading skill but also a skill used in everyday life. Think of at least three situations in which you would use predicting.

VOCABULARY CHECK

A. Review the vocabulary items in the Vocabulary Preview. Write their definitions and add examples. Use a dictionary if necessary.

B. Complete each sentence using the correct vocabulary item from the box. Use the correct form.

employee	guide	journey	partner	reflect	state	update

1. In order to stay competitive, technology companies must .... their product often because technology is quickly outdated.

2. Your career should .... your interests. Like the saying goes, how you spend your days is how you spend your life.

3. The spokesperson in the TV ad very clearly .... that everything would be on sale on Friday.

4. A mission statement can .... a business along the path toward success.

5. All three of the business .... agreed to sell the business. It was a group decision.

6. Starting a business is not an overnight process. It is a(n) .... that takes many months.

7. Companies that offer benefits such as vacation and health insurance are valued by their ....

TIP

Add the Vocabulary Check vocabulary items and any other useful items from the reading to your vocabulary flashcards, journal, or study list.

○ Go to MyEnglishLab to complete vocabulary and skill practices, and to join in collaborative activities.

INTEGRATED SKILLS

IDENTIFYING PARTS OF A LECTURE

WHY IT'S USEFUL By recognizing the signals a speaker uses when introducing parts of a lecture, you can be ready to receive and note that information.

In an academic lecture, speakers often discuss information not in the assigned textbook. So it's important for you to recognize **signal words**—words that tell you to get ready for certain kinds of information.

Speakers usually organize their talks into parts:

- a beginning, where they introduce the topic(s) to be discussed,
- a middle, where they explain those ideas by adding details and examples,
- an end, where they summarize their talk.

Speakers use expressions like these to signal parts of a talk:

To Introduce Main or Important Ideas	A major development … Before we go on … Let's begin with … Let's look at … Now we will discuss … Pay special attention to …	The basic idea is … The first point we'll discuss … The three main ideas of … We're going to examine … What we will cover …
To Introduce Supporting Details	Also … As an example … As a result, … For example, … For instance, … However, …	In contrast, … Most importantly … Similarly, … This is an important point to remember … Two effects of this …
To Introduce a Conclusion	In conclusion, … Remember that …	To conclude, … To sum up, …

Other Ways to Introduce Parts of a Lecture

- Speakers might use **visuals** (write sentences on a board, show slides, use graphs).
- They might use **verbal cues**: stress keywords, pause before and after saying a keyword, speak louder or slower on key details.
- They might use **repetition** of a key concept.
- They might **give a definition** of a key concept.
- They might use **body language** (pointing to details mentioned on a board or slide, making facial expressions).

TIP

Here are some best practices for taking lecture notes:

- Preview the course outline or textbook.
- Complete any assigned readings or homework.
- Get rid of distractions (turn off text notifications, silence your phone).
- Watch the speaker and listen carefully.
- Listen for signal words.
- Take notes on main ideas and important details.
- Use symbols (for instance: *mi* for main idea, *ex* for example) to help you keep up.
- Ask questions if anything is unclear.
- If there is a summary at the end, review your notes as you listen.
- Review your notes after class.
- Compare notes with a study partner.

VOCABULARY PREVIEW

Read the vocabulary items in the box. Circle the ones you know. Put a question mark next to the ones you don't know.

resources	proper	in regard to	significantly	make sure	influence (n)

EXERCISE 7

A. Look at the title and image on the professor's opening slide on the next page. What do you think the lecture is about? Check (✓) your idea.

☐ Unilever's products and where they are sold

☐ Unilever's corporate social responsibility plan

☐ Unilever's plan to sell products around the world

Glossary

Vitality: excitement and energy

Good nutrition: a healthy diet

Good hygiene: keeping the body clean

Well-being: a feeling of being comfortable, healthy, and happy

Enhance: to improve something

Oral: relating to the mouth

CULTURE NOTE

Unilever is a multinational brand that sells over 1,000 brand-name products. These products include Lipton®, Dove®, Breyers Ice Cream®, Knorr®, and Vaseline®. In 2016, Unilever's pretax profit was $8 billion.

B. Listen as the professor introduces the lecture. Then check (✓) the main idea of the lecture.

☐ to show how Unilever meets people's everyday needs

☐ to explain Unilever's worldwide connections and resources

☐ to examine the details of Unilever's successful CSR program

☐ to make a connection between Unilever and nutrition

C. Now listen to the whole lecture. Listen for words that signal important information. Complete the outline. Why is Unilever's CSR plan important?

Meeting Everyday Needs—Unilever's CSR Action

Class: Intro to Business

Date: ....

Lecture Title: ....

Topic: An examination of Unilever's successful .... :

    Unilever's Sustainable ....

        1st Goal: Improving .... & ....

          (Supporting Details) ....

        2nd Goal: Reducing ....

          (Supporting Details) ....

        3rd Goal: Enhancing ....

          (Supporting Details) ....

D. Read each statement and circle *T* (True) or *F* (False). Correct the false statements.

T / F   1. Unilever is a multinational company that primarily sells products for nutrition.

T / F   2. Unilever's Sustainable Living Plan is the name of its CSR plan.

T / F   3. Unilever's CSR plan is mainly focused on the environment.

T / F   4. Unilever's oral health plan is an example of how CSR can be beneficial to both the world and the business.

T / F   5. The expression "strict employee standards" means that employees are treated severely.

T / F   6. The author suggests that Unilever's CSR plan could encourage other businesses to work on their CSR plan.

CULTURE NOTE

Many dental diseases can be prevented if people brush their teeth twice a day with fluoridated toothpaste; however, in many countries people only brush once a day, if at all. In fact, toothaches and other dental problems often cause students to miss school. Unilever, in partnership with World Dental Federation (FDI), has established educational programs, as well as other "fun" campaigns, to teach and promote proper dental care. Children, in turn, have helped to educate their parents on the importance of brushing.

E. With a partner, compare notes from Part C. Then discuss these questions and be prepared to share your answers with the class.

1. Did you identify all of the key ideas? If so, what verbal cues helped?

2. Did the lecturer use a lot of signal words to indicate new ideas? What were some of the phrases she used?

3. When you listen to a lecture, do you take notes? If so, how do you organize those notes?

4. When you listen to a lecture, do you compare notes with a classmate? How might this be useful?

VOCABULARY CHECK

A. Review the vocabulary items in the Vocabulary Preview. Write their definitions and add examples. Use a dictionary if necessary.

B. Complete each sentence using the correct vocabulary item from the box. Use the correct form.

influence	in regard to	make sure	proper	resource	significantly

1. The number of businesses with CSR plans today is .... higher than it was 20 years ago.

2. The company is rich in .... , including smart employees and modern technology.

3. The report contained a lot of worrisome financial findings. But .... the company's customer satisfaction, the report could say only good things.

4. A manufacturing business should .... that its employees are well trained by offering safety classes.

5. A manager has a big .... on the culture of the office. A creative and easygoing manager, for example, usually means a relaxed workplace.

6. The .... technique for cleaning your teeth involves brushing for two minutes.

⟩ **Go to MyEnglishLab to complete a skill practice and to join in collaborative activities.**

LANGUAGE SKILL
INTERPRETING HEDGING LANGUAGE

> **WHY IT'S USEFUL** By noticing when a writer is using hedging language, you can better evaluate the strength of the writer's statements.

○ Go to MyEnglishLab **for the Language Skill presentation and practice.**

VOCABULARY STRATEGY
COMPILING A VOCABULARY JOURNAL

> **WHY IT'S USEFUL** By using vocabulary journals, you can better organize and grow your word knowledge.

Vocabulary journals provide a place for recording new words and their meanings. In class, you will encounter a lot of new vocabulary, and while it's important to read fluently and not stop to look up every new word, there may be times when you want to know an exact definition of a word. A vocabulary journal allows you to record those words and study them. A simple vocabulary journal contains the target word and its definition.

A more complex journal might include the following:

- the part of speech (noun, verb, adjective, adverb, etc.)

- a synonym (word with a similar meaning)

- an antonym (word with an opposite meaning)

- the word families (prefixes, suffixes, etc.)

- some context (the sentence that the word appeared in)

- a visual representation of the word (a drawing or a picture of the word)

- an example sentence (created by you) with the word

Consider this vocabulary journal entry for the word *sustainable*:

Word:	sustainable
Definition:	able to continue without causing damage to the environment
Part of Speech:	adjective
Word Family:	sustainability, sustain, unsustainable
In Context:	Unilever believes in <u>sustainable</u> practices, including using sustainably sourced raw materials.
Example Sentence:	More and more companies are using <u>sustainable</u> business practices.

Knowing the word, noticing how it is used, and learning related forms will help grow your vocabulary knowledge. Be sure to review your vocabulary journal often.

EXERCISE 8

A. Complete the vocabulary journal entries with the descriptions from the box.

Definition	Word	Synonym	Part of Speech
Word Family	In Context	Example Sentence	

1. Word: **guarantee**

    .... : If a company guarantees something, it promises it.

    Part of Speech: verb

    .... : guarantee, guaranteed

    .... : Unilever <u>guarantees</u> that workers in its supply chain are treated fairly.

    .... : ....

2. Word: **key**

    .... : adjective

    .... : A <u>key</u> goal of business is making a profit.

    Definition: very important or necessary

    .... : significant

    Antonym: unimportant

    .... : ....

3. .... : **influence**

  In Context: In many parts of the world, multinational companies have more <u>influence</u> than local governments.

  .... : noun

  Definition: the power to affect the way someone or something behaves without using direct force or action

  .... : influential, influence (verb)

  .... : ....

B. Create journal entries with other vocabulary words that you want to learn. Skim the readings in this unit for ideas. Use a dictionary if necessary.

C. Work with another student. Teach each other three words from Part B. Add them to your vocabulary journal.

◊ Go to MyEnglishLab to complete a skill practice.

APPLY YOUR SKILLS

> **WHY IT'S USEFUL** By applying the skills you have learned in this unit, you can gain a better understanding of this challenging reading about the United Nations' Global Compact and Sustainable Development Goals.

BEFORE YOU READ

A. Discuss these questions with one or more students.

1. A business's goal is to make a profit. However, many companies are also interested in social responsibility. From what you know, is corporate social responsibility practiced around the world? Or is it more popular in certain places and types of companies?

2. The United Nations (UN) is an international organization that supports peace and security around the world. Imagine a relationship between the UN and large companies. Why would they work together?

3. What are some of the big problems facing people around the world today? What solutions have you heard about?

B. You will read an article about the United Nations' Global Compact and Sustainable Development Goals. As you read, think about these questions.

1. What is the Global Compact? What are the Sustainable Development Goals (SDGs)?

2. What benefits do companies receive from working with the UN?

3. What benefits do communities enjoy as a result of the Global Compact?

C. Review the Unit Skills Summary. As you read the article, apply the skills you learned in this unit.

UNIT SKILLS SUMMARY

ENGAGE IN THE TOPIC BY USING THESE SKILLS:

Make inferences

• Use your own knowledge to understand information not directly stated in the text.

Predict

• Use facts, ideas, and inferences to make guesses about what will come next.

Identify parts of a lecture

• Recognize nonverbal and verbal behaviors that signal the different parts of a lecture.

Interpret hedging

• Notice when writers use certain language to distance themselves from their stated claim.

Compile a vocabulary journal

• Understand different techniques for learning and remembering new vocabulary.

READ

A. Read the article. Annotate and make notes in the chart.

Question	Information You Know from the Text	Information You Know from Other Sources or Experiences	Your Inferences
How can businesses benefit from the Global Compact?			
How can the sustainable development goals benefit the world?			

Working Together for a Better World

1. The most influential corporate social responsibility initiative in the world may, in fact, not be corporate at all. Since 2000, the United Nations has organized a series of corporate sustainability initiatives under the heading of the UN Global Compact. With ten principles, including ending child labor and workplace discrimination, the UN's goals are far reaching. The UN has worked to achieve these goals by partnering with businesses around the world, using their resources to help make a difference. Not only do people in the developing world benefit from these initiatives, but businesses have much to gain as well; over 9,000 companies have joined the Global Compact, with more signing on every year.

2. What makes businesses want to sign up for additional, unpaid work? Many businesses are encouraged by both opportunities to work in new markets and the ability to engage in meaningful philanthropy. It is also generally agreed that sustainability initiatives improve global stability, which helps businesses be successful. The UN is usually quite flexible when it comes to working with businesses; a business agrees to assist the UN in one or more areas, and the UN works with that business. Often, multiple businesses work together under the direction of the UN to achieve specific sustainability goals.

PRINCIPLE 10

Businesses should work against corruption in all its forms, including extortion and bribery.

PRINCIPLE 1

Businesses should support and respect the protection of internationally proclaimed human rights, within the scope of their influence.

PRINCIPLE 9

Businesses should encourage the development and diffusion of environmentally friendly technologies.

PRINCIPLE 2

Businesses should make sure that they are not complicit in human rights abuses.

PRINCIPLE 8

Businesses should undertake initiatives to promote greater environmental responsibility.

PRINCIPLE 3

Businesses should uphold the freedom of association and the effective recognition of the right to collective bargaining.

THE GLOBAL COMPACT

10 — 1 — 2 — 3 — 4 — 5 — 6 — 7 — 8 — 9

ANTI-CORRUPTION · HUMAN RIGHTS · LABOUR STANDARDS · ENVIRONMENT

PRINCIPLE 7

Businesses should support a precautionary approach to environmental challenges.

PRINCIPLE 4

Businesses should uphold the elimination of all forms of forced and compulsory labour.

PRINCIPLE 6

Businesses should uphold the elimination of discrimination in respect of employment and occupation.

PRINCIPLE 5

Businesses should uphold the abolition of child labour.

Sustainable Development Goals

3 While the early years of the Global Compact saw success in terms of networking and progress reports, by 2015 many in the UN General Assembly hoped to achieve more concrete results. This led to the implementation of 17 Sustainable Development Goals, concrete and measurable achievements—with a strict deadline. The 17 goals, each with difficult yet measurable action platforms,

(Continued)

were created in the hopes of making significant gains by 2030. This 2030 Agenda for Sustainable Development has goals that complement the Global Compact's ten principles. The primary difference, however, involves just how clearly worded these goals are. For example, Goal 13—"Take urgent action to combat climate change and its impacts"—includes specific targets with language like " ... mobilizing jointly $100 billion annually by 2020 from all sources to address the needs of developing countries ... " and "Integrate climate change measures into national policies, strategies, and planning."

4   Businesses were encouraged by the specificity of the goals and immediately began working to achieve them. Some businesses have already found success in doing so even though the sustainable development goals were only put in place recently. Goal 4—"Ensure inclusive and equitable quality education and promote lifelong learning opportunities to all"—is looking to make sure that education is for everyone, everywhere. Targets for this goal include training more teachers in critical-needs countries and providing better access to educational resources. Microsoft, one of the world's leading technology companies, was quick to help. Microsoft has a long history of educational philanthropy. With the support of the British Council, Project Badiliko works to provide technology to areas without dependable tech infrastructure. Using solar-powered computer hardware, Microsoft has worked to build a variety of learning and training centers for both students and teachers. Microsoft hopes to use this equipment to improve teacher training in underserved developing areas.

5   Goal 5 is to "achieve gender equality and empower all women and girls." This includes issues ranging from equal access in schooling to more representation in elected office. The UN has long advocated for gender equality, noting that on a practical level, businesses with more equal representation are usually better performing. Unilever, an enormous multinational business, has been working with the group UN Women to protect women working in one specific industry: tea and tea growing. As part of an effort to ensure safety and fair treatment throughout the supply chain, Unilever is helping to expand women's safety programs beyond Kenya, where it originally began. Given Unilever's significant presence in the industry, its behavior could easily influence other businesses to do the same.

6   Goal 9 focuses on infrastructure, resolving to "build resilient infrastructure, promote inclusive and sustainable industrialization, and foster innovation." The more focused targets of the goal emphasize how infrastructure of all types contributes to both economic growth and sustainability. Qualcomm, a US-based telecommunication company, is using its expertise to build up wireless infrastructure throughout the world. While the specifics of the program vary by region, initiatives include supporting small businesses in developing areas through microfranchising and building Internet connections to hard-to-reach areas. Such initiatives support local industries, as they can better do business themselves instead of depending on a larger company to do everything for them.

This also demonstrates how all the sustainable development goals support one another—improved infrastructure typically leads to more opportunities for women and better available education resources. If progress continues, the businesses operating under the UN's Global Compact are on track to make significant advances in sustainable business by the 2030 deadline.

CULTURE NOTE

The United Nations was formed in 1945 following the Second World War to maintain peace and security in the world. Currently it is made up of 193 member states who work together on issues from protecting human rights to promoting sustainable development. The UN is headed by a secretary general who is selected by the member states and can serve a five-year term, which is renewable, but generally lasts two terms. In 2017, a new secretary general was chosen, António Guterres.

Glossary

Infrastructure: the basic systems that a country or organization needs in order to work in the right way, for example, roads, communications, and banking systems

Microfranchising: a business model that applies traditional franchising methods to small businesses in developing countries

B. Compare notes with a partner.

C. Reread the questions in Before You Read, Part B. With your partner, use your notes and opinions to answer the questions.

⬥ Go to MyEnglishLab to read more closely, answer the critical thinking questions, and complete a summarizing activity.

THINKING CRITICALLY

Use information from the reading to answer these questions.

1. Why do you think there is a deadline for the achievement of the SDGs? How might a deadline be helpful?

   ....

   ....

2. Things such as war, poverty, and lack of resources present a challenge to Goal 4. What can governments, companies, and individuals do to help everyone receive a quality education?

   ....

   ....

THINKING VISUALLY

Use information from the visual to answer the following questions.

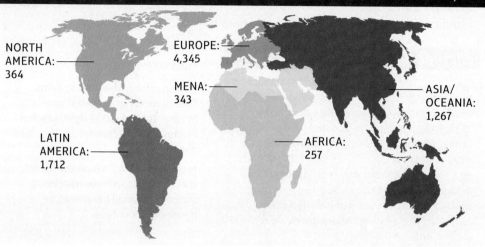

UN GLOBAL COMPACT: NUMBER OF BUSINESS PARTICIPANTS BY REGION, 2013

NORTH AMERICA: 364

EUROPE: 4,345

MENA: 343

ASIA/OCEANIA: 1,267

LATIN AMERICA: 1,712

AFRICA: 257

1. What does the map suggest about the popularity of the Global Compact? What might account for the difference in numbers from region to region? What do you think will happen in the next 15 years, especially considering that the Sustainable Development Goals has a deadline of 2030?

2. Make a bar graph indicating the regions, the numbers in the map, and your predictions for 2030.

THINKING ABOUT LANGUAGE

A. Read these excerpts from "Working Together for a Better World." Is hedging used? If so, underline it. Then complete the vocabulary journal entry for the bolded word.

> For help with interpreting hedging language, go to MyEnglishLab, Business and Design, Part 2, Language Skill.

1. The most influential corporate social responsibility initiative in the world may, **in fact**, not be corporate at all.

Definition: ....

Part of Speech: ....

2. Many businesses are encouraged by both opportunities to work in new markets and the ability to **engage** in meaningful philanthropy.

Definition: ....

Part of Speech: ....   Word Family: ....

3. It is also generally agreed that sustainability initiatives improve global **stability**, which helps businesses be successful.

Definition: ....

Part of Speech: .... Word Family: .... Antonym: ....

4. The UN is usually quite **flexible** when it comes to working with businesses; a business agrees to assist the UN in one or more areas, and the UN works with that business.

Definition: ....

Part of Speech: .... Word Family: .... Antonym: ....

5. The UN has long advocated for gender equality, noting that on a **practical** level, businesses with more equal representation are usually better performing.

Definition: ....

Part of Speech: .... Word Family: .... Antonym: ....

6. Given Unilever's **significant** presence in the industry, its behavior could easily influence other businesses to do the same.

Definition: ....

Part of Speech: .... Word Family: .... Antonym: ....

7. This also demonstrates how all the sustainable development goals support one another—improved infrastructure typically leads to more opportunities for women and better available education **resources**.

Definition: ....

Part of Speech: .... Word Family: ....

8. If progress continues, the businesses **operating** under the UN's Global Compact are on track to make significant advances in sustainable business by the 2030 deadline.

Definition: ....

Part of Speech: .... Word Family: ....

❶ Go to MyEnglishLab to watch Juli Sherry's concluding video and to complete a self-assessment.

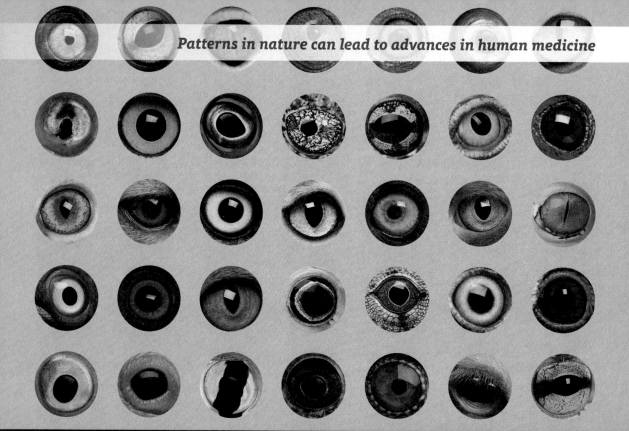

Patterns in nature can lead to advances in human medicine

ZOOLOGY

Classification

UNIT PROFILE

In this unit, you will learn about how elephants communicate and the parts of the body they use to do so. In the final reading of the unit, you will study seismic communication and its usefulness to elephants.

Look at the reading "Elephant Listening: A Feeling in Their Bones" on page 220. Skim Paragraph 2. What two examples could you list under the heading "Ways that elephants communicate"?

OUTCOMES

- Classify information
- Distinguish points of view
- Support a presentation with visuals
- Identify the language of parts and wholes
- Recognize connotative language

For more about **ZOOLOGY**, see ❶❸. See also Ⓦ and ⓄⒸ **ZOOLOGY** ❶❷❸.

GETTING STARTED

⊙ Go to MyEnglishLab to watch Professor O'Connell-Rodwell's introductory video and to complete a self-assessment.

Discuss these questions with a partner or group.

1. What is the difference between hearing and listening? For a human, what body parts are needed to hear information? Do all animals hear in the same way? Explain.

2. Besides listening to spoken information, how else can you get information? How do you best remember new information? Does it depend on the context (personal, business, educational, etc.)?

3. In her introduction, Professor O'Connell-Rodwell explains that elephants use different parts of their body to communicate. Think about your own communication. Do you use different parts of your body for different kinds of communication? Why?

SKILL 1
CLASSIFYING INFORMATION

WHY IT'S USEFUL By understanding classification, you can better see the relationship between information in a text—how things are similar or different.

Classification is a way of grouping things by a characteristic. For instance, notice how in this T-chart the animals are classified by their skin covering—feathers versus fur.

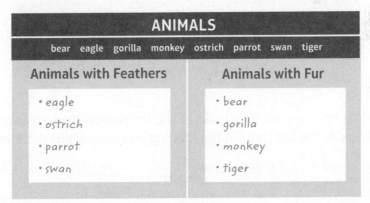

ANIMALS	
bear eagle gorilla monkey ostrich parrot swan tiger	
Animals with Feathers	**Animals with Fur**
• eagle	• bear
• ostrich	• gorilla
• parrot	• monkey
• swan	• tiger

After classifying the information, you might notice that all of the feathered animals have wings and beaks, lay eggs, and are birds, whereas all of the animals with fur have claws and teeth, and are mammals that give birth to their young—all of which are other kinds of classification.

Language can also be classified. When you sort words into parts of speech such as nouns, verbs, and adjectives, you are classifying information. Study this T-chart.

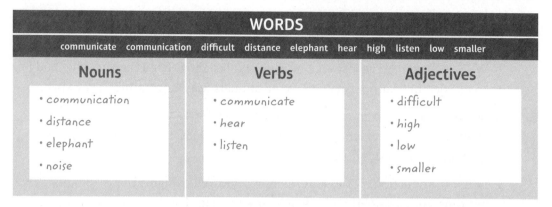

WORDS
communicate communication difficult distance elephant hear high listen low smaller

Nouns	Verbs	Adjectives
• communication	• communicate	• difficult
• distance	• hear	• high
• elephant	• listen	• low
• noise		• smaller

Classification makes it easier to see a common feature of a group as well as relationships between groups.

TIP

To recognize when someone is writing about classes or categories, look for classification signal words such as *divisions, groups, kinds, types,* and *varieties.*

VOCABULARY PREVIEW

Read the vocabulary items in the box. Circle the ones you know. Put a question mark next to the ones you don't know.

| organs | suitable | tool | pay attention | a great deal of | be aware of |

EXERCISE 1

A. The reading on the next page looks at the frequency at which animals hear sound. Look at the bar chart in the reading and answer the questions.

1. What classes of sound does it show?

2. Which animals can hear frequencies in each class?

B. From the bar chart, what can you tell about elephant hearing? How does it compare to human hearing? How does it compare to the hearing of other animals?

EXERCISE 2

A. When you communicate with someone, what sense (sight, hearing, smell, taste, touch) is most useful? Explain.

B. Read the passage. Then read the statements that follow. Circle *T* (True) or *F* (False). Correct the false statements.

All Ears: How an Elephant Hears

1 Among mammals, the elephant is one of nature's best listeners. Elephants tilt (or move to one side) their heads to better hear far-away sounds. The African savanna elephant's enormous ears are especially well designed for this. Even smaller elephants, like African forest elephants and Asian elephants, still benefit from these large sensory organs. Additionally, an elephant's skull size keeps its ears widely spaced—which helps it better triangulate, or determine the location of, sounds. Finally, the elephant's inner ear shape is suitable to picking up seismic (underground) vibrations—which is not a common feature in mammals.

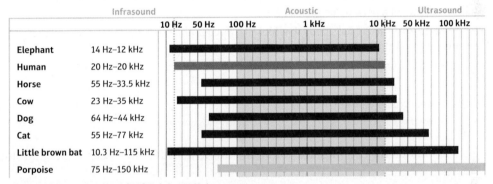

The range between 100 Hz and 10 kHz is in 100 Hz increments.

2 But elephants don't listen with just their ears. An elephant's whole body can be used for listening. One category of elephant calls is known as rumbles. Rumbles are vocalized infrasounds, low frequencies that humans cannot hear. Usually under 20 hertz, these sounds can travel as far as 10 kilometers under perfect conditions. However, elephants don't put their ears to the ground. Instead, they listen to these seismic vibrations through both skin and bone. The bones in an elephant's feet and legs can feel the vibration—right up to their ears—through a process called *bone conduction*. Elephants will carefully position one of their front legs, letting the sound better carry through their bone structure. The elephant's skin, specifically its nerves, is also a listening tool. Nerves in the elephant's feet can "hear" seismic infrasound, and elephant trunks contain many other nerves that are sensitive to infrasound. Male elephants in musth will often use their trunks to pay attention to the rumbles of responsive females. The males will travel for miles at a time to find a female elephant during the mating process.

(Continued)

3 Elephants can also hear categories of calls other than low-frequency rumbles. The most common is acoustic (sound) communication. These include trumpets, roars, and barks, all of which are at a higher frequency than rumbles. These are elephant sounds that humans can hear and typically associate with elephant calls.

4 Elephants face a few communication challenges, however. For one, they can't hear some of the higher frequencies that humans can. Also, for elephants, it takes a great deal of work to triangulate the location of a sound. For instance, forest elephants and Asian elephants sometimes have a difficult time locating other elephants because trees and hills block the sound. Lastly, elephant calls are loud. This can be dangerous at certain times of day, when predators—including lions, tigers, and hyenas—are looking for an unprotected elephant calf or hurt adult. Despite these things, elephants' anatomy helps them communicate with each other and be aware of the world around them.

Glossary

Mammal: a type of animal that drinks milk from its mother's body when it is young

Skull: the bones of a person's or animal's head

Nerve: parts inside an animal's body that look like threads and carry messages between the brain and other parts of the body

Musth: when bull (male) elephants have higher levels of testosterone and are more aggressive

Calf: a baby elephant

Anatomy: the structure of a body

T / F 1. Elephant rumbles are loud and can be heard by both elephants and humans.

T / F 2. An elephant has one category of call, which is called a rumble.

T / F 3. If an elephant were looking for a mate, its ability to hear infrasounds could be useful in finding one within 10 kilometers.

T / F 4. Trumpets and barks are examples of infrasounds.

T / F 5. The nerves in an elephant's skin are used for hearing infrasounds through the ground.

T / F 6. In addition to hearing low-frequency sounds, elephants can hear all the high-frequency sounds that a human can hear.

T / F 7. Mountains and trees can interfere with an elephant's ability to triangulate sounds.

T / F 8. An elephant that is hurt and calling out for help is an easy target for a predator.

C. Reread the passage. Then check your answers in Part B.

D. Work with a partner to answer these questions.

1. Notice the three categories of elephants in the Venn diagram. Use what you have read and do light research to complete the diagram.

   - In the areas where the circles overlap, write the shared (similar) sensory features and abilities.

   - In the other circles, write the specific (different) sensory features and abilities.

   - Study your completed diagram. Which elephants are most similar? Most different? Explain.

2. What classification could be used to identify the types of elephant calls? Which calls could be grouped into each category? Create a Venn diagram or T-chart showing elephant calls.

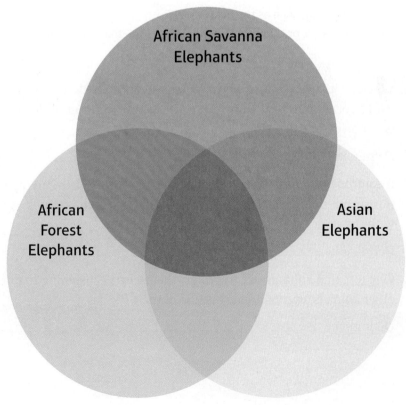

EXERCISE 3

Discuss these questions with a partner.

1. How can classifying information, such as different elephant calls, help you better understand it?

2. Classification is used as a way to organize information in everyday life as well as in academics. For instance, history can be classified into regional history (e.g., South American, African, European), and math can be classified into types of properties (e.g., addition, subtraction, multiplication, addition). What are some other examples of classification used in academic and everyday life?

VOCABULARY CHECK

A. Review the vocabulary items in the Vocabulary Preview. Write their definitions and add examples. Use a dictionary if necessary.

B. Read each sentence. Then write the correct definition of the underlined vocabulary item. Use the definitions from the box.

> something used to do a task or meet a goal
> right or acceptable
> to know about
> a part of the body, such as the heart or liver
> to watch, listen to, or think about someone or something carefully
> a lot

1. When a vital part of your body—such as your kidneys or lungs—no longer works correctly, it's called <u>organ</u> failure. This can result in death if treatment is not given immediately.

   Definition: ....

2. If someone is experiencing organ failure, one treatment is an organ transplant, but that involves finding a <u>suitable</u> match—that is, someone with the same blood type.

   Definition: ....

3. One <u>tool</u> that animals use to protect themselves is listening to the calls of other animals, even animals outside of their species.

   Definition: ....

4. Students who don't <u>pay attention</u> in class often end up confused and struggle to do well.

   Definition: ....

5. Scientists spend <u>a great deal of</u> time doing research. That is why patience is an important characteristic to have if you want to be a scientist.

   Definition: ....

6. In the wild, smaller animals must always <u>be aware of</u> their surroundings, for example, noticing movement and listening for a larger predator.

   Definition: ....

◐ Go to MyEnglishLab to complete vocabulary and skill practices, and to join in collaborative activities.

SKILL 2
DISTINGUISHING POINTS OF VIEW

WHY IT'S USEFUL By distinguishing points of view, you can better evaluate information in a text.

Academic textbooks and articles are, generally speaking, meant to be neutral—not for or against a topic. They should be factual. Various people—writers, experts, editors—review such material to make sure the information is correct. As part of that review, they look to see that the text presents a fair **point of view**, that it doesn't include personal opinions, and that it doesn't include only information that supports a particular point of view. As a result, these kinds of materials are considered credible— factual, truthful, and accurate.

Other publications, however, may not receive serious review. Not only might the information be incorrect, but also it may not be presented fairly.

As a reader, it's important for you to think about point of view as you read. As you read a text, consider these factors:

FACTORS	
Kind of publication	• Who published the information? (a government organization, the author himself or herself, a well-known publishing house, an educational institution) • What is the reputation of the publisher? What do your professors or other people you respect think about the source? • What is the genre (type) of the publication? (academic textbook, journal, magazine, website, personal blog)
Author's biography	• Who is the author? Who does the author work for? What are the author's credentials? (educational background, work experience, record of publishing / research) • Does the author have experience in the area he or she is writing about? • Is the author's identity relevant? (gender, nationality, race, culture, religious and personal beliefs) **Note:** Identity should not automatically be considered a factor in point of view. An author may directly or indirectly show that it is, however.
Purpose of text	• What is the text trying to do? (entertain, persuade, inform)
Sources in text	• Who is quoted in the text? What is the source's experience with the subject? • Where did the statistics come from?
Opinion language	• Does the author include his or her own ideas? Are there expressions signaling a personal opinion? (*In my view … , As far as I'm concerned … , It seems that … , It's worth noting that … , It's reasonable to assume that …*)
Descriptive language	• Does the author include descriptive language that shows opinion? For example, these two sentences report the same event, but the first one has opinion language and the second one does not: *The experience ruined his life.* *The experience changed his life.*

Note: Some textbooks will refer to point of view as *bias*. *Bias* is more negative in tone—suggesting a personal and unfair opinion about something.

Read these examples. Think about the point of view of the quoted sources. What is each person's point of view? What are the factors?

A. "The main cause of hearing loss in young people is prolonged listening to loud music on their smartphones," reported Dr. Beth Easterly, an audiologist in Boston, Massachusetts.

B. "My husband, who used to do construction without ear protection, now has difficulty hearing. That's what inspired me to run for office. I want to protect workers and prevent hearing loss in this noisy world," said Nora Blanco, candidate, House District 2.

C. "I believe that listening to music through earbuds not only damages your hearing but distorts the quality of the sound, making it an unpleasant listening experience," explained Jake Kuhns, owner of Jake's Home Stereo Store.

In (A) the source is a doctor who has expertise in audiology. Her point of view has been shaped by her work and educational experience. (author's biography)

In (B) the source is a public health advocate, politician, and wife of someone who has difficulty hearing. Her point of view has been influenced by her personal experience and political interests, and is anecdotal. (author's biography, opinion language)

In (C) the source is the owner of stereo business. His point of view has been shaped by where he works. Perhaps he sells stereo equipment, including speakers, and the information could be biased because of it. (author's biography, opinion language, descriptive language)

TIP

When reading, pay attention to signal phrases. An expression like *according to (speaker's name, title / profession)* will often give the credentials of the speaker, which may give you an idea about point of view.

VOCABULARY PREVIEW

Read the vocabulary items in the box. Circle the ones you know. Put a question mark next to the ones you don't know.

back and forth	rate (n)	in turn	exception
concerns (n)	immediate		

EXERCISE 4

A. Read each passage. Each includes a point of view. Describe the point of view in your own words. Then identify the factors. Use the Factors chart on page 204 to help you.

1. Ethan Jones, a 32-year-old teacher and cat owner, is amazed by his cat's hearing. "It's so much better than the neighbor dog's hearing. I've seen Spice jump on something that the dog didn't even hear coming!" (from an article in *Cat and Canoodle* magazine)

   Point of view: ....

   Factors: ....

2. According to Dr. Sarah Nystrom, large animal veterinarian, "Cows can hear sounds at higher and lower frequencies than humans. From the cows I treat, I can see that their hearing is superior to—that is, far better than—humans'." (from an article in the monthly newsletter *Veterinarian Journal*)

   Point of view: ....

   Factors: ....

3. A ferret's hearing is more advanced than a human's. Based on research, a ferret's range is between 16 and 44,000 hertz. A human's range is between 20 and 20,000 hertz. (from an article in the academic journal *Audition Quarterly*)

   Point of view: ....

   Factors: ....

B. In your daily reading, do you think about point of view? Do you look at the author's credentials? Or evaluate the type of publication? Do you examine the reading for descriptive language that may suggest the point of view? Explain to a partner.

EXERCISE 5

A. The article on the next page discusses how insects and animals hear. From the diagram, what details might the article include? What do you already know about how animals hear?

B. Read the article. Then choose the correct answers to the questions that follow.

BiosciencesNow   YOUR VIEW   WORLD VIEW   CONNECT   MORE

Blog | Comments | Tags

LISTENING AND LEARNING ABOUT OUR FASCINATING WORLD

1   Every sound we hear, from the buzz of bees to the roar of a plane's engine, is a series of vibrations. The ringing of a guitar string, for example, is simply the result of the string vibrating back and forth rapidly. The buzzing sound of insects is similar—they vibrate themselves. Dr. Laurel Symes, an evolutionary biologist at Dartmouth College, has studied male tree crickets and learned that they make vibrations by rubbing their wings together. Larger animals will create sounds too, of course. Mammals like humans create sound by sending air through their vocal cords, which makes the cords vibrate.

2   Hearing is the act of interpreting, or receiving and understanding, the vibration. Insects have ears that are small and simple, not large and complex like those of mammals. So they feel vibration through different appendages and hairs. In some environments, insects have very specific ranges of hearing—this means that each insect "hears" only other insects of the same species. For instance, Symes discovered that the rate at which male crickets rub their wings together changes depending on the species of cricket. And as Symes noted, female crickets have become very good at picking out the sound of a potential mate in a forest filled with a variety of competing sounds.

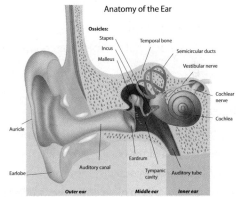

Anatomy of the Ear

Ossicles:
Stapes
Incus
Malleus
Temporal bone
Semicircular ducts
Vestibular nerve
Cochlear nerve
Cochlea
Auricle
Eardrum
Earlobe
Auditory canal
Tympanic cavity
Auditory tube
Outer ear
Middle ear
Inner ear

3   Most mammals hear using a combination of an eardrum, bones, and cochlea. Unlike insects, our "hearing hairs" are contained inside the cochlea. Sound is passed to the cochlea by a series of small bones, which, in turn, get their sounds from the eardrum. Most mammals don't "hear" through their body—though elephants are an important exception. Elephants can produce low, rumbling calls that are far below any frequency humans can hear. According to Dr. Caitlin O'Connell-Rodwell, a respected ecologist and consulting assistant professor in otolaryngology at Stanford University School of Medicine, these low sounds travel long distances. Other elephants can hear and interpret these calls as the vibrations travel through the ground. Elephants can hear like other mammals— the usual eardrum, ear bones, and cochlea method—but they can also conduct sound to their cochlea through skin and bone.

(Continued)

4 O'Connell-Rodwell has noticed that elephants will use both methods to communicate. The higher-pitched, close-range calls that travel through the air are used for more immediate concerns—for example, calves asking their mother for food, an elephant calling for help with a lion, or even one elephant complaining about another. These can all be communicated with normal "speaking." Rumbling calls are used for information that needs to be sent far away. Need to tell your sister elephants that you found some fresh fruit trees? Use long-distance rumbling. Elephants will turn themselves toward the sound, stand on one leg, and tilt their bodies to better triangulate the location of the sound. It seems that elephants are "good listeners."

> **ABOUT ME:**
>
> My name is Karen Vega, and I have a bachelor's degree in audiology. I also love to travel, hike, and spend time in nature. Check out my blog each week for a new article about hearing.

Glossary

Vibration: a continuous slight shaking movement

Appendage: part of the body that extends from the main part, such as an arm

Ecologist: a person who studies the relationship between organisms (plant, animal) and their environment

Otolaryngology: a field of medicine that studies problems related to ears, nose, and throat

1. What is the main idea of the text?
   a. Insects and animals make and hear sounds in different ways.
   b. Vibrations are necessary to make sounds.
   c. Crickets hear very differently than elephants.
   d. The science of hearing is easy to understand.

2. Crickets will create sound by _____ .
   a. rubbing their wings together
   b. putting air into their vocal cords
   c. vibrating their eardrums
   d. vibrating a part of a tree

3. Which factors probably influence Dr. Laurel Symes's point of view? Choose TWO.

    a. her education

    b. the number of publications her research appears in

    c. her gender

    d. her work experience

4. The purpose of mentioning Symes's work with crickets is to _____ .

    a. explain how vibrations cause sounds

    b. give an example of how an insect can distinguish sounds

    c. show how mammals hear

    d. prove that larger animals hear differently than smaller animals

5. Which best summarizes the main idea of Paragraph 4?

    a. Dr. Caitlin O'Connell-Rodwell has a lot of experience studying the communicative habits of elephants.

    b. An elephant can communicate by "speaking" or with body language.

    c. Elephants are good at communicating because they can hear information over long distances.

    d. Elephants have developed two effective methods of communicating information; one more suited for short distance and one better for long distance.

6. The author probably includes Symes and O'Connell-Rodwell in order to _____ .

    a. make her reading longer

    b. give credible support to her writing

    c. define animal hearing

    d. explain the complicated subject of sounds

C. Reread the passage and check your answers in Parts A and B.

D. Discuss these questions with a partner.

1. What do you know about the author? What might influence the author's point of view?

2. Why is Dr. Laurel Symes a credible source to speak about how insects produce sounds? What might influence her point of view?

3. How is Dr. Caitlin O'Connell-Rodwell qualified to speak about elephants' hearing?

4. What is the author's attitude about O'Connell-Rodwell? What adjectives convey her opinion?

5. How credible (trustworthy) is the blog post? What could you do to check the facts?

EXERCISE 6

Discuss your reading experience with one or more students.

1. Do you have any experience with the topic of hearing? What's your point of view? How does that influence how you respond to the information?

2. What was the purpose of the article: to entertain, to inform, or to persuade? In what types of texts do you think more opinion language can be found?

VOCABULARY CHECK

A. Review the vocabulary items in the Vocabulary Preview. Write their definitions and add examples. Use a dictionary if necessary.

B. Read each sentence. Then choose the correct definition of the underlined vocabulary item.

1. During the exam, the professor walked <u>back and forth</u> among the students to make sure that everyone was working.

   in one direction and then another   in the middle   on the side   quickly

2. Recent studies have shown that women are attending US colleges and universities at a higher <u>rate</u> than men, with women representing 55 percent of the student body in four-year colleges.

   evaluate   value   frequency   speed

3. An elephant can communicate over long distances with another family member, who, <u>in turn</u>, can communicate to even more distant relatives.

   similarly   as a result   go   move in one direction

4. Because of their size, elephants are not scared of most things. An <u>exception</u> to this is bees, which they are terrified of.

   problem   addition   compromise   exclusion

5. A <u>concern</u> of ecologists is global warming. They think that it might be causing damage to animals' habitats, which would have terrible results.

   involvement   effect   interest   worry

6. An <u>immediate</u> effect of short-term hearing loss may be confusion and disorientation. But with time, normal hearing will return.

   near   delayed   instant   late

🔊 Go to MyEnglishLab to complete vocabulary and skill practices, and to join in collaborative activities.

INTEGRATED SKILLS

SUPPORTING A PRESENTATION WITH VISUALS

WHY IT'S USEFUL As a student, you will be asked to give in-class presentations. By supporting your presentation with visuals, you can help your audience better understand and be interested in your message.

Many studies have shown that people remember information best when they both hear and see it. **Visuals** such as photographs, maps, graphic organizers, timelines, video, slides, and realia (objects) can help make your presentation memorable while supporting your points.

Visuals

- offer a different form of explanation
- engage the audience
- emphasize a point
- create interest
- build confidence in the speaker (reduces anxiety of forgetting information)

Tips for Using Visuals

- **Slide presentations:** Use clear language. Use easy-to-read type. Include interesting images.
- **Poster board presentations:** Use clear language. Have a mix of text and images (photos, diagrams).
- **Video clips:** Make sure the clip supports your point—don't let it take over your presentation.
- **Handout (fact sheets, brochures):** Unless your audience is using the information on the handout during the presentation, give it out after your presentation. Otherwise, it will be distracting.

VOCABULARY PREVIEW

Read the vocabulary items in the box. Circle the ones you know. Put a question mark next to the ones you don't know.

database	defend	beats	sense of humor
pretend	apology		

EXERCISE 7

A. Body language shows our feelings. What gestures do people make when they are happy? Angry? Sad? Do you think animals, like elephants, have similar gestures? Explain.

Glossary

Flirt: to show interest in someone in a small or fun way

🎧 **B.** Listen to the first half of a lecture about elephant gestures. As you listen, look at the four slides from the lecture. What do you understand from these slides?

Elephant Talk

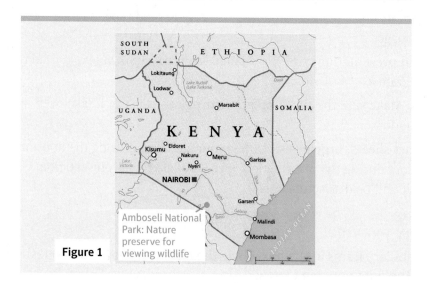

Figure 1 — Amboseli National Park: Nature preserve for viewing wildlife

Figure 2

Figure 3

C. Work with a partner. Discuss these questions about the first half of the lecture.

1. What is one thing an elephant will do when it wants to frighten a person or animal?

2. Did the visuals help you understand the spoken information? If so, how?

D. Listen to the second half of the lecture. Based on what you hear, create a visual (slide) that complements the information in the lecture. Share it with the class.

E. Answer the following questions. Then discuss your answers with a partner. Are any of the answers mentioned in your slide?

1. What is an example of something an elephant will do when it is playing?

   ....

2. Explain how male and female elephants show interest in each other.

   ....

3. What parts of an elephant's body are used when elephants communicate nonverbally?

   ....

4. Why is knowing about elephant gestures important?

   ....

VOCABULARY CHECK

A. Review the vocabulary items in the Vocabulary Preview. Write their definitions and add examples. Use a dictionary if necessary.

B. Complete each sentence using the correct vocabulary item from the box. Use the correct form.

apology	beat	database	defend	pretend	sense of humor

1. While humans have developed weapons like guns and swords to
   .... themselves, animals have to use their body to protect
   themselves from threats.

2. The earbud manufacturer issued a(n) .... after an investigation
   found that its product caused hearing damage.

3. In order to organize all the information she had collected about elephant
   calls, the researcher created a(n) ....

4. Elephants are not the only animals with a(n) .... Koko,
   a gorilla in California who knows sign language, once asked her researcher
   to play chase after tying the researcher's shoes together!

5. To frighten the lion, the elephant .... its trunk against the
   ground, causing the whole area to vibrate.

6. To avoid being noticed by predators, some animals will .... to
   be asleep when they are actually awake.

○ **Go to MyEnglishLab to complete a skill practice and to join in collaborative activities.**

LANGUAGE SKILL
IDENTIFYING THE LANGUAGE OF PARTS AND WHOLES

WHY IT'S USEFUL By understanding how certain words indicate the concepts of "parts" versus "wholes," you can be a more accurate speaker and writer.

◑ Go to MyEnglishLab for the Language Skill presentation and practice.

VOCABULARY STRATEGY
RECOGNIZING CONNOTATIVE LANGUAGE

WHY IT'S USEFUL By understanding connotative meaning in addition to literal meaning, you can be clearer in your understanding of words.

Words not only have definitions, but they can also carry feelings. "Denotation" is the dictionary definition of a word. For some words, this is the end of the story—they are neutral. But some words can have a layer of meaning beyond their dictionary definition. That is, they carry a **connotation**, or emotional meaning. There are positive and negative connotations.

It's important to choose your words carefully, depending on the context. In academic writing, it's important to use neutral, or unbiased, language. In persuasive situations, more positive or negative connotative language might be used, depending on your purpose.

Notice the following chart of words and their connotations. Compare words that have the same meaning but different connotations. Is anything surprising to you? **Note:** Big factors in connotation are context and the speaker's tone.

Negative Connotation	Neutral or Positive Connotation	Positive Connotation
skinny / gaunt	thin	slender
cheap	inexpensive	
childish		youthful
bossy		confident
miserly	economical	thrifty
	conversational / talkative	chatty
mutt	dog	
scheme	plan	
pushy	aggressive	
greedy		ambitious

(Continued)

Negative Connotation	Neutral or Positive Connotation	Positive Connotation
hyperactive		energetic
cowardly	shy / reserved / timid	
nosy	curious	inquisitive
stench	smell	aroma
tree hugger	environmentalist	
riot	protest	
guerilla / terrorist	soldier	freedom fighter
novice	student / learner	
snicker	laugh	
nerdy	serious	

EXERCISE 8

A. Choose the word with the neutral or positive connotation. Use a dictionary if needed.

1. An important trait for scientists is to be **curious / nosy**; they need to have a desire to find answers or solutions to big questions or problems.

2. The new research student is very **hyperactive / energetic** and is quick to volunteer for any task.

3. At our company, there is a push to recruit more **nerdy / serious** researchers.

4. The lab ordered **cheap / inexpensive** equipment in order to have enough money to cover other costs.

5. The scientist's **scheme / plan** was to study the elephants' behavior for at least two years to be able to compare statistics from one season to another.

6. Although extremely confident when doing work privately in the lab, the scientist was more **timid / cowardly** when having to give presentations.

B. Sort these words into pairs that have similar meanings. Complete the chart.

lazy	unusual	outdated	stubborn	vintage
weird	smirk	trudge	glare	walk
mushy	smile	persistent	strange	foreign
look	relaxed	sentimental		

Negative Connotation	Neutral / Positive Connotation
lazy	relaxed

C. Discuss these questions with a partner.

1. Compare your answers in Parts A and B. Discuss any differences. Were you surprised by any of the negative connotations? If so, which ones?

2. Nouns—colors and animals, for example—can also be used to connote certain feelings. For example, in some cultures, the color *red* is used in language to express anger, passion, and love. The word *snake* is used to talk about a person you can't trust. Think of other colors or animals that have connotations attached to them.

❯ Go to MyEnglishLab to complete a skill practice.

APPLY YOUR SKILLS

WHY IT'S USEFUL By applying the skills you have learned in this unit, you will have a better understanding of this challenging reading about how elephants respond to seismic signals.

BEFORE YOU READ

A. Discuss these questions with one or more students.

1. What do you know about elephant listening? How is it similar to and different from the way that humans listen?

2. Is it important for scientists to study animal behavior in the wild as well as in captivity? Why?

3. Most countries have national parks. Why are national parks important for people as well as for animals?

B. You will read an article about Caitlin O'Connell-Rodwell's research on how elephants listen and communicate. As you read, think about these questions.

1. What is the focus of O'Connell-Rodwell's research?

2. What did her experiment show about how elephants respond to various seismic signals?

3. How can O'Connell-Rodwell's research findings be useful to nonscientists?

C. Review the Unit Skills Summary on the next page. As you read the article, apply the skills you learned in this unit.

UNIT SKILLS SUMMARY

CLASSIFY INFORMATION BY USING THESE SKILLS:

Classify information

• Sort information into groups by shared qualities.

Distinguish points of view

• Think about how an author's work experience, education, and personal beliefs may influence his or her point of view.

Support a presentation with visuals

• Decide what visual material can reinforce your spoken information.

Identify the language of parts and wholes

• Examine how specific language is used for concepts of parts and wholes.

Recognize connotative language

• Be aware of how words convey positive and negative meanings.

READ

A. Read the article on the next page. Annotate and take notes. Think about how an elephant's skeletal and nervous systems are involved in listening. Note the information in the T-chart.

ELEPHANTS	
Skeletal System	Nervous System

Elephant Listening: A Feeling in Their Bones

1 Observing a family of elephants in the wild, you may be surprised to see the whole family suddenly freeze in place. The elephants may even change direction, all facing the same way, and then freeze. A few elephants in the family might touch their trunks to the ground or lift one leg into the air. What, exactly, are the elephants doing? Researcher Dr. Caitlin O'Connell-Rodwell wondered about this, too—and has spent the past several years trying to find out.

2 Dr. O'Connell-Rodwell is an ecologist, elephant researcher, and ENT specialist. She is also the scientist who realized that elephants listen not just to sounds in the air but also to sounds in the ground. It turns out that sound carried in the air, the way humans or birds communicate, is only a part of how elephants say things. Elephants are also listening to seismic sound waves, which travel through the ground. A few years before O'Connell-Rodwell began examining elephants, other research showed that elephant communication included vocalizations far below the range of human hearing. Before studying elephants, O'Connell-Rodwell studied planthopper insects, which communicate seismically through trees. What if elephants were doing the same thing?

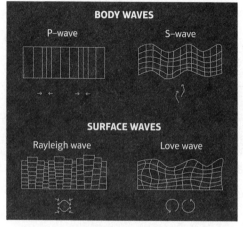

Kinds of seismic waves. Rayleigh waves are the vibration used in elephant communication.

3 O'Connell-Rodwell did a series of experiments, including both elephants in captivity and in the wild. Her wild-elephant-focused experiments were at a watering hole in Namibia's Etosha National Park. Her equipment included microphones as well as geophones—devices that measure seismic vibrations in the earth. By pairing microphones and geophones across a wide area, she discovered that low-frequency elephant rumbles can travel seismically—and over surprisingly long distances.

4 O'Connell-Rodwell studied how elephants responded to various seismic signals. By playing recordings of the rumbles of both Namibian and Kenyan elephants, O'Connell-Rodwell learned that the Etoshan elephants would immediately respond to well-understood warning calls by grouping up defensively and leaving the area. Interestingly, recorded warning calls of elephants from the other side of the continent would still bother the elephants, but not as much as the "local" calls did. The team also included calls made up of just low-frequency noise, to see if the elephants could tell the difference between real calls and gibberish. (They could.)

5 These experiments allowed O'Connell-Rodwell's team to document how elephants listened. "Freezing"—listening through their feet—was one way. The elephants could even close their ear canals, blocking out airborne noise, so they could better "listen" through skin and bone. Interestingly, this behavior could explain how elephants seem to be able to predict the weather—they may be hearing it through the ground.

6　Studying the calls of wild elephants also showed just how widely elephant activities were "broadcast," or sent to others. Many behaviors, like angry, threatening behavior toward predators, would have low-frequency rumbling included with clear gestures and trumpeting. It turns out that when dealing with dangerous situations, elephants use seismic communication to broadcast their situation to all other elephants in the surrounding area. This helps tell the whole group what each member of the group is doing.

7　O'Connell-Rodwell wanted to better understand the anatomy involved in seismic communication. How much seismic listening involved the bones? What part of the process involved the nervous system? The research team used the next set of recordings—which consisted of a warning call, a greeting call, and a call to move—to closely study listening habits. This helped O'Connell-Rodwell discover that bone conduction—in which sound waves are carried to the cochlea through the skeletal system—was more important than anything felt by the skin. Almost all elephants studied would, when repositioning themselves, do so for better bone conduction when "listening" to seismic activity.

8　One group of elephants, however, often used the trunk's nerves to listen better. Male elephants would not just position their bodies to better hear female elephants but would also often use their trunks. Wild elephants can be far apart; adult male elephants live far from matriarchal social units. Since female elephants are only fertile, or in estrus, for short periods of time, males need to find them quickly. Males in musth—a time when males are aggressive and interested in reproduction—will travel long distances listening for the estrus calls of female elephants. Interestingly, males not in musth still seem to hear these calls but ignore them—much to the confusion of juvenile males that see each of the older male elephants responding differently.

9　After discovering many new features of elephant communication, O'Connell-Rodwell is now trying to use this information to help both elephants and humans. Seismic signals can, hopefully, help farmers keep elephants away from their crops. And geophones may be useful in tracking elephant migration—and finding poachers who seek to harm vulnerable herds.

CULTURE NOTE

Namibia's Etosha National Park was established in 1907 and is visited annually by about 200,000 people. Lions, elephants, rhinoceroses, and giraffes live in the 20,000 square kilometers of park. Namibia is located in southwest Africa and is bordered by South Africa, Botswana, Angola, and the Atlantic Ocean.

Glossary

ENT specialist: the short name for ears, nose, and throat doctor

Gibberish: something you write or say that has no meaning

Ear canal: a tube, made up of skin and bones, in the ear that goes from the outer ear (what you see) to the inner ear (eardrum)

Behavior: the way that someone or something acts in different situations

Nervous system: a connection of nerves and cells that carries messages to and from the brain to parts of the body

Skeletal system: the bones and tendons that provide support, protection, and movement to a body

B. Compare notes with a partner. Did you identify similar details about how elephants use their skeletal and nervous systems for listening?

C. Reread the questions in Before You Read, Part B. With your partner, use your notes and opinions to answer the questions.

◐ Go to MyEnglishLab to read more closely, answer the critical thinking questions, and complete a summarizing activity.

THINKING CRITICALLY

Use information from the reading to answer these questions.

1. Scientific research can take years and require a lot of funding to cover the work and material expenses. How can scientists get funding for their research projects, and should governments be responsible for covering any of those costs? Explain.

   ....

   ....

2. Dr. Caitlin O'Connell-Rodwell applied her knowledge of treehopper insect communication to elephant communication. How does this support the argument that scientists should vary their research? How could changing research focus be detrimental (negative) to a scientist's research?

   ....

   ....

THINKING VISUALLY

Do light research to identify the parts of the human foot and the elephant foot. Add details and the labels from the box to the diagram. Then answer the questions on the next page.

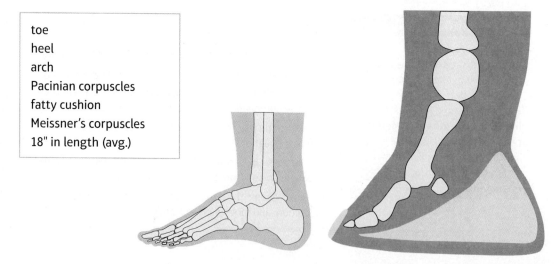

toe
heel
arch
Pacinian corpuscles
fatty cushion
Meissner's corpuscles
18" in length (avg.)

1. Look at the diagram on the previous page. What does it show? What are the similarities? What are the differences? Which would be better at feeling sound in the ground? Why?

   ....

   ....

2. Sketch a similar comparison showing the same part of two other species. Label your sketch and make notes about which is better at sensing (hear, smell, taste, feel, see) things.

THINKING ABOUT LANGUAGE

A. Read each excerpt. Then choose the correct answers.

For help with identifying parts and wholes, go to MyEnglishLab, Zoology, Part 2, Language Skill.

1. Which noun is considered the "whole"?

   > Her equipment included microphones as well as geophones—devices that measure seismic vibration in the earth.

   a. equipment
   b. microphones
   c. geophones
   d. vibration

2. Which nouns are considered the "parts"?

   > Her equipment included microphones as well as geophones—devices that measure seismic vibration in the earth.

   a. equipment / vibration
   b. microphones / geophones
   c. microphones / devices
   d. geophones / vibration

3. Notice the bolded word. Is it positive, negative, or neutral? Which word could best replace it?

   > Interestingly, males not in musth still seem to hear these calls but ignore them—much to the confusion of **juvenile** males that see each of the older male elephants responding differently.

   a. young
   b. childish
   c. infantile
   d. immature

4. Notice the bolded word. Is it positive, negative, or neutral? Which word could best replace it?

> Interestingly, males not in musth still seem to hear these calls but ignore them—much to the confusion of juvenile males that see each of the **older** male elephants responding differently.

a. elderly
b. senior
c. ancient
d. strong

5. Notice the bolded word. Is it positive, negative, or neutral? Which word could best replace it?

> And geophones may be useful in **tracking** elephant migration—and finding poachers who seek to harm vulnerable herds.

a. shadowing
b. obeying
c. trailing
d. following

6. Notice the bolded word. Is it positive, negative, or neutral? Which word could best replace it?

> And geophones may be useful in tracking elephant migration—and finding poachers who seek to harm **vulnerable** herds.

a. sensitive
b. helpless
c. healthy
d. at risk

7. In this sentence, which noun is the "whole" and which noun is the "part"?

> Other research showed that elephant communication included vocalizations far below the range of human hearing.

a. whole: research; part: vocalizations
b. whole: communication; part: hearing
c. whole: communication; part: vocalizations
d. whole: elephant; part: vocalizations

8. In this sentence, which noun is the "whole" and which noun is the "part"?

> The research team used the next set of recordings—which consisted of a warning call …

a. whole: set; part: recordings
b. whole: team; part: warning
c. whole: call; part: recordings
d. whole: team; part: set

B. Practice using connotative language. Follow these steps:

1. Choose a topic from the list.

2. Prepare a visual about the topic.

3. Share your mini-presentation with a small group. Use language that is positive, negative, or neutral to explain your topic.

Threats to Elephants	Elephant Behavior
Elephant Habitat	Elephant Communication

◑ Go to MyEnglishLab to watch Professor O'Connell-Rodwell's concluding video and to complete a self-assessment.

HISTORY

Specialized Vocabulary

UNIT PROFILE

In this unit, you will read about the city of Troy and the tomb of Tutankhamun, and the archaeologists behind those discoveries. In the final reading of the unit, you will learn how archaeology impacts popular culture.

Look at the reading "The Influence of History on Pop Culture" on page 253. Skim the reading. Highlight any words you don't know but seem important. How can you figure out their meanings?

OUTCOMES

- Find definitions and explanations in a text
- Deal with specialized vocabulary
- Respond in an online forum
- Demonstrate civil discourse online
- Use graphic organizers

For more about **HISTORY**, see ❶❸. See also Ⓦ and OC **HISTORY** ❶❷❸.

GETTING STARTED

○ Go to MyEnglishLab to watch Dr. Hunt's introductory video and to complete a self-assessment.

Discuss these questions with a partner or group.

1. Why is archaeology important to our understanding of historical time periods and events?

2. In order to carry out a successful archaeological excavation, what is necessary? Explain.

3. In his introduction, Dr. Hunt mentions two places of archaeological importance—the city of Troy and the tomb of Tutankhamun. Why do you think people were surprised by those two discoveries? How do you think these discoveries may have changed people's feelings about literature and the life of pharaohs?

SKILL 1

FINDING DEFINITIONS AND EXPLANATIONS IN A TEXT

WHY IT'S USEFUL By recognizing how writers define or explain vocabulary, you can improve your reading comprehension.

With over a million words in English, it's unlikely that most readers know the exact meaning of every word. So writers use various strategies to define or explain difficult or technical vocabulary. Meanwhile, readers can do their part to **find definitions and explanations in a text**. By looking at the context (the surrounding words, phrases, and sentences), they can make logical guesses to figure out the meaning of difficult words.

TIP

To help figure out the meaning of new vocabulary, good readers will ask questions while reading. For example: What are the surrounding words? Do those words give me clues? What does it mean in this context?

For strategies on finding definitions and explanations in a text, study the chart.

Strategy	Example	Explanation	Signal Word / Phrase
Look for definition / synonym context clues. Sometimes a writer will state the definition of the word or use a synonym (a word with the same meaning) immediately after a difficult word.	*A desire to **loot**—in other words, steal— the city's riches, and anger at over-taxation could have easily made neighboring nations attack the city for profit and revenge.*	In this sentence, the signal *in other words* introduces the word *steal*, which is a synonym for *loot*.	*in other words* *to say it another way* *or* *which means* *similarly* *like* *in the same way*
Look for contrast / antonym context clues. Sometimes a writer will use words with an opposite meaning to explain a word.	*While the stories of the Trojan War may have been a **myth**, it looks like there really was an ancient city in northwestern Turkey that was once a busy trading center.*	In this sentence, *While* in the first clause indicates a contrast, and the second clause stresses there really was an ancient city. So we can conclude that *myth* refers to something that is not real.	*while* *although* *whereas* *on the other hand* *yet* *but* *however* *in contrast*
Look for example / explanation context clues. Sometimes a writer will give an example to explain a word.	*Archaeologists have discovered many ancient **relics** that have given us new insights into the past. For instance, the remains of very old buildings and objects in Pompeii showed historians what ancient Pompeiians used and valued.*	Examples are sometimes introduced with expressions such as *for instance*. In this sentence, *for instance* gives the reader an example of ancient relics—remains of very old buildings and objects.	*for instance* *for example* *such as* *specifically* *to illustrate*
Use previous knowledge / logic. Often readers will use what they already know about the topic to make a logical guess about a word's meaning.	*Homer, the Greek poet whose Iliad recorded part of the Trojan War **legend** almost 500 years later, was likely putting his own mark on a very, very old story.*	Homer is a famous poet known for his epic poems, the *Iliad* and the *Odyssey*. Also, the writer mentions that Homer was putting his own mark on an old story. So we can conclude that *legend* is a story.	

VOCABULARY PREVIEW

Read the vocabulary items in the box. Circle the ones you know. Put a question mark next to the ones you don't know.

claimed	destination	rare	passed down
work (n)	amazed		

EXERCISE 1

A. Read the excerpts from the upcoming reading "Troy: A Legend or a City?" Each word in bold is explained by a context clue, which is underlined. Check (✓) the type of context clue. Then write the definition of the bolded word.

1. For centuries, European intellectuals believed the city of Troy was **fictional**, or <u>imaginary</u>.

   ☐ antonym   ☐ logic   ☐ synonym   ☐ example

   Definition of *fictional*: ....

2. As a safe **harbor** in the eastern <u>Aegean Sea</u>, Troy would have been the final destination for traders bringing goods from far to the east.

   ☐ antonym   ☐ logic   ☐ synonym   ☐ example

   Definition of *harbor*: ....

3. This <u>story</u> kept "Troy" alive in the imaginations of readers for centuries. By the 19th century, people were wondering if an **actual** Troy could be located.

   ☐ contrast   ☐ definition   ☐ synonym   ☐ example

   Definition of *actual*: ....

B. Check your definitions with the ones in a dictionary. Did you come up with similar definitions? Did looking at the context clues help you figure out an approximate meaning of each word?

A. Read the title and look at the image. From this information, what can you tell about the reading?

☐ It will describe the city plan of Troy.

☐ It will explore the question of whether the city of Troy was imaginary or real.

☐ It will explain Homer's story of the Trojan War.

B. Read the passage. Then read the statements that follow. Circle *T* (True) or *F* (False). Correct the false statements.

Troy: A Legend or a City?

1   For centuries, European intellectuals believed the city of Troy was fictional, or imaginary. In 1872, when an amateur German archaeologist claimed to have found the ancient city, many did not believe it. While the stories of the Trojan War may have been a myth, it looked like there really *was* an ancient city in northwestern Turkey that had once been a busy trading center. What was the real story? As time went on and archaeological science improved, researchers were better able to understand the facts.

2   The city today referred to as Troy began during the early Bronze Age, around 2400 BCE. For the next 1,200 years, the city grew through trade and taxation. As a safe harbor in the eastern Aegean Sea, Troy would have been the final destination for traders bringing goods from far to the east; rare, expensive goods would be shipped off to the greater Mediterranean from Troy's harbor. Forensic evidence shows that the population included a mix of both Hittites, ancient inhabitants of the Anatolian peninsula, and Mycenaeans, who were early ancestors of the Greeks. A desire to loot—in other words, steal—the city's riches, and anger at over-taxation could have easily made neighboring nations attack the city for profit and revenge.

3   At some point around the 12th century BCE, the city was attacked and fell to ruin. The story of the beautiful city near the ocean on a hill survived, passed down from generation to generation in the form of song, poetry, and legend. Homer, the Greek poet whose *Iliad* recorded part of the Trojan War legend almost 500 years later, was likely putting his own spin on a very, very old story. There is even evidence of this Trojan War story across many cultures in the region. It is Homer's version of the story

that survived—due to being an excellent work of literature and one of the first to be written down. This story kept "Troy" alive in the imaginations of readers for centuries. By the 19th century, people were wondering if an actual Troy could be located.

4 Businessman and self-trained archaeologist Heinrich Schliemann, using the work of previous writers and scholars, found evidence of an ancient city at Hisarlik mound, a built-up hill in northwestern Turkey overlooking the Aegean Sea and the Dardanelles. Back in 1870, the idea that Schliemann used ancient literature as a way to find the ruins of an *actual* city amazed people. Archaeology was still quite a young discipline; this was a clearly successful application of investigative techniques. Ancient stories might be more than fiction; those tales could be doorways to the past. Archaeologists used Troy to develop modern techniques of investigation and cataloguing to keep accurate track of discoveries. United Nations Educational, Scientific and Cultural Organization (UNESCO) would go on to make the ruins of Troy a World Heritage Site, noting its importance both as an ancient civilization and as a valuable, fascinating archaeological site.

Glossary

Myth: an ancient story, especially about gods, that tries to explain a natural or historical event

Taxation: the system of charging taxes, or the money that is collected

Safe harbor: a place that offers protection

Inhabitant: a person living in a specific place

Civilization: a developed and organized society

T / F 1. Troy is a fictional city made famous by Homer in his poem the *Iliad*.

T / F 2. Troy was discovered by archaeologists in the late 19th century.

T / F 3. The ancient city of Troy had been a prosperous community.

T / F 4. In the 12th century, the city of Troy was attacked.

T / F 5. Homer's story was written as the ancient city of Troy was being attacked.

T / F 6. Heinrich Schliemann used Homer's story to help figure out where the ancient city of Troy was located.

T / F 7. Schliemann was a long-time archaeologist whose discovery of Troy was based on his own original research.

T / F 8. Prior to Schliemann's discovery, people imagined Troy was a mythical city.

C. Reread the passage. Then check yours answers in Parts A and B.

D. Read each excerpt and make annotations about the meaning of the bolded word. Use the strategies you have studied in this section.

1. Forensic evidence shows that the **population** included a mix of both Hittites, ancient <u>inhabitants</u> of the Anatolian peninsula, and Mycenaeans, who were early ancestors of the Greeks.

   group of people
   ~ "inhabitants"

2. Forensic evidence shows that the population included a mix of both **Hittites**, ancient inhabitants of the Anatolian peninsula, and Mycenaeans, who were early ancestors of the Greeks.

3. Homer, the Greek poet whose *Iliad* **recorded** part of the Trojan War legend almost 500 years later, was likely putting his own spin on a very, very old story.

4. It is Homer's version of the story that **survived**—due to being an excellent work of literature and one of the first to be written down. This story kept "Troy" alive in the imaginations of readers for centuries.

5. By the 19th century, people were wondering if an actual Troy could be **located**. Businessman and self-trained archaeologist Heinrich Schliemann, using the work of previous writers and scholars, found evidence of an ancient city at Hisarlik mound, a built-up hill in northwestern Turkey overlooking the Aegean Sea and the Dardanelles.

6. Businessman and self-trained archaeologist Heinrich Schliemann, using the work of previous writers and scholars, found evidence of an ancient city at Hisarlik **mound**, a built-up hill in northwestern Turkey overlooking the Aegean Sea and the Dardanelles.

EXERCISE 3

Discuss these questions with a partner.

1. Compare definitions from Exercise 2, Part D with a partner and explain what strategies helped you to figure out each word.

2. When reading in your first language, do you often encounter unknown vocabulary? If so, what do you do to figure out meaning?

TIP

Add the Vocabulary Check vocabulary items and any other useful items from the reading to your vocabulary notecards or journal.

VOCABULARY CHECK

A. Review the vocabulary items in the Vocabulary Preview. Write their definitions and add examples. Use a dictionary if necessary.

B. Read each sentence or passage. Then choose the correct definition of the underlined vocabulary item.

1. Heinrich Schliemann <u>claimed</u> to have found ancient treasures from King Priam, the king of Troy during the Trojan War. But others disputed this and believed that he had buried them himself.

   When someone <u>claims</u> to have done something, _____ .

   a. he or she says something is true even though it might not be
   b. he or she demands that something be done

2. Scholars who have studied Homer and his epic poems can travel on organized tours in Turkey. One available <u>destination</u> is the UNESCO site at Hisarlik.

   A <u>destination</u> is a place someone _____ .

   a. is from
   b. travels to

3. With technology, we can search the earth for ancient things. In the future, new discoveries will become <u>rare</u> because we will have found most everything.

   If something is <u>rare</u> it is _____ .

   a. unusual
   b. common

4. In many cultures, stories are <u>passed down</u> from the elders to a younger generation so that traditions are not forgotten.

   When something is <u>passed down</u>, people _____ .

   a. tell or give it to someone else
   b. stop talking about it

(Continued)

5. The <u>works</u> of Homer are very well known and are part of many college courses.

A <u>work</u> is a _____ .

a. job
b. play, book, painting, and so on

6. It's perhaps surprising that Homer's stories can still <u>amaze</u> students with their description and emotion, considering that they were written between the 7th and 8th centuries BCE.

If something <u>amazes</u> someone, it _____ .

a. makes the person feel great
b. makes the person feel surprised

◐ Go to MyEnglishLab to complete vocabulary and skill practices, and to join in collaborative activities.

SKILL 2

DEALING WITH SPECIALIZED VOCABULARY

WHY IT'S USEFUL By learning how to manage specialized vocabulary, which is an essential part of university textbooks and courses, you can increase your chances of academic success.

Every academic discipline—history, economics, physics, engineering, computer science, and so on—has vocabulary specific to that field. As opposed to vocabulary found on the Academic Word List (AWL), the **specialized vocabulary** of those fields is not high frequency. That means it's rare to encounter it outside of that discipline. The meaning of some of this specialized vocabulary can be figured out through context clues (definitions, synonyms, antonyms, examples, affixes), and some textbooks will also include marginal glosses, footnotes, or even a glossary. However, what do you do if there are no context clues or other vocabulary help? Which words do you choose to focus on, and how do you learn their meaning?

When deciding which words to learn, think about these questions:

- Which words are repeated often?

- Which words are important to the meaning of the passage?

- What are the content words in the questions? (This is especially useful to consider if there are questions at the beginning or end of chapters.)

Learning Specialized Vocabulary

Because specialized vocabulary is specific to a certain field, you will need to take an active role in its acquisition. It's not enough to notice a new word, record it on a vocabulary card, and look at it a few times. Studies have shown that in order to acquire a new word, you have to encounter it at least eight times in content-rich, meaningful ways. In other words, you improve your chances of acquiring it if, for example, you read it in a textbook and make a note of it, come across it in a visual, later hear it during a classroom lecture, and use it in writing or speaking.

Steps for Acquiring New Words

1. Identify the word, find its definition, check that the definition is correct for its context, and record it in a vocabulary journal.
2. Paraphrase the definition (i.e., explain the definition in your own way to yourself, either aloud or in writing).
3. Associate the word to something you know (background knowledge) or visualize it (go online to look at images).
4. Compare the word to other words (e.g., synonyms or antonyms).
5. Use the word in an example sentence.
6. Talk about the word and its definition with a classmate or friend. Teach each other new vocabulary as you review your course notes.

VOCABULARY PREVIEW

Read the vocabulary items in the box. Circle the ones you know. Put a question mark next to the ones you don't know.

briefly	mask (n)	related	references
barely	contents	recovered	possession

EXERCISE 4

A. Scan the article "Who Was King Tutankhamun?" on page 237 for the following specialized vocabulary. Write how often each appears. Which vocabulary items are important to know in order to understand the article? Underline two more.

___5___ pharaoh .... tomb .... Theban priests .... Tutankhamun

.... sarcophagus .... death mask .... obsidian statues

B. Add your two other vocabulary items from Part A to the chart. For now, write just the definition for each item. In your own words, explain each item to a partner.

Specialized Vocabulary Word	Definition	Paraphrase of Definition	Association	Synonym / Antonym	Example Sentence
pharaoh	a ruler of ancient Egypt	someone with power in Egypt; back in history	a documentary I saw about the pyramids	king	Many different pharaohs had ruled Egypt before King Tut.

EXERCISE 5

A. The article on the next page introduces the Egyptian pharaoh King Tutankhamun. What do you know about him?

B. The article contains specialized vocabulary. How can you deal with it? Follow these steps:

> **TIP**
>
> *Content words* have meaning. They are often subjects or objects (nouns), or actions (verbs). *Function words* have a grammatical role. They are usually articles, prepositions, or pronouns.

1. Read the questions that follow the article. Mark the content words.

2. Read the article. Mark and try to define any words that are important for understanding the article and answering the questions.

3. Add those words to the chart above.

Who Was King Tutankhamun?

1 King Tutankhamun was relatively unimportant in his day. He was royalty, but he ruled only briefly during his childhood and teens; Tutankhamun died around the age of 19. Why, then, is he one of the most famous pharaohs? Tutankhamun's fame is due to the discovery of his tomb—undamaged and undisturbed. In 1922, after years of searching, an archaeological team led by Howard Carter discovered Tutankhamun's tomb near Luxor, Egypt. Ancient Egyptian rulers were buried with their treasures, and Tutankhamun was buried with everything appropriate for a pharaoh. His golden bejeweled death mask, polished stone sarcophagus, and an assortment of luxury items filled his final resting place— which remained untouched by human hands for centuries.

Howard Carter and an assistant examining King Tut's sarcophagus

CULTURE NOTE

During the ages of the pharaohs, the Egyptians worshipped many gods, but Amun was regarded as the king of gods. Tutankhamun's father led a campaign against the Egyptians' singular devotion to Amun, which caused political problems with the powerful Theban priests. Thebes was the capital of Egypt at this time, and the priests—as much if not more than the pharaohs—held considerable power.

2 How had Tutankhamun's grave gone unnoticed? When he died, around 1320 BCE, Tutankhamun was a lesser ruler of a very unpopular family. Akhenaten, who may have been Tutankhamun's father, had ruled Egypt in ways that the priestly caste disliked. This led to a great deal of political instability. Tutankhamun's parents would have been very closely related, as Egyptian royalty of the time married within families; years of doing so likely contributed to health problems that, research shows, affected the young king. As a very young, very sickly ruler disliked by the powerful Theban priests of Amun, Tutankhamun's position was mostly ceremonial.

3 In any case, Tutankhamun was still buried "properly," with all of the gold, benedictions, inscriptions, and other items of a pharaoh. Soon after, further political instability caused the Theban priests to try to "erase," or forget, various heretical[1] pharaohs from the historical record. Tutankhamun was mostly forgotten. By the 19th century, references to Tutankhamun were few. This relative unimportance allowed Tutankhamun's tomb to remain undisturbed for many years; no one thought to find and loot the barely known tomb of an unimportant king.

4 This situation greatly benefitted modern research; Tutankhamun's tomb became one of the most important discoveries in modern archaeology. The discovery of a complete tomb has allowed us to know the true wonder of the pharaohs. From obsidian statues to finely polished quartzite, the stonework is incredible. Tutankhamun's tomb contains an enormous amount of gold—which would have been even more difficult to get in the ancient world than it is today. No single find has done more for the field of Egyptology. The contents of Tutankhamun's tomb provided archaeologists with large amounts of information regarding life in ancient Egypt. At museums in Egypt and around the world, the relics recovered from the tomb of Tutankhamun fascinate people to this day; even the smallest of Tutankhamun's possessions prove to be incredibly popular museum exhibits.

[1]having beliefs that are considered against the beliefs of a particular religion

C. Choose the correct answers.

1. What is the main idea of the article?
   a. Howard Carter's discovery of Tutankhamun's tomb was incredible because it uncovered many treasures.
   b. Tutankhamun was a boy king who had limited power during his rule.
   c. Although Tutankhamun was a minor ruler in his day, the discovery of his tomb contributed enormously to our understanding of ancient Egyptian society.
   d. Tutankhamun is the best known pharaoh of ancient Egypt even though he died when he was young.

2. What was NOT mentioned as being buried in Tutankhamun's tomb?
   a. a jeweled death mask
   b. obsidian statues
   c. gold
   d. swords and other weapons

3. According to the article, what may have contributed to Tutankhamun's health problems?
   a. the stress of being ruler of Egypt
   b. the fact that his parents were related to each other
   c. the dry, hot temperatures of Egypt
   d. the poor medical care at that time

4. The purpose of explaining Tutankhamun's poor relationship with the Theban priests is to _____ .
   a. explain how his tomb might have been forgotten
   b. give an example of how he was a poor leader
   c. show how Egyptians worshipped during Tutankhamun's time
   d. prove that Tutankhamun was an ineffective leader

5. Why did Theban priests want to erase "heretical pharaohs from the historical record"?
   a. because the pharaohs, by disagreeing with the Theban priests' religion, threatened the priests' influence and power
   b. because the priests believed that Tutankhamun had been too powerful in Egypt
   c. because the pharaohs believed that the ancient Egyptians would no longer believe in religion
   d. because the priests wanted to protect the tombs of the ancient Egyptian pharaohs

6. In the last sentence of Paragraph 2, the word *ceremonial* most closely means _____ .

    a. powerful
    b. luxurious
    c. attractive
    d. without power

D. Reread the article. Then check your answers in Part C.

EXERCISE 6

Discuss your reading experience with one or more students.

1. Did scanning the reading and identifying the specialized vocabulary help you understand the article? Explain.

2. To help remember the specialized vocabulary, complete the chart in Exercise 4, Part B.

VOCABULARY CHECK

A. Review the vocabulary items in the Vocabulary Preview. Write their definitions and add examples. Use a dictionary if necessary.

B. Complete each sentence using the correct vocabulary item from the box. Use the correct form.

barely	briefly	contents	mask
possession	recover	reference	related

1. A burial practice for ancient Egyptian rulers was to make a .... that would be placed over the face of the deceased when he or she was buried.

2. Compared to his father who ruled Egypt for 17 years, Tutankhamun was .... in power, ruling ceremonially for just ten years, with most of the political power in the hands of the Theban priests.

3. The ancient Egyptians' belief in an afterlife explained why people were buried with many of their ....—such as gold, furniture, and artwork— since it was thought that they would need these items in their afterlife.

4. Because Amun was considered the king of gods and was chiefly worshipped during ancient Egyptian times, there are many .... to him that appear in writings, statutes, and other relics.

5. When Howard Carter uncovered the .... of Tutankhamun's tomb, he must have felt overwhelmed by the number of treasures that had been undisturbed for centuries.

6. In ancient Egypt, it was not uncommon for Egyptian royalty to marry within the family, as it was considered that people who were .... would enjoy greater political stability.

7. During excavations, it was not uncommon for relics to go missing, and in the past, not much effort was taken to .... these items. However, nowadays, if an item goes missing, much attention is placed on finding and returning it.

8. Even though Tutankhamun was .... an adult when he died at the age of 19, his name is now recognized worldwide.

⬤ Go to MyEnglishLab to complete vocabulary and skill practices, and to join in collaborative activities.

INTEGRATED SKILLS
RESPONDING IN AN ONLINE FORUM

WHY IT'S USEFUL By understanding what professors expect and what is considered appropriate behavior in online forums, you can be successful in responding to online prompts.

More university classes are being offered online, and many "traditional" classes have an online component where students are expected to **respond in online forums**.

The goal of online forums (such as blogs and discussion boards) is to engage students in a meaningful conversation about an issue. When responding to others, you shouldn't simply write, "I agree" or "Great idea" (or their opposites)—you should explain *why* in a constructive and respectful way.

Questions

Professors will typically avoid *yes / no* questions, as the goal is to get students thinking and responding in a meaningful way. Some question types you may encounter include the following:

Question Type	Example
Personal experience: These kinds of questions require you to apply your experience to the topic or reading. It's OK to use *I, me, my* in your writing. Also explain how your experience is connected to the reading or the discussion.	What artifacts have you seen? Were they from King Tutankhamun's tomb or from another archaeological dig? Explain what you saw, discuss whether it relates to what we've read, and explore the relationship between museums and archaeologists.
Problem-solving: These questions ask you to come up with a solution to a problem. Your solution may directly relate to a problem outlined in the text or be on the same topic.	Howard Carter, the archaeologist who discovered King Tut's tomb, spent years searching in Egypt. His primary financier, the Earl of Carnarvon, was about to end his financial support, but Carter found the tomb. If Carter had lost this financial support, what other ways could he have financed his exploration?
Interaction: These questions invite you to interact with your classmates' ideas. Remember to engage thoughtfully and respectfully.	Howard Carter has been criticized for how he damaged the mummy of King Tutankhamun when he was removing it from its sarcophagus. In 1922, archaeological techniques were not as advanced as they are today. According to recent standards, how should the mummy have been handled? Your first response should give your ideas on the best techniques for handling ancient relics, such as a mummy. Your second response should relate to a classmate's ideas.
Synthesis: These questions ask you to think about other readings or assignments and connect the information to come up with a new understanding of the topic.	The first reading explained the archaeological discovery of Troy by Heinrich Schliemann, and the second reading explained the archaeological discovery of Tutankhamun's tomb by Howard Carter. In what ways are the two discoveries similar, and how does this inform your understanding of the field of archaeology?

Responses

When responding, remember to do the following:

- Understand what kind of question it is (problem-solving, etc.) and what specifically it is asking.

- Take a few minutes to think about your response, and then write it.

- Use academic English.

- Be polite.

- Use correct grammar, punctuation, and spelling.

- If you have facts (evidence) that can back up your opinion, cite them.

- Make sure your evidence is connected to your point (be concise).

- Check that you wrote your response clearly and correctly.

- Take a moment before you hit the Send or Submit button to make sure that your response accurately reflects your ideas.

Consider this possible response to the problem-solving question in the chart:

Egypt4eva: If Carter had lost his financial backing from the Earl of Carnarvon, he could have gone to the first king of Egypt, King Fu'ad I, and asked for financial assistance, promising that in return, Egypt would be able to keep any artifact that was found. This might have been attractive to the king, since according to the encyclopedia, Egypt had just become independent of Great Britain, and the discovery could have shown the world that Egypt was willing to do something that Britain wasn't—financially support one of its countrymen.

VOCABULARY PREVIEW

Read the vocabulary items in the box. Circle the ones you know. Put a question mark next to the ones you don't know.

attracted	poor	resumed	quit
chance (n)	look for	realized	lived up to

EXERCISE 7

A. Read a professor's discussion question about the upcoming reading "Searching for King Tut's Tomb." Check (✓) the question type(s).

> Being an archaeologist requires great skill and much patience. Howard Carter had spent many years unsuccessfully looking for King Tut's tomb before he found it in 1922. Based on today's lecture and the assigned reading, what motivated him to be persistent (to keep looking)? Clearly explain your idea. Also, include a reaction to another student's idea.

☐ personal experience

☐ problem solving

☐ interaction

☐ synthesis

B. Now read two students' answers to the question. Check (✓) the one you think is better. Tell a partner why.

☐ **Mummy4life**

My response: Archaeologists like Howard Carter may be motivated because they are fully invested in their research and have spent years of their lives researching and searching for something, giving up would signal that all those years of work were in vain.

Reaction to another student: I really like what **Herstory2** said about how archaeologists are motivated.

☐ **Herstory2**

My response: From the lecture we know that people who choose to go into archaeology are very patient people who understand the chance of uncovering a great "discovery" is slim and that it takes a great deal of careful research and work. However, since we know from the reading that Carter spent a considerable amount of time researching Egyptology, he probably had a very good idea of where such "a discovery" would exist, and all he needed was the time and money to uncover it.

Reaction to another student: While I can understand **TashaK's** point that some may be motivated by money, I think the thrill of discovery and the excitement of knowing that your ideas were proven correct are more motivating than simply the economic aspect of it.

C. Now read the passage. Then read the statements that follow. Circle *T* (True) or *F* (False). Correct the false statements.

Searching for King Tut's Tomb

1 Howard Carter found himself attracted to archaeology from an early age. Growing up, his poor health kept him indoors; he used this time to study art and history. Carter was born in London in 1874. When he was eight years old, the British Empire occupied the nation of Egypt. Carter was fascinated by news reports and research studies discussing the relics of ancient Egypt. When he became an adult, Carter convinced his family that instead of an *ordinary* career, he should travel to Egypt to study ancient history.

2 Carter found success as an archaeological artist. He had the right mix of artistic and academic talent needed to accurately draw findings, draft tomb layouts, and transcribe hieroglyphs. Carter's excavations were successful, but he was no longer happy with ordinary crypts. Any "discovery" made by archaeologists was usually centuries too late; the graves of the pharaohs had been robbed, often thousands of years earlier.

3 By 1907, Carter was working with George Herbert, the Earl of Carnarvon. Herbert was both a friend and a financial backer, constantly delighted by Carter's discoveries. Carter was convinced that there could yet be an undiscovered tomb—that of the "boy king" Tutankhamun. Carter set off to find the tomb in 1914 but found his research interrupted by the Great War. He resumed the search later, only to meet with years of failure.

4 Even the Earl of Carnarvon wasn't one to throw money away; by 1922, Herbert was forced to give Carter an ultimatum: Find the tomb this year or quit. Carter had returned to the Valley of the Kings, near Luxor. This seemed his best chance to find an undiscovered tomb, though many were unsure; why did Carter think he would find an undisturbed tomb in the most obvious of locations? The Valley of the Kings is where most of Egypt's pharaohs were buried. Carter's idea was simple—Tutankhamun was not an important king. His short lifespan, combined with the unpopularity of his family, meant that there were few records of his life *or* death. Grave robbers, being less scholarly than archaeologists, likely did not even think to look for lesser-known pharaohs.

Howard Carter (left) with Lord Carnarvon at the entrance to the inner chamber of Tutankhamun's tomb in the Valley of the Kings, Egypt, 1923

5 In November of 1922, Carter found what he had been searching for. An accidental discovery in a worker encampment area led to a door that, in turn, led to an atrium, or larger space. While parts of the entrance had been disturbed, the tomb itself was sealed. Once Lord Carnarvon arrived, the tomb was opened; Carter looked at the untouched treasures of a pharaoh, which had been left alone for thousands of years.

6 There are sources that claim that, at some point in the excavation, Carter began to act unethically. Stories include everything from theft to carelessly breaking walls. There is even a conspiracy theory that says Carter made up evidence of grave robbing in the entranceway in front of the tomb. This is a serious charge, as agreements at the time required Egyptian government representatives to be present at specific types of excavations. These conspiracy theorists think that Carter would have done anything to claim the riches of the tomb for himself; however, there is no meaningful evidence to support this position. Carter was, above all, dedicated to bringing this history to the world.

7 That dedication sometimes went beyond his own capabilities; archaeologists agree that Carter could have done a better job of removing the mummy of King Tut from its sarcophagus. This is regrettable, but the technology to perform the procedure had not been developed at the time. Carter did the best he could with the tools available to him.

8 After discovering Tut's tomb, Carter spent years studying its contents. Later, he would travel the world, giving lectures and meeting with museums. He may have realized that no other archaeological discovery could have lived up to what he had already accomplished. Finally, his poor health caught up with him; he died of cancer and was, fittingly, buried under an epitaph translated from the tomb of Tutankhamun.

Glossary

The Great War: an old-fashioned phrase for *World War I*

Sarcophagus: a decorated stone box for a dead body, used in ancient times

T / F 1. While sick as a child, Howard Carter developed an interest in history.

T / F 2. Carter was skilled at drawing and used this talent in his job.

T / F 3. Carter searched continuously for the tomb of King Tut from 1914 to 1922.

T / F 4. It can be inferred that the Earl of Carnarvon was getting frustrated that Carter hadn't found King Tut's tomb after searching for it over a number of years.

T / F 5. The Valley of the Kings was where the ancient pharaohs had ruled and lived.

T / F 6. Because of Carter's careful attention to detail, nothing was destroyed during the excavation of King Tut's tomb.

T / F 7. Some conspiracy theories suggest that Carter took some treasures from the tomb and falsely accused grave robbers of the crime.

T / F 8. After finding the tomb, Carter retired to his estate in England.

D. Write a 100-word response to the following online discussion prompt. After you have written your first draft, review it against the checklist below.

> According to the passage "Searching for King Tut's Tomb," some people believe that Carter acted unethically and took some of the treasures, and then invented stories about grave robbers. These theories have never been proven, but they do pose an interesting question. Should archaeologists be allowed to keep any ancient relics that they find? What rules should an archaeologist follow when making an archaeological discovery? Explain.

☐ I identifed the question type as ....

☐ I used academic English.

☐ My tone is polite.

☐ I checked for grammar, punctuation, and spelling.

☐ I supported my opinion and cited the source(s).

☐ My ideas relate to the question.

☐ My ideas are clear and concise.

☐ My response represents what I believe.

E. Compare responses with a partner. Give a reaction to your partner's response. Be sure to state whether you agree or disagree and explain why.

VOCABULARY CHECK

A. Review the vocabulary items in the Vocabulary Preview. Write their definitions and add examples. Use a dictionary if necessary.

B. Complete each sentence using the correct vocabulary item from the box. Use the correct form.

attract	chance	live up to	look for
poor	quit	realize	resume

1. After hundreds, if not thousands, of years of being buried, many archaeological relics are in .... condition—maybe chipped or broken—but many of the treasures of King Tut's tomb were in surprisingly good shape.

2. Many of the pharaohs' tombs had .... grave robbers, who had come looking for an easy way to get rich quick.

3. Some archaeologists will _____ their search if they can't find anything after a few years, but many others are persistent and will spend a lifetime searching.

4. George Herbert died from an infection shortly after King Tut's tomb was discovered, but Howard Carter _____ his work of documenting and studying all the findings after taking a short break for the funeral.

5. Many people believed there was a good _____ that Howard Carter would also suffer an early death since they thought that anyone who had entered the tomb would be affected by the so-called "pharaoh's curse."

6. Archaeologists continue to _____ mythical cities, such as the Lost City of Atlantis, which is mentioned by Plato in some of his work.

7. Carter _____ that he had discovered a pharaoh's tomb when he looked through a small opening in the tomb's door and saw rooms filled with statues and gold.

8. Even though it took many years to find King Tut's tomb, Carter _____ the promise that he had made Herbert to find the tomb.

◑ Go to MyEnglishLab to complete a skill practice and to join in collaborative activities.

LANGUAGE SKILL
DEMONSTRATING CIVIL DISCOURSE ONLINE

WHY IT'S USEFUL In an online forum, it is important to use civil discourse (polite language) when expressing your ideas and responding to others. Learning how to use civil discourse online can help you engage with others in a respectful and constructive manner.

◑ Go to MyEnglishLab for the Language Skill presentation and practice.

VOCABULARY STRATEGY
USING GRAPHIC ORGANIZERS

WHY IT'S USEFUL By using a graphic organizer, you can organize idea and vocabulary, which can help you study and learn new information.

Graphic organizers are a way to visually represent information. There are many different graphic organizers to help acquire vocabulary. You should choose the one that best suits your needs.

Alphabox

This type of graphic organizer is similar to a word wall where you record all the words you know about a certain topic or field. You simply fill in the boxes with the vocabulary starting with the letter for that box. For example, *excavation* would fit in the *E* box. As the semester goes on, you add to the boxes. Alphaboxes can remind you of the words you have learned, but if you need more specific information (e.g., definitions, parts of speech, antonyms), you will need to consult another graphic organizer.

A	B	C	D
E *excavation*	F	G	H
I	J	K	L
M *mummy*	N	O	P *pharaoh*
Q	R	S *site*	T
U	V	W X	Y Z

Vocabulary Cluster

With this type of graphic organizer, you write a vocabulary word in the middle oval and then search for antonyms (that you write in the squares) and synonyms (that you write in the circles) for that word.

Study this example:

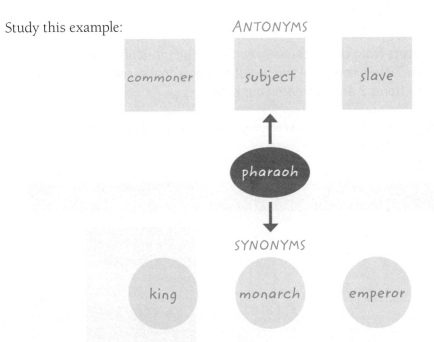

Visual and Personal Association

This type of graphic organizer uses images as well as personal associations to help you learn new vocabulary. You can go online to find an image of the word, or you can sketch a quick representation.

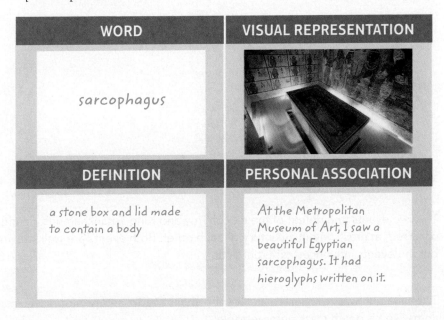

Knowing a word, noticing how it's used, and learning related forms will help expand your vocabulary knowledge.

EXERCISE 8

A. Read the excerpts from the upcoming reading, "The Influence of History on Popular Culture." Then complete the visual and personal association organizer for "mask." For Items 2 and 3, create your own.

1. Tutankhamun was revealed to us recently; mass media and photography made items like his death **mask** unforgettable.

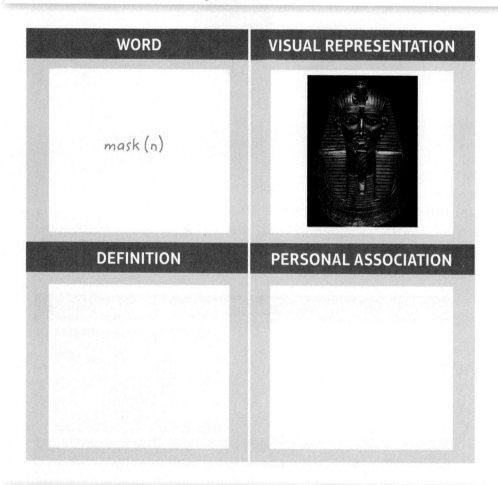

WORD	VISUAL REPRESENTATION
mask (n)	
DEFINITION	**PERSONAL ASSOCIATION**

2. The two events [the defeat of the city of Troy and King Tutankhamun's death] occurred, at most, within a century of each other. Both events are well known, but the events influenced different **arts**.

3. Tutankhamun was revealed to us recently; **mass media** and photography made items like his death mask unforgettable.

B. Complete the vocabulary cluster for "resume." Then create your own for Items 2 and 3. Use a dictionary if necessary.

1. Carter **resumed** the search later, only to meet with years of failure.

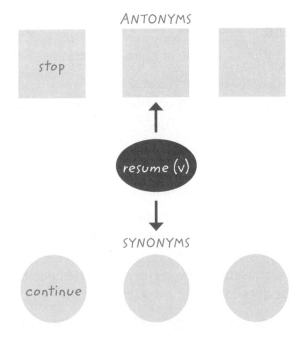

ANTONYMS

stop

resume (v)

SYNONYMS

continue

2. Some of these writings were meant to honor the dead, while others were meant to **terrify** the living.

3. Growing up, Carter's **poor** health kept him indoors.

C. Complete the alphabox graphic organizer with vocabulary you have learned in this unit. Then choose three of those terms and explain them to a partner.

A	B	C	D
E	F	G	H
I	J	K	L
M	N	O	P
Q	R	S sarcophagus	T
U	V	W X	Y Z

❷ Go to MyEnglishLab to complete a skill practice.

APPLY YOUR SKILLS

WHY IT'S USEFUL By applying the skills you have learned in this unit, you will have a better understanding of this challenging reading about the influence of history on pop culture.

BEFORE YOU READ

A. Discuss these questions with one or more students.

1. *Pop culture* refers to movies, television shows, books, art, and music that interest and are enjoyed by the general population. What effect might historical events have on pop culture?

2. Have you ever read about, seen, or heard of the fall of Troy or King Tut and ancient Egypt in popular culture (not in academic readings, but in fictional accounts, commercial products, or architectural designs)? Give examples.

3. When you close your eyes and visualize Egypt, what comes to mind? Why do you think you have those associations with Egypt?

B. You will read an article about how history influences pop culture. As you read, think about these questions.

1. How has the fall of Troy been represented in popular culture?

2. How have King Tut and ancient Egypt been represented in popular culture?

3. Why is the fall of Troy mainly represented through literary works (fiction), while King Tut's influence is more commonly seen in the visual arts?

C. Review the Unit Skills Summary. As you read the article, apply the skills you learned in this unit.

UNIT SKILLS SUMMARY

MANAGE SPECIALIZED VOCABULARY BY USING THESE SKILLS:

Find definitions and explanations in a text

- Look for context clues in the text to understand new vocabulary.

Deal with specialized vocabulary

- Decide which words to learn and then use strategies to make them a permanent part of your knowledge.

Respond in an online forum

- Recognize the expectations for communicating in an online forum.

Demonstrate civil discourse online

• Communicate with others online in an intelligent and respectful manner.

Use graphic organizers

• Use a variety of graphic organizers to help review and retain new vocabulary.

READ

A. Read the article. Annotate and take notes. As you read, mark new vocabulary. After reading, note that vocabulary in an alphabox.

The Influence of History on Pop Culture

1 Ancient history influences popular culture in some surprising ways. The people and places of history can suddenly appear as characters in a Hollywood movie; the art and architecture of history can be used to make a new hotel vibrant and exciting. What's odd is that ancient civilizations that existed at the same time can be viewed differently in the popular imagination. Consider this—King Tutankhamun died around 1323 BCE while the city of Troy fell around the 13th century BCE. The two events occurred, at most, within a century of each other. Both events are well known, but the events influenced different arts. The fall of Troy is mostly an object of literary interest, while the death of Tutankhamun is celebrated in the arts. Why? Why do we tell stories of Troy and make Tutankhamun-inspired jewelry, yet rarely speak of Tut stories or Trojan architecture? It is actually quite simple—both events, while based in reality, entered popular culture in very different ways.

An art deco structure with Egyptian influence, in Paris, France

2 Troy is remembered primarily through fiction; the ancient Greek poet Homer described the fall of Troy in the *Iliad* in the 8th century BCE, almost 500 years after the city fell. The poem was an enormously popular literary influence. To this day, expressions like *Achilles heel* and *Trojan horse* survive in common language; the hidden danger of a Trojan horse has even been adapted to technology—a Trojan virus is a harmful computer file pretending to be something else! Soon after Homer, the Roman poet Virgil put his own spin on the Trojan War with the *Aeneid*, relating the fall of Troy to the rise of Rome. Western literature regularly retells and reinterprets the *Iliad*; even in the age of cinema, multiple movies and television shows have retold the same story as Homer. Oddly, these artistic efforts were almost entirely divorced from the *reality* of Troy—the ancient city was thought to be *fictional* until archaeological discoveries of the 19th century.

(Continued)

3   On the other hand, the reality of ancient Egypt's existence was never questioned. From the enormous pyramids to mysterious hieroglyphs, ancient Egypt remained a strong *visual* image, even as its culture and stories were lost to time and change. Ancient Egypt's history remained told primarily by outsiders who made it their own or chronicled their interactions with it. From Shakespeare's *Anthony and Cleopatra* to Elizabeth Taylor's starring role in the 1963 film *Cleopatra*, stories of ancient Egypt were really stories of Greeks and Romans *set* in ancient Egypt and *decorated* with its aesthetic.

4   The stunning discovery of King Tutankhamun's tomb by Howard Carter in the 1920s changed this, but only slightly. Ancient Egypt remained a *visual* spectacle. Suddenly, American movie theaters were decorated in the style of ancient Egypt; people wore jewelry inspired by the possessions of the pharaohs. Everything from horror films to quickly written novelty songs referenced ancient Egypt, but purely in an ornamental capacity. The difference is that while the story of Troy had been passed down through oral history, the beauty of Tutankhamun was expressed *visually* in an age of photography. Works responding to Tut's discovery revolved less around the history itself than the visual spectacle of that history.

> **CULTURE NOTE**
>
> Art deco is a style of visual arts that was seen in architecture and interior design beginning in the early 20th century. The design was based on geometric shapes and angular forms, and it incorporated arts from Africa and ancient Egypt. After the discovery of King Tut's tomb in 1922, Egyptian-inspired ornamentation in art deco architectural details and jewelry design flourished. Buildings built during this time often incorporated elements from ancient Egypt. For example, the elevator doors in the Chrysler Building in New York City have a design reminiscent of reeds found on ancient Egyptian scrolls, and many famous jewelry designers used ancient Egyptian designs in their jewelry.

5   One might disagree with the idea that ancient Egypt's history is a visual spectacle. After all, Hollywood produces stories about a "mummy's curse" with regularity. The problem is, those stories are less about ancient Egypt than they are a distortion of modern archaeology. Mummy stories are really about brave archaeologists coming across monsters; these monsters have the style and fashion sense of ancient Egypt, but the stories are entirely modern tales of horror.

6   On the other side of the equation, the Trojan War has a consistent story that is reinterpreted by popular culture through artists and writers retelling it. In the Roman Empire, Odysseus was "wise" in ways that emphasized the patrician values of ancient Rome. In Tennyson's *Ulysses*, Ulysses (the Latin name for Odysseus) is constantly searching for greater truth because Tennyson was an *aging romantic*—like the poets Tennyson was responding to. In modern film and TV, actors go out of their way to portray Odysseus as funny and personable because these are the qualities that represent cleverness and success to modern audiences. The character of Helen receives a similar treatment; the Romans, the Renaissance, the Romantics, and Hollywood all portray her as beautiful by *their* standard of beauty, not Homer's.

> **CULTURE NOTE**
>
> **Odysseus**, also known as Ulysses, was a Greek king of Ithaca and the hero of the *Odyssey*, the poem by Homer. He was portrayed as a great speaker and thinker, but also as a great warrior who was vital in the Greek victory in the Trojan War.

7. The difference between Tutankhamun and Troy is all due to how the subjects entered popular culture. Tutankhamun was revealed to us recently; mass media and photography made items like his death mask unforgettable. Troy survives in memory through Homer's fictionalized retelling, which is retold and adapted every generation. The actual discovery of a real, physical ancient city in the 19th century is little more than a formality. The real Troy could have remained buried; the popular, fictional Troy would have been unaffected. Tutankhamun, though, was lucky enough to have been discovered at a time when the entire world could appreciate his treasures in the same instant. That is how two civilizations that existed at the same time have had such widely different effects on the popular imagination.

Glossary

Fall: (n) a situation when someone loses power or is defeated

Fiction: writing that is from the imagination

Achilles heel: a weak part of someone's character, which could cause him or her to fail at something

Trojan horse: someone or something that is accepted because it seems good or harmless but that is really intended to cause harm

Patrician: characteristics typical of people from the highest social class

B. **Compare notes with a partner. Were there definitions or explanations you didn't understand? Ask your partner.**

C. **Reread the questions in Before You Read, Part B. With your partner, use your notes and opinions to answer the questions.**

◑ Go to MyEnglishLab to read more closely, answer the critical thinking questions, and complete a summarizing activity.

THINKING CRITICALLY

Use information from the reading to answer these questions.

1. You read how Odysseus's portrayal in literature has been shaped by the values (what is important) of the age. For instance, in modern TV and film, he is portrayed as funny and personable because these are characteristics popular today; however, in earlier works, he was portrayed differently—always searching for truth—which was important at that time. Do you think pop culture always represents the values of the age? Explain using evidence from pop culture now. Give some examples of what is popular now (use examples from sources like television, films, songs) and examine what values are being represented in those works.

....

....

2. Homer's story of the *Iliad*, and subsequent stories about the fall of Troy, are fictional accounts of an historical event. Homer was not alive during the fall of Troy; it happened 500 years before he wrote his work. What responsibility does an author have when telling a story about an historical event? Should he or she tell a story about an historical event if he or she doesn't have all the facts? Think of another story or movie (popular today) that is also based on historical events. Do you think it is a 100 percent accurate representation of the events that occurred, or do you think the author made up some events to make the story more exciting? Do you think popular values are represented in the story or film? Explain.

....

....

THINKING VISUALLY

Use the information in this timeline to answer the questions.

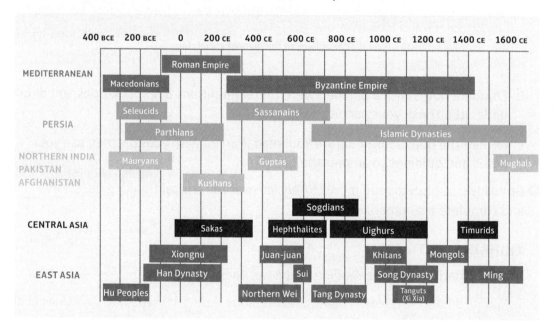

1. Look at the timeline showing the rise and fall of different empires. What patterns do you see?

....

....

2. Based on the current balance of power in the world, what do you predict will happen in the next 100 years? Create a continuation of the timeline, starting in 1700, going 100 years into the future. Do light research to add facts. Then add your predictions.

THINKING ABOUT LANGUAGE

A. Reread the passage "The Influence of History on Pop Culture" and use civil discourse to respond to three points that the author made. For instance, you could disagree with his idea that the actual Troy could have stayed buried yet still have remained popular in fiction. Follow the prompts. Be respectful in tone and use academic English. Use these expressions and vocabulary from the unit:

For help with demonstrating civil discourse online, go to MyEnglishLab, History, Part 2, Language Skill.

To Express Your View	• My point of view is … • In my experience … • I strongly believe … • I'd like to point out that …	• Personally, I believe / think … • Speaking for myself, I think that … • I'd like to point out that …
To Agree and Expand on Someone's Post	• I definitely agree with your point about … In fact, … • I couldn't agree with you more. In addition, … • I see what you mean, and what I've found is … • That's a good point, and I'd like to add that …	
To Respectfully Disagree with Someone's Post	• Although / While / Even though I understand your point, I believe … • I respectfully disagree with your point that … • I see what you're saying, but I don't entirely agree. I think … • I'm afraid I disagree. I believe that … • I'm not so sure of your point. I think that … • I agree with you to a point, but I think …	
To Ask for Clarification	• I don't understand your post … Could you clarify? • Could you explain it in a different way? • Could you explain what you mean by … ?	

1. Agree and expand: ....

....

2. Respectfully disagree: ....

....

3. Ask for clarification: ....

....

B. Choose three words from your alphabox in Read, Part A. Create a mind map or other graphic organizer with each word. Then compare with a partner.

◐ Go to MyEnglishLab to watch Dr. Hunt's concluding video and to complete a self-assessment.

CHEMICAL ENGINEERING

Processes

UNIT PROFILE

In this unit, you will learn about processes including how solids change to liquids and liquids change to gas. You will also read about relationships between different forms of energy. In the final reading of the unit, you will discover the meaning of "entropy."

Scan the reading "Ice, Eggs, and the Second Law of Thermodynamics" on page 282. Can you find two words that signal time? Can you identify two words that signal space or condition? What does this tell you about the reading?

OUTCOMES

- Analyze time and space descriptions
- Examine conditions
- Use passive voice
- Make use of conditionals
- Identify collocations

For more about **CHEMICAL ENGINEERING**, see ❶❸.

See also ⟦W⟧ and ⟦OC⟧ **CHEMICAL ENGINEERING** ❶❷❸.

GETTING STARTED

Go to MyEnglishLab to watch Professor Spakowitz's introductory video and complete a self-assessment.

Discuss these questions with a partner or group.

1. Water can change from solid to liquid to gas. When something changes form, it's called *phase change*. What is something in your day-to-day life that you notice changes form—say, from a solid to a liquid or from a liquid to a gas?

2. Energy is defined as the ability to do work, and there are many different types of energy. For instance, electrical energy creates light (and heat) in lightbulbs. What other types of energy can you think of, and what "work" do they do for you?

3. In his introduction, Professor Spakowitz gives two examples of phase transitions. What are they? How do they show changes in the state of matter?

SKILL 1

ANALYZING TIME AND SPACE DESCRIPTIONS

WHY IT'S USEFUL By following a description, you can better understand the order and location of ideas in a process.

Process writing is the description of, or instructions for, a series of steps. In academic writing, process writing is common, especially in the fields of science and technology. For example, a writer may describe the stage of research that resulted in a particular discovery. In their writing, authors will typically include signals, such as time signals and space signals, to help the reader follow the process.

Time signals indicate when something occurs. These words alert the reader to the order of events in a process description. Study this example:

$$1 \qquad\qquad\qquad\qquad 2$$

<u>**Almost as soon as** the rods were removed from the ice bath, they **began** to heat up again.</u>

$$3 \qquad\qquad\qquad\qquad 4$$

<u>**When** the researcher noticed this, she **immediately** returned them to the bath.</u>

Space signals tell where something is. These words are often used to help the reader visualize the steps in a process or the arrangement of parts. Consider this example:

> On the **outside** of the electric panel is a safety latch. The technician flips the latch **down** and swings the hinged panel door **up**. **Inside**, the panel features a column of switches on the **left** and labels on the **right**. Wires exit the box **at the top** and **bottom**.

Review the list of time and space signals.

Time Signal		Space Signal
after, afterward(s)	last	above, overhead, at the top, on top, over, up
another	later	below, beneath, at the bottom, under, down
as, as soon as	meanwhile	across
at first, at last	most important	adjacent to
at the same time	next	along the edge (side)
before	often	around, outside, surrounding
currently, now	previously	behind, in back
during the morning (day, week)	rarely	beside, next to, side by side
	since	between, in the middle, center
eventually	soon	beyond, far
finally	then	close to, near, nearby
for a minute (hour, day)	thereafter	here, there
first (second, third)	to begin with	in, out
generally	until	in front of
immediately	usually	inside, within
in order to	when	left, right
in the end		north, south, east, west
in the meantime		on
Verbs		opposite
begin, start		straight ahead
conclude, end		

TIP

Time signals are also known as *temporal* or *sequential* expressions. Space signals are also known as *spatial* expressions. Both categories are also referred to as *transitions* or *connectives*, or *cohesive devices*, as they connect two or more ideas.

VOCABULARY PREVIEW

Read the vocabulary items in the box. Circle the ones you know. Put a question mark next to the ones you don't know.

basic	weak	unlike	steam (n)	boiling	required

EXERCISE 1

A. Read the following description on how to expand your vocabulary in English. Underline the time and space signals. Then record them in the chart.

Many English language learners want to expand their English vocabulary skills but are not sure of the best way to go about it. If you're one of those students, here are some tips on what you can do. First, find a topic of interest and read as much as possible. When you select a topic that is of interest, you are more likely to be engaged and want to spend time reading. When faced with a new vocabulary word, don't look it up immediately in a dictionary or translator. Read the entire sentence, and the sentences before and after, to guess the meaning from the context. If the meaning can't be guessed, then consult a dictionary. After reading, select five new words and use them. Write them down in a vocabulary journal, include them in an email or essay, and practice saying them in conversation. The more you practice, the more likely you'll be to retain the new words as part of your permanent English vocabulary.

Time Signal	Space Signal

B. Think about your reading experience. How did the time and space signals help you? Discuss with a partner.

EXERCISE 2

A. Consider these questions.

1. Why is water so important? What do you already know about the chemistry of water?

2. Based on the title of and image in the article on the next page, predict what the author might cover.

B. Read the article and the questions that follow. Then reread the article and mark the paragraphs where you found the answers.

Matter and Its States

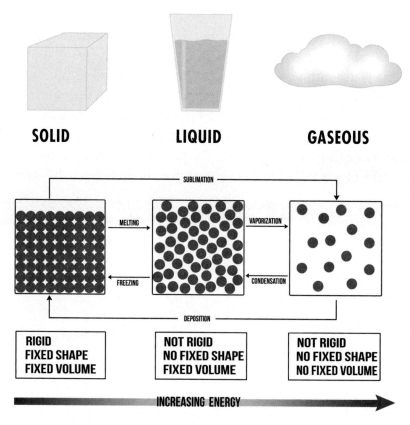

SOLID   LIQUID   GASEOUS

1 The book you are reading, the glass of water on your table, the clothes you are wearing, in fact all the "stuff" out there that you can touch, see, and smell is matter. *Matter* is defined as anything that has mass and takes up space. It is found in three main states: solid, liquid, and gas.

2 If everything physical is matter, then what is matter itself made of? The basic building blocks of matter are atoms. Atoms are extremely small, so they cannot be seen, even with most microscopes. For instance, a piece of paper is a million atoms thick. When atoms combine together, they form molecules.

Glossary

Solid: an object or substance that has a firm shape

Atom: the smallest part of an element that can exist alone

Molecule: one or more atoms that form the smallest unit of a particular substance

Substance: a type of solid, liquid, or gas that has particular qualities

3 Water is a combination of two hydrogen atoms and one oxygen atom, which together form the molecule H_2O. The state of a substance is determined by how its atoms behave. For example, at $0°C$ or below, water molecules do not move much; they are held together by strong bonds at this low temperature.

4 This solid form of water is ice. If the ice's temperature rises to above $0°C$, then the bonds between the water molecules become weak, and the atoms begin to move. This eventually causes the ice to change into liquid. Unlike its solid form, the liquid does not hold its shape. Instead, it takes on the shape of whatever container is holding it, like a cup or bowl.

5 As the water's temperature is raised to $100°C$ or higher, the water undergoes another change of state. Now the molecules move around even more, and there is greater space between them. The water is now in its gas state: steam. Like liquids, gases take on the shape of their container.

6 The point at which matter changes its state depends on the substance, the temperature, and the surrounding atmospheric pressure. For example, substances such as candle wax and butter remain solids at room temperature ($20–25°C$), while substances such as water and mercury are liquids, and substances like oxygen and carbon dioxide are gases. If the atmospheric pressure changes substantially, the temperature at which all of these substances change their state (i.e., the freezing point, the melting point, and the boiling / evaporation point) will be changed. For example, if water is boiled at a high elevation—where the atmospheric pressure is higher—it has a lower boiling point. That explains why water boiled on top of Mount Everest boils at around $71°C$, not the normal $100°C$ required at lower elevations.

1. What is matter? ....

2. What are the states of matter? ....

3. What is an atom? ....

4. What is a molecule? ....

5. How does temperature affect the states of water? ....

....

6. How does atmospheric pressure affect the boiling point of water?

....

7. Order the steps. Write ordinals *1ˢᵗ*, *2ⁿᵈ*, etc. If two things happen at the same time, write the same ordinal.

.... Ice's temperature goes above 0°C.

.... The atoms begin to move.

.... The bonds between the water molecules become weak.

8. Assume each pot of water starts at the same temperature and is heated at the same rate. Which would happen first? Write ordinals *1ˢᵗ*, *2ⁿᵈ*, etc. If two things happen at the same time, write the same ordinal.

.... The pot of water on Mount Kilimanjaro begins to boil.

.... A pot of water on Miami Beach begins to boil.

C. Underline the time and space signals in these excerpts. Label them as *T* (time) or *S* (space) signals. Then check (✓) the sentences that describe a process.

☐ 1. The book you are reading, the glass of water on your table, the clothes you are wearing, in fact all the "stuff" out there that you can touch, see, and smell is matter.

☐ 2. If the ice's temperature rises to above 0°C, then the bonds between the molecules become weak, and the atoms begin to move.

☐ 3. This eventually causes the ice to change into liquid.

☐ 4. As the water's temperature is raised to 100°C or higher, the water undergoes another change of state.

☐ 5. Now the molecules move around even more, and there is greater space between them.

☐ 6. That explains why water boiled on top of Mount Everest boils at around 71°C.

D. Check your answers to Parts C and D.

EXERCISE 3

Work with a partner. Give examples of when having time signals in a reading is important to understanding it. What about space signals? In what types of readings are they most helpful?

VOCABULARY CHECK

A. Review the vocabulary items in the Vocabulary Preview. Write their definitions and add examples. Use a dictionary if necessary.

B. Read each sentence. Then choose the correct definition of the underlined vocabulary item.

1. The most <u>basic</u> part of matter is the atom. Atoms are the simple building blocks in structures.

   a. rare   c. simple

   b. clear   d. open

2. As temperatures rise, the ice on lakes and streams grows thin and <u>weak</u>.

   a. small   c. unwilling

   b. not strong   d. tired

3. <u>Unlike</u> ice, water does not hold its form.

   a. similar to   c. completely different from

   b. the same as   d. in the same way as

4. Anyone who has taken a hot shower has seen <u>steam</u> rising off the hot water.

   a. boiling water   c. liquid that gathers on glass

   b. hot mist   d. droplets

5. Water <u>boils</u> at a lower temperature at high elevations.

   a. becomes hot and bubbles   c. turns to ice

   b. gets warm   d. stops moving and becomes a solid

6. Freezing temperatures are <u>required</u> for water to become ice. This occurs at 0 degrees Celcius.

   a. allowed   c. made

   b. needed   d. requested

⬥ Go to MyEnglishLab to complete vocabulary and skill practices, and to join in collaborative activities.

SKILL 2

EXAMINING CONDITIONS

> **WHY IT'S USEFUL** By learning to identify the language used for conditions, you can better understand process descriptions.

Scientific writing often discusses the **conditions** under which certain events can or can't occur. Words signaling conditions, listed below, help readers anticipate not only the condition but the outcome.

Signal Word or Phrase	Example
as long as	**As long as** the temperature is above 32°F, the pipes won't freeze.
if	**If** the temperature is below 0°C, the experiment will be canceled.
in the event that	**In the event that** the lake dries up, the fishing community will go elsewhere.
on (the) condition (that)	**On (the) condition (that)** everyone be respectful, we will open the floor to questions.
only if	**Only if** the petroleum company apologizes publicly will the county not sue.
when	**When** the temperature drops suddenly, a storm front is coming in.
even if	**Even if** the temperature outside dips below 32°F, we won't freeze because the house is insulated.
unless	**Unless** we hear otherwise, let's assume we still have class.
given that	**Given that** the temperature is below 32°F, I think I'll wear an extra layer.
granted,	**Granted,** the temperature is above 50°F, but it still feels cold because of the wind.

These examples show **real**—true or possible—conditions and outcomes:

	Condition	Outcome
Future:	If you heat an ice cube to 0°C,	it <u>will melt</u>.
Present:	When the lever is pulled,	a bell <u>rings</u> in the other room.
Past:	Given that the ground temperature reached 33°F,	it's not surprising that the snow on the lawn <u>melted</u>.

These examples show **unreal**—untrue or impossible—conditions and outcomes:

	Condition	Outcome
Present:	If a large asteroid struck Earth,	people <u>would panic</u>.
Past:	If the drug trials had resulted in deaths,	the drug <u>would not have gone</u> on the market.

TIP

An **empirical article** (a type of process description found in science) typically follows the following structure:

- Introduction: outlines the topic and the questions being researched
- Literature review: presents an overview of the research that has been conducted on this topic
- Methodology: explains the steps taken in the research. Gives an explanation of the experiment, an overview of the group studied, the conditions of the experiment, and the methods of data analysis
- Results: presents the findings of the experiment and the analysis of the data
- Discussion: looks at the effects that the results might have on the topic and explores the strengths and weaknesses of the findings

VOCABULARY PREVIEW

Read the vocabulary items in the box. Circle the ones you know. Put a question mark next to the ones you don't know.

disappear	policies	lack of	completely	contributes	level (n)

EXERCISE 4

A. Read the sentences. Underline the condition. Circle the outcome. Then identify the situation as real (R) or unreal (U).

.... 1. When water is put in a freezer, it slowly becomes solid.

.... 2. If you heat a pan of water, sooner or later the water will evaporate.

.... 3. If global warming continues, some regions of the world may go under water.

.... 4. Even if the telescope were on sale, we would not buy it.

.... 5. If the experiment had failed, the university would have lost its funding.

.... 6. As long as we have sunlight, we can generate solar power.

B. When students first study words of conditions, they usually learn *if* and *when*. Why is it important to know other words that express condition?

EXERCISE 5

A. The following article is about the disappearance of Lake Poopó. What might cause a lake to disappear?

B. As you read the passage, underline conditions and outcomes.

Phase Change: Liquid to Gas

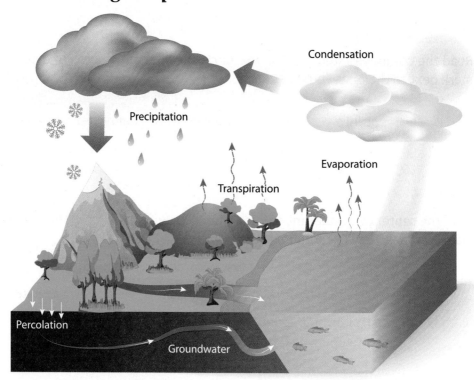

1   Lake Poopó was once Peru's second largest lake, but in its place now there is only dry land. How and why did this lake disappear? To answer this question, we need to look at one of the basic physical processes of water, evaporation.

2   Since 1985, slow increases in temperature and water diversion policies, along with a lack of rain (the lake was in one of the driest areas of Peru) eventually resulted in all the water in Lake Poopó completely evaporating. Evaporation, the process by which a liquid becomes a gas, happens to liquids. This process is often seen in water, and in fact, the evaporation that occurs in lakes, rivers, and oceans accounts for about 90 percent of the moisture in the atmosphere, which contributes to our water cycle.

3   The same process of water evaporation can happen in your home. When a small amount of water is left in a dish in your house for a day or two, it slowly disappears. This is because water slowly evaporates at room temperature. Repeat the experiment, but also turn up the heat or leave the dish next to the fire, and watch what happens. The water will evaporate more quickly. In the same way, if you put water in a pan and turn on the heat, eventually the water will boil and evaporate, i.e., change into steam. In all of these examples the process is the same. Energy (heat) makes the water molecules move around more quickly, and then space between them increases. A phase change (matter going from one state to another) will occur when the energy in a molecule reaches a specific level. More energy (heat) will speed up the process. In the event that a drop of water falls on a very hot iron, it will evaporate immediately, while a dish of water at room temperature evaporates much more slowly.

TYPES OF PHASE TRANSITION

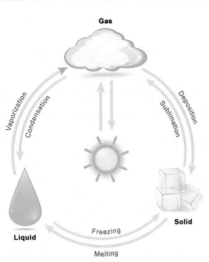

4   This change in the state of water from a liquid to a gas involves a large amount of heat exchange. This is why we sweat only if our body is hot: The water on the surface of our skin (sweat) evaporates and makes us cooler. And this same process occurred with the Peruvian lake. Given that not enough moisture was replenishing the water that was lost with evaporation, it slowly disappeared.

C. Answer these questions about conditions, based on the reading. Use your own words.

1. Under what condition will a small amount of water slowly disappear?

   It will slowly disappear if it is left in a dish in your house for a day or two.

2. Under what condition will a pan of water boil and change into steam?

   ....

3. Under what condition does phase change occur?

   ....

4. What's a condition under which a drop of water will evaporate immediately?

....

5. What condition(s) caused Lake Poopó to disappear?

....

D. Read the questions. Then reread the passage and mark the paragraphs where you find the answers to the questions. Discuss answers with a partner.

1. What is evaporation?

....

2. How is evaporation connected to the water cycle?

....

3. What can speed up the process of evaporation?

....

4. What is a phase change?

....

5. When does a phase change occur?

....

6. What is the relationship between phase change and the disappearance of Lake Poopó?

....

EXERCISE 6

Discuss your reading experience with one or more students.

1. Evaporation is a key component of the water cycle. Using the diagram on page 268, explain what happens once evaporation occurs.

2. Using condition words from the reading, as well as other time / sequence words, write an explanation of the water cycle. Read it aloud with the transition words and without the transition words. Which sounds better?

VOCABULARY CHECK

A. Review the vocabulary items in the Vocabulary Preview. Write their definitions and add examples. Use a dictionary if necessary.

B. Complete each sentence using the correct vocabulary item from the box. Use the correct form.

completely	contribute	disappear	level	lack of	policy

1. If the .... outlined in the Paris Climate Agreement are not followed, more severe effects of global warming will occur.

2. Humans .... to global warming by using cars and electricity, both of which can emit carbon into the atmosphere, which is a leading factor of climate change.

3. As ocean temperatures increase, the Greenland ice sheet .... slowly.

4. Because of warmer water, the algae in the coral is expelled, and this .... algae results in coral bleaching.

5. One cause of rising sea .... is melting ice from glaciers. But the height of the water changes for other reasons, too.

6. The water had not .... evaporated, as the ground was a little muddy. If the water had totally evaporated, the ground would be dry.

🔾 Go to MyEnglishLab to complete vocabulary and skill practices, and to join in collaborative activities.

INTEGRATED SKILLS

USING PASSIVE VOICE

WHY IT'S USEFUL By using passive voice construction in your writing, you can restate others' ideas and direct the reader to important information in a process.

In scientific writing, **passive voice** allows the writer to describe a process without using personal pronouns or the names of researchers. The focus is on the action or event, not on the doer.

The passive voice is formed with *be* + a past participle. It can be used in all tenses (past, present, future). Review the chart. Notice that the person doing the boiling is not mentioned because it is not important.

PASSIVE VOICE			
Tense	**Example**		
simple present		**is boiled**	
present progressive		**is being boiled**	
present perfect		**has been boiled**	
simple past	In this first stage of the experiment, water	**was boiled**	for one minute.
past progressive		**was being boiled**	
past perfect		**had been boiled**	
simple future		**will be boiled** **is going to be boiled**	
future perfect		**will have been boiled**	

If the doer were important, the writer could indicate that by including *by* + name / noun, or by using active construction.

> In this first stage of the experiment, the water was boiled for one minute **by the researcher.**

> In this first stage of the experiment, **the researcher boiled** the water for one minute.

VOCABULARY PREVIEW

Read the vocabulary items in the box. Circle the ones you know. Put a question mark next to the ones you don't know.

ties (v)	simply	law	design (n)	transfer (n)	consistent

EXERCISE 7

A. Read the title of the following article and look at the image. What process do you expect to read about?

☐ how electrical energy works

☐ how lightbulbs waste energy

☐ how thermodynamics is related to radiant energy

☐ how lightbulbs are made

B. Read the article. Notice what process is being described and if the "doer" of the process is mentioned.

> **Glossary**
>
> Vibrate: to move back and forth quickly

Thermodynamics: The Relationship Between Different Kinds of Energy

1   When it gets dark, what do you do? Easy answer: You hit the light switch and the lights go on—a simple process that makes modern life possible. But how does the switch create the light in a lightbulb? It is the result of both energy and thermodynamics. Thermodynamics is an area of physics that studies the energy and work of a system.

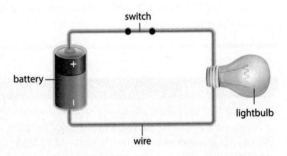

A simple electric circuit

2   Energy is a complicated thing. First, it comes in many forms: thermal energy (heat), radiant energy (light), chemical energy, electrical energy (electricity), and so on. What is the string that ties all of these types of energy together? Simply put, it is *work*. Energy measures the amount of work that one thing can do to another. These things can be objects (a ball) or systems (all of the H_2O molecules in a glass of water). Thermal energy, for example, is the transfer of heat from one system to another, like fire heating water when you make tea; the fire works on the water to make it hot.

(Continued)

3 A lightbulb works with all sorts of energy: thermal, radiant, and electrical. When you hit the switch on your wall to turn on a light, that switch allows electricity (electrical energy) to go into the lightbulb. But the light that you see is not electricity, or it would cause a lot of pain to your eyes. Light energy comes in a different form: photons. How does electricity become photons?

4 To answer this question, we must understand two things: 1) the first law of thermodynamics, and 2) the design of a lightbulb. The first law of thermodynamics says that energy cannot be created or destroyed. However, energy can transform from one form to another. And that is what makes a lightbulb work: Electrical energy becomes radiant energy. How does this happen? To begin with, when you turn on a light, electricity moves quickly through the wire that connects the switch and lightbulb. Inside the lightbulb, the electricity passes through the filament—the small metal piece in the center of a lightbulb's glass—and makes the filament's atoms vibrate. This is the *work* that the electrical energy is doing. This vibration causes the filament to create light. Therefore we have electrical energy transforming into radiant energy: electricity changing into light.

5 But there is even more to it. Anyone who has ever touched a lightbulb knows that it becomes hot when turned on. The reason is that as the filament's atoms are vibrating, they create heat. So the lightbulb produces both thermal energy—the transfer of the lightbulb's heat to the air in the room—and radiant energy, the photons of light that allow you to see. The electrical energy, electricity, does not disappear. Instead, it becomes something else, which is consistent with the first law of thermodynamics.

CULTURE NOTE

Although Thomas Edison often gets credit for inventing the lightbulb, there were many scientists busy working on it before he patented his lightbulb in 1879. However, the lightbulb that he and his team of researchers worked on burned for at least 13 hours, much longer than the few minutes previous scientists were able to deliver. Nowadays, incandescent lightbulbs can last about 1,000 hours, while LED lightbulbs can last at least 10,000 hours.

C. Reread the article. Then answer these questions.

1. What are some of the different forms of energy?

....

2. What is energy?

....

3. The first law of thermodynamics is that energy cannot be created or destroyed. What does this mean?

....

4. Without a filament, would a lightbulb be able to create light? Why or why not?

....

5. What happens to the lightbulb when the filament vibrates?

....

6. Based on the reading, is thermodynamics best explained as the science of energy or the science of light?

....

D. Reread Paragraphs 3–4. As you read, complete the process diagram, a kind of graphic organizer. Use passive voice in each step. Compare organizers with a partner and discuss any differences. Then write a summary of the process. Use your own words and passive voice.

MAIN IDEA: HOW A LIGHTBULB PRODUCES ENERGY

STEP 1:

The lamp, with a lightbulb, ... (plug) into an electrical socket by a wire.

STEP 2:

The light .... (turn on). The electricity goes through the wire, through the lamp, into the lightbulb.

STEP 3:

Light energy .... (generate) when the electricity goes through the filament and makes the filament's atoms move quickly.

STEP 4:

As the filament's atoms vibrate, they also make heat, which .... (transfer) to the lightbulb's glass exterior and then the air.

STEP 5:

Radiant energy, or light, ... (produce) and those photons of light .... (observed).

E. Discuss these questions in a small group.

1. When you were reading, how did you annotate the article? (For example, did you: highlight / underline the steps, use numbers to detail what happened first, second, third, etc.?) How can annotating a reading help you if you have to write a summary?

2. Have you ever written a process description? When writing a process description, should you emphasize the process or the person doing the process? Is it ever appropriate to mention the person?

VOCABULARY CHECK

A. Review the vocabulary items in the Vocabulary Preview. Write their definitions and add examples. Use a dictionary if necessary.

B. Read each sentence. Then choose the correct definition of the underlined vocabulary item.

1. What is the string that <u>ties</u> all types of energy together?
   a. to restrict something
   b. to finish with equal points
   c. to connect two or more things
   d. to have a strong relationship

2. What is the first law of thermodynamics? <u>Simply</u> put, energy never disappears.
   a. However
   b. Clearly
   c. Therefore
   d. Quickly

3. Sir Isaac Newton's so-called first <u>law</u> of motion is familiar to most people: An object in motion stays in motion, and an object at rest stays at rest.
   a. rule
   b. study
   c. belief
   d. objective

4. The <u>design</u> of a traditional lightbulb is simple: incoming electric wire, a filament, a glass bulb.
   a. the construction of something
   b. the planning of something
   c. a drawing of something
   d. a decoration on something

5. It's dangerous to be in the water during a lightning storm because water conducts, or <u>transfers</u>, electricity.
   a. to move from one place to another
   b. to sell something to someone
   c. to electrify something
   d. to exchange something for something else

6. The patient's symptoms were <u>consistent</u> with a lightning strike: His heartbeat was irregular and his skin was burned.
   a. in agreement with
   b. ongoing
   c. contradictory to
   d. different from

◐ Go to MyEnglishLab to complete a skill practice and to join in collaborative activities.

LANGUAGE SKILL

MAKING USE OF CONDITIONALS

WHY IT'S USEFUL By using conditionals, you can better understand the possibility or probability of something occurring.

◐ Go to MyEnglishLab for the Language Skill presentation and practice.

VOCABULARY STRATEGY

IDENTIFYING COLLOCATIONS

WHY IT'S USEFUL By learning which words frequently go together, you can express yourself more fluently, making your ideas easier to understand.

Collocations are pairs or groups of words that commonly appear together. In English, there is a predictability of words appearing together. They can be combinations of many parts of speech: adjective + noun, verb + noun, noun + noun, and so on.

Examples

adjective + noun

black coffee, cold water, light rain, low temperatures, brown eyes

verb + noun

eat dinner, make breakfast, do homework, take a test, boil water, make a promise, give advice

noun + noun

cell membrane, blood test, health professional, water cycle

> **CULTURE NOTE**
>
> Collocations were not typically taught in language classes until recently, but most dictionaries will now list common collocations after the definition. When using a dictionary, take time to take note of collocations as they can help expand your vocabulary.

EXERCISE 8

A. Choose the word that best collocates with the boldfaced word. Use a dictionary if necessary.

1. All of the students _____ **the homework** and were prepared for class.

   a. made   b. did   c. kept   d. put

2. If students don't learn to manage their time, they will _____ **difficulty** in class.

   a. put   b. make   c. do   d. have

3. University students typically take a(n) _____ **exam** at the end of the semester.

   a. ending   b. end   c. final   d. last

4. Professors will _____ **homework** every day.

   a. dispense   b. assign   c. transfer   d. detail

5. Some _____ **believe** that homework is essential for learning.

   a. powerfully   b. heavily   c. solidly   d. strongly

6. To _____ **understand** collocations, use a dictionary and review them frequently.

    a. better   b. good   c. well   d. improve

7. Some students' study habits are **influenced** _____ their classmates.

    a. for   b. in   c. by   d. with

8. Many believe that in the _____ **future**, college students won't come to a classroom but will learn everything online.

    a. close   b. nearby   c. next   d. near

B. Use a dictionary to come up with additional collocations for each word.

homework	exam	difficulties	future
do the homework hand in homework	final exam	have difficulties	the near future

C. Write original sentences with some of the collocations from Part B. Include context to show that you understand the meaning.

1. As the bell rang, I handed in my homework, setting it on the teacher's desk.

2. ....

3. ....

4. ....

5. ....

6. ....

🔵 Go to MyEnglishLab to complete a skill practice.

APPLY YOUR SKILLS

WHY IT'S USEFUL By applying the skills you have learned in this unit, you can gain a better understanding of this challenging reading about entropy and the second law of thermodynamics.

BEFORE YOU READ

A. Discuss these questions with one or more students.

1. When you drop a glass on a tiled floor, it shatters into many pieces. Is it easy to predict the exact direction that those pieces of glass will go? Explain.

2. When water is in a solid state (ice), the water molecules are bound together in a specific pattern. When ice melts and eventually evaporates, what do you think happens to all those water molecules?

3. Do you like surprises and the unexpected? Or are you more comfortable with a predictable schedule and familiar events? Explain.

B. You will read an article about entropy and the second law of thermodynamics. As you read, think about these questions.

1. Explain the difference between a system that has high entropy and a system with low entropy, using the example of an egg.

2. What is the second law of thermodynamics?

C. Review the Unit Skills Summary. As you read the article, apply the skills you learned in this unit.

UNIT SKILLS SUMMARY

ENGAGE IN PROCESSES BY USING THESE SKILLS:

Analyze time and space descriptions

• Recognize time and space signals to understand how ideas are connected.

Examine conditions

• Develop your understanding of how vocabulary and grammar are used in explanations of experiments and empirical studies.

Use passive voice

• Write summaries of process descriptions that emphasize the process being described, and not the agent of the action.

Make use of conditionals

- Understand how real and unreal conditional sentences express real or hypothetical situations in the present or past.

Identify collocations

- Notice how certain words collocate with each other.

READ

A. Read the article on the next page. As you read Paragraphs 2–4, highlight words that indicate time and make notes about the events they signal. Then, on the timelines, write the signals and events.

> **Glossary**
>
> Concept: general idea
> Constant: unchanging
> Feature: part of something

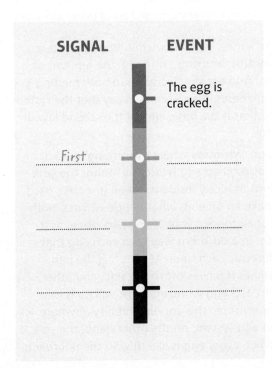

SIGNAL — EVENT

The egg is cracked.

First ....

....

....

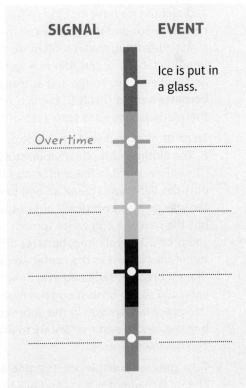

SIGNAL — EVENT

Ice is put in a glass.

Over time ....

....

....

....

Ice, Eggs, and the Second Law of Thermodynamics

1 The second law of thermodynamics is a complicated concept, if you have never heard of it. So let's start with ice and eggs, two things that are quite familiar to us. We break eggs to make omelets, and ice melts as it cools our drinks. But what do broken eggs and melting ice have in

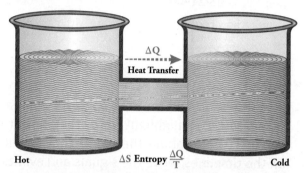

A demonstration of the second law of thermodynamics

common? For one thing, they can make a mess on your kitchen floor. But there is also something that is a bit more scientific: *entropy*. Entropy is the amount of unpredictability or disorder in a system. And entropy increases in both melting ice and broken eggs. To say that entropy increases in a system is to say that the system becomes more difficult to predict. And that is the basic idea of the second law of thermodynamics. Let's take a closer look.

2 Think of an egg. If we look inside an egg, we know where everything inside it is: The albumen (the clear white stuff, also called *egg white*) surrounds the yolk (the yellow stuff) in the center, and both fit nicely inside the shell (the thin, hard outside). When you break an egg to make an omelet, what happens? First, both the yolk and egg white fall out of the shell toward your frying pan. Then, as it hits the pan, the egg white spreads out, in a different way with each egg that you break. The yolk, too, behaves differently each time. After it hits the pan, sometimes it stays in the center, sometimes it moves off to the side, and other times it breaks. Predicting exactly where the egg white and yolk will go is not easy, and so the broken egg has higher entropy: the unpredictability of where things are in a system. In the unbroken egg system, on the other hand, the yolk is in the center, and that is easy to predict; every egg is like this. So the unbroken egg has lower entropy.

3 Take another example: ice. Imagine an ice cube dropped into a glass of water. The ice is made of billions and billions of water molecules stuck together in a solid state. Over time, the ice in the glass begins to melt. Meanwhile, the cube gets smaller. This is because the water slowly makes the ice cube's molecules warmer. Subsequently, the melted ice molecules mix with the water. In the end, those molecules end up all over the glass of water.

4 The result is that it is difficult to predict where the water from the melting ice is; some molecules might move to the bottom of the glass, while others might stay at the top. This means that entropy is increasing. Meanwhile, there is still ice floating at the top of the glass. Since the ice is solid, we can easily predict where its molecules are. Unlike liquid water, the H_2O molecules of ice do not move to different parts of the ice cube—they stay in the same place. But, as long as no one puts the glass in the freezer, eventually the ice melts and entropy prevails.

5 Now, we never see a broken egg become an unbroken egg, and we do not see an ice cube suddenly form in a glass of water at room temperature. The reason for this is that entropy in a system either stays the same or increases—if there is a constant temperature. This is another feature of the second law of thermodynamics. It says that heat can move only one way, from hot things to cold things; a cold object cannot heat a warmer object naturally. Have you ever become warm after touching a glass of ice water? Of course not. But you have likely experienced growing warmer after holding something hot, like a cup of tea or coffee.

B. Compare notes and timelines with a partner.

C. Reread the questions in Before You Read, Part B. With your partner, use your notes and opinions to answer the questions.

◯ Go to MyEnglishLab to read more closely, answer the critical thinking questions, and complete a summarizing activity.

THINKING CRITICALLY

Use information from the reading to answer these questions.

1. How do the examples of an egg and an ice cube in various states illustrate entropy? Explain.

   ....

   ....

2. Use an example of a frozen ice cream sandwich in your hand to explain entropy and the second law of thermodynamics.

   ....

   ....

THINKING VISUALLY

Use information from the reading and the graph to answer the questions.

1. Look at the graph. What can you say about the relationship between temperature and entropy? What can you say about the relationship between entropy and phase changes (solid, liquid, gas)?

2. Do a little research and create a new visual with a different substance. Show some aspect of change.

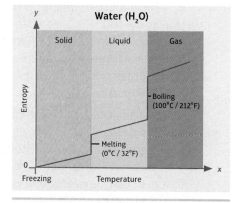

THINKING ABOUT LANGUAGE

A. Match the conditions with the outcomes.

For help with conditionals, go to MyEnglishLab, Chemical Engineering, Part 2, Language Skill.

.... 1. As long as no one puts the glass in the freezer,

.... 2. When you break an egg to make an omelet,

.... 3. If there's a constant temperature,

.... 4. When there is a shortage of rain,

.... 5. Agricultural crops suffer and food prices generally increase

.... 6. The glass of water would boil at a higher temperature

a. droughts are more likely to occur.

b. entropy increases.

c. the ice melts and entropy prevails.

d. if it were at a lower elevation.

e. if there is a drought.

f. entropy in a system either stays the same or increases.

B. Complete the collocations. Scan the reading to check your answers.

1. Cold-climate cultures have a lot .... **common**.

2. When conducting an experiment, you sometimes have to .... **a mess**.

3. We fry eggs in a **frying** .... , of course.

4. A couple of .... **cubes** will cool your drink.

5. When you're thirsty nothing sounds better than a simple **glass of** ....

6. The carpet seller poured his guest a small .... **of tea** with mint and sugar.

⭕ Go to MyEnglishLab to watch Professor Spakowitz's concluding video and to complete a self-assessment.

Part 3 presents authentic academic content written and delivered by university professors. Academically rigorous application and assessment activities allow for a synthesis of the skills developed in Parts 1 and 2.

BIOETHICS

Right and Wrong

UNIT PROFILE

In this unit, you will read about the medical process of whole genome sequencing (WGS): what it is, what it can do, and what challenges it presents. You will also read about cognitive enhancements—ways to improve our ability to think.

You will research the strengths and weaknesses of a government program that uses WGS and present an argument for or against it.

EXTENDED READING

BEFORE YOU READ

Think about these questions before you read the essay "Whole Genome Sequencing: Uses and Challenges." Discuss them with another student.

1. What do you already know about DNA? What can doctors learn from studying a patient's DNA?

2. Which is more important: creating technology that prevents diseases or finding cures for existing diseases?

3. Whole genome sequencing (WGS) gives patients a complete record of their DNA, including their risk for some genetic diseases. Would you get your genome sequenced? Explain.

READ

Skim Paragraphs 1–7. Use the T-chart that follows to write the main ideas. Then read and annotate the passage, add details to the chart, and answer the questions in Check What You've Learned.

> **TIP**
>
> Skim (looking quickly at a text before reading) to get the main idea. Scan (looking for specific information) to find specific information quickly—such as answers to questions.

For more about skimming and scanning, see Bioethics, Part 1, Skills 1 and 2, pages 3 and 8.

Whole Genome Sequencing: Uses and Challenges
By Professor Henry T. (Hank) Greely

Introduction

1 In 2003, a human's DNA was "sequenced" for the first time in history. It had taken over a decade and cost about $500 million. By 2008, Stanford University's Stephen Quake sequenced his own DNA in a few weeks for about $100,000. By 2017, a person's genome could be sequenced for about $1,500, roughly 0.0003 percent of the price from less than 15 years earlier. Tomorrow's price, though never $0, will be lower still.

2 As genome sequencing has become cheaper, using it in patients' medical care has become plausible; in some cases, it is already happening. When whole human genome sequencing becomes sufficiently inexpensive, its medical uses will explode, bringing both benefits and challenges.

3 This essay will first describe the human genome and its sequencing. It will then discuss its uses, present and future, in healthcare, before ending with the practical and ethical challenges such use will bring.

(Continued)

What Is Whole Genome Sequencing (WGS)?

4 The answer to this question starts with the answer to another question—what is the whole genome sequence? All living things on Earth, including humans, are largely built according to instructions in a molecule called deoxyribonucleic acid (DNA). In humans this DNA is found almost entirely in structures called *chromosomes* inside our cells. Humans almost always have 46 chromosomes, a pair of the chromosomes named 1 through 22, along with two so-called sex chromosomes, X and Y. (Women have two X chromosomes, men an X and a Y.) Our mothers and fathers gave us one copy each of those 22 pairs of chromosomes and one copy of a sex chromosome.

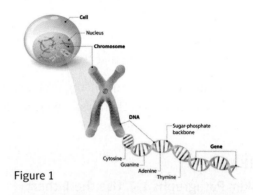

Figure 1

5 Each chromosome is one very long DNA molecule. This DNA molecule takes the form of the famous "double helix." Think of a ladder that has been twisted into a spiral. The sides of the ladder are the sides of the DNA molecule; the rungs of the ladder make DNA special. Each rung is made up of two small molecules, one attached to each side of the DNA ladder. These small molecules are always one of four types: adenine, cytosine, guanine, and thymine (called A, C, G, and T). The secret of DNA is that A is always attached to T, and C to G. These two molecule combinations—the ladder's rungs—are called "base pairs." The discovery of this double helix structure in 1953 made Francis Crick and James Watson famous, particularly because, as they noted at the end of their very short article announcing their discovery, the structure, and its possible "unzipping," provided a clear mechanism for DNA to be copied accurately as cells grow and divide.

> **CULTURE NOTE**
>
> Francis Crick (English) and James Watson (American) won the Nobel Prize for Medicine in 1962 for this discovery of DNA's structure. They had been working together at Cambridge University in England, where they discovered the double helix structure. Crick later moved to California, where he studied brain research and died in 2004. Watson also moved to the United States and was instrumental in the Human Genome Project.

6 The "whole genome sequence" lists all of the As, Cs, Gs, and Ts in a person's chromosomes, starting with the two copies of chromosome 1 and ending with the two sex chromosomes. You can consider it a book made up only of four letters (A, C, G, and T) but about 6.4 billion of them.

> **CULTURE NOTE**
>
> *The Lord of the Rings* trilogy, written by J.R.R. Tolkien in 1937, is a fantasy novel. It is made up of three books: *The Fellowship of the Ring, The Two Towers,* and *The Return of the King.* In total, a combined edition is about 1,200 pages long.

Think of a real book and consider each letter, punctuation mark, or space as being an A, C, G, or T. To be as long as your whole genome sequence, the book would have to have about 2 million pages. Or, to put it another way, "reading" your whole genome sequence would be like reading the full *The Lord of the Rings* trilogy about 1,500 times.

7 But that is what is now possible for about $1,500 through WGS. And reading that whole genome sequence can tell us things about you. The sequence is almost identical across all humans—we differ in one out of a thousand letters. But that is 6.4 million differences, and they can tell us things about individuals. Sometimes they are very powerful things. For example, unless you die first from something else, you will be diagnosed with and die from Huntington disease sometime in your middle age. Sometimes they are weak things. For example, you have a 10 percent higher risk of being diagnosed with type 2 diabetes than most people. Sometimes they are unimportant things. For example, your earwax is wet and not dry. But each whole genome sequence will contain some important information. At today's prices, WGS is already being used in medicine. As its price falls, its uses will grow explosively, with good and possibly bad consequences.

Glossary

deoxyribonucleic acid (DNA): an acid found in the cells of living things, that carries genetic information

Sequence: to find the order of the molecules in a piece of DNA

Genome: all the genes in one type of living thing

Chromosome: a part of every living cell, contains the genes that control the size, shape, etc., that a plant or animal has

TOPIC ....

Main Ideas:	Details:
DNA sequencing has become faster and cheaper.	2003—first human DNA sequenced; time: decade; cost: $500 million
	2008—time: few weeks; cost: $100,000

CHECK WHAT YOU'VE LEARNED
PARAGRAPHS 1–7

A. Think about the section you just read and refer to your notes.
   Answer these questions.

1. What three main ideas will be covered in this essay?

   ....

   ....

   ....

2. What information is in the 23rd chromosome?

   ....

3. What is the definition of whole genome sequencing (WGS)?

   ....

4. What medical information can be learned from WGS?

   ....

   ....

5. Why does the author compare a genome sequence to *The Lord of the Rings* trilogy?

   ....

B. Read the section again. Check your answers and add details to your notes.
   Then continue to the next section.

"WHOLE GENOME SEQUENCING: USES AND CHALLENGES," *CONTINUED*
PARAGRAPHS 8–14

Read, annotate, and use a
T-chart or other organizer
to take notes.

TIP

Create your own graphic organizer or find one online by searching
for "graphic organizer" or a specific kind, such as "T-chart."

Current and Future Medical Uses of WGS

8 Doctors have used DNA tests in medical decisions for nearly 50 years, but those tests
have been limited to a few specific bits of that patient's DNA. WGS gives doctors
information about *all* the patient's DNA, and, with the continuing development
of WGS, it allows access to *all* the information for less than the cost of looking
specifically at two or three DNA regions. It is already being used regularly in at least
two medical contexts; more will follow inevitably.

9   WGS is being used to try to diagnose children who appear to have genetic conditions that do not fit obviously into those that are now known. Some genetic or chromosomal conditions, like Down syndrome, come with very characteristic symptoms or features, but others are more complicated. In confusing cases physicians will use WGS on the child, looking for something different or unusual in the child's genome that might explain the symptoms. If the WGS leads to identifying a DNA sequence that is the likely cause of the condition, it might, occasionally, lead to a hopeful treatment option. More often, it will give parents information about the child's condition and their chances of having another child with the same problems.

10 WGS is also being used today, to some extent, in cancer treatment. Cancer is always a disease of DNA though it is rarely of inherited DNA. Instead, DNA in cells mutates during a cell's lifetime. Sometimes those mutations lead to the uncontrolled growth that is cancer. Scientists have realized that each patient's cancer has a different mix of mutations, whether the cancer started in lung, prostate, breast, or colon tissue, and doctors know that certain drugs work well against cancers with particular mutations. Today, tens of thousands of cancer patients each year get WGS of their tumors, in the hope that it will lead to more effective treatment. It is not clear how often a patient's condition actually improves as a result, but as sequencing prices fall, this use will expand.

11 WGS will not just grow in its existing uses, but new uses will flourish. Three important ones will be screening for genetically predictable disease risks in children and adults, in newborn babies, and in embryos and fetuses before birth.

12 WGS will soon become a routine part of a child's or adult's medical care. Just as a physician takes a medical history and runs some routine blood tests, she will order a WGS to look for medical risks. Sometimes this will be helpful to take preventive measures. For example, some people have a genetic predisposition to a serious lung condition called *berylliosis*. Berylliosis only strikes people who both have the genetic predisposition *and* are exposed to beryllium, an uncommon element that can be largely avoided. Other times it will be helpful to alert doctors and patients to the possible onset of a disease, allowing for early diagnosis and treatment. I expect most people with good healthcare to have WGS within the next 20 or possibly 10 years.

13 WGS will also be used for newborn babies. In many countries newborns have been tested for some genetic diseases for over 40 years. Phenylketonuria was one of the first. This disease causes severe intellectual disability, but babies with affected brains can be saved if they are put on a special diet shortly after birth. Today all American states require some genetic tests for newborns, with most states testing for 30 to 50 different rare conditions. When WGS becomes less expensive, it will probably be used for newborn screening, providing information on not just 50 conditions but thousands.

(Continued)

14 Similarly, fetuses and embryos have been subject to genetic tests for several decades but only for specific diseases known to run in the parents' families. WGS has already been used experimentally before birth; this kind of use will certainly expand as it becomes less expensive.

Glossary

Access: the right to enter a place, use something, see someone

Diagnose: to find out what illness a person has

Physician: a doctor

Symptom: a sign that a serious problem exists

Treatment: medical help for someone who is sick or injured

Mutate: to change because of a change in the genes

Tumor: a group of cells in the body that can grow quickly and cause health problems

Predisposition: a tendency to behave in a particular way or suffer from a particular health problem

Screening: a medical test that is done on a lot of people to make sure that they do not have a particular disease

Fetus: a human or animal before it is born

CHECK WHAT YOU'VE LEARNED

PARAGRAPHS 8–14

A. Think about the section you just read and refer to your notes. Answer these questions.

6. How is today's WGS testing today different from DNA testing in the past?
   a. It is more controversial in the medical community.
   b. It provides a more complete look at a patient's DNA.
   c. It provides information that is difficult to understand.
   d. It is a less dangerous procedure.

7. How is WGS being used today?
   a. to diagnose children with known genetic conditions and to prevent cancers
   b. to identify genetic diseases in fetuses and as part of routine medical exams
   c. to stop genetic diseases in newborns and to identify cancer risk
   d. to diagnose children with unusual genetic conditions and in cancer treatments

8. In Paragraph 10, the author writes that "Cancer is always a disease of DNA though it is rarely of inherited DNA." He is _____ .

    a. suggesting that cancer is usually not a genetic disease that is passed down from one's parents
    b. showing that WGS is not an effective part of cancer treatments
    c. comparing inherited diseases with other diseases
    d. supporting the funding of cancer research

9. Which idea is implied in Paragraph 12?

    a. All people who are treated at hospitals will receive WGS in the near future.
    b. Children who do not have a genetic predisposition for disease will receive WGS.
    c. People with good health insurance will receive WGS in the near future.
    d. All doctors will order WGS for their patients very soon.

10. In Paragraph 13, it can reasonably be inferred that all US states require some genetic testing because _____ .

    a. nurses want to have an accurate record of newborn diseases
    b. the government and public support the idea
    c. parents demand more information about their newborns
    d. testing provides more jobs for people

B. Read the section again. Check your answers and add details to your notes. Then continue to the next section.

"WHOLE GENOME SEQUENCING: USES AND CHALLENGES," *CONTINUED*
PARAGRAPHS 15–20

Read, annotate, and use a T-chart or other organizer to take notes.

Challenges from WGS

15 Like all new technologies, WGS brings challenges that might both limit its benefits and cause some harm. Four deserve particular attention: its accuracy, conveyance of its results meaningfully, non-medical information, and privacy.

(Continued)

TIP

When reading a passage on a new or unfamiliar topic, annotate the text. In the margins, note key information, questions, connections, and opinions. After you finish annotating, you may want to transfer some of those ideas to a graphic organizer like a T-chart, or to your notebook. A T-chart helps you to classify information. Use different headings based on the categories of information in the text.

For more about annotating, see Bioethics, Part 1, Integrated Skills, page 13.

16 Information is only useful if it is accurate. Currently WGS is very accurate in some ways and less accurate in others. Today WGS reads the base sequence correctly about 99.9 percent of the time. That's very accurate, but making a mistake one time in a thousand in a whole genome means making 6.4 million mistakes. Even worse, WGS is not currently very accurate at looking for some kinds of problems in DNA, including short insertions or deletions of base pairs and the length of DNA repeats. These can be clinically crucial; WGS accuracy will have to improve and methods will be needed to double-check important WGS results. Even if WGS correctly reads the sequence, for it to be useful we need to know what those sequences *mean*. For some diseases we understand that very well; for others our understanding is quite uncertain, quite weak, or both. For example, every person carries thousands of bits of DNA sequence that are unusual but whose meaning is unknown: variants of unknown significance (VUSs). We must not assume DNA can tell more than it can; wrong information can often be worse than no information.

17 Even today, though, WGS can provide a large amount of fairly accurate information— an amount so large that conveying the information is itself a huge challenge. After Stephen Quake sequenced himself, a team looked (with his permission) at his sequence for medical insights about him. It found about 100 things he should know. If it took just three minutes to tell him about each condition, that would be five hours of counseling. Who will be able to provide that counseling, who will be able to listen to and understand it, and who will be willing to pay for it? And yet counseling is crucial. Even good information, if misunderstood, can do harm. If a woman mistakenly thinks having a mutation in the BRCA1 gene means she will get breast cancer, she may take drastic but unnecessary action. If she thinks a "no mutation" test result means she cannot get breast cancer (when her lifetime risk is actually the US average of 12 percent), she might stop breast examinations, with fatal consequences.

18 Third, WGS will provide not only medical information but also information on other things. Some will be unimportant, such as the type of a person's earwax. Some may be more important, such as the likelihood of particular physical or mental traits. And some may be deeply personal, such as who are a person's genetic relatives or where her ancestors came from. And that WGS information could be used by the police or others to determine whether someone's DNA was present at a crime scene. None of these is a medical use, but because WGS picks up all the base pairs, it can provide all of this information as well.

19 Finally, what about privacy? A person's WGS results must be stored somewhere. Some people may have legal access to them, for criminal, civil, or public health investigations. Others may be able to gain access surreptitiously and illegally. No one can promise that the information can always be kept confidential. How much of your DNA would you want subject to possible hacking and exposure? It may not be as important as credit card records or web searches—but it may be.

Conclusion

20 WGS has gone from a dream to a medical reality in less than 30 years; in the next 10, it will become routine. It offers substantial benefits but, like all new technologies, comes with real risks. We must strive to use this technology wisely, to maximize its benefits and to minimize its harms.

Glossary

Accuracy: the ability to do something in an exact way without making a mistake

Convey: to communicate a message or information, with or without using words

Privacy: the protection of information; keeping it secret, not available to others

Assume: to think that something is true, although you have no proof

Permission: the act of allowing someone to do something

Insight: a useful understanding that you did not have before, or the ability to understand something clearly

Counseling: advice given by a counselor to people about their personal problems or difficult decisions

Fatal: causing death

Confidential: secret and not intended to be shown or told to other people

---

CHECK WHAT YOU'VE LEARNED

PARAGRAPHS 15–20

A. Think about the section you just read and refer to your notes. Answer these questions.

11. Which of the following best summarizes the main idea of this section?

   a. The benefits of WGS currently are far greater than its challenges.
   b. In order for WGS to become more routine, its accuracy must be improved.
   c. One harm is that more counselors will be needed to share the results of WGS.
   d. Accuracy, counseling, non-medical information, and privacy are areas of concern.

12. If WGS is correct about 99.9 percent of the time, why is the author worried about accuracy?

   a. because he is a scientist, and his job demands that results be 100 percent accurate
   b. because of the size of a genome, the .1 percent translates into millions of possible mistakes
   c. because he doesn't approve of WGS and wants to persuade others of his opinion
   d. because the medical community will lose respect if the information is untrue

13. What are variants of unknown significance (VUSs) and how do they relate to the issue of accuracy?

   ....

   ....

14. In Paragraph 17, the author, when giving an example of a woman who gets information that she has the BRCA1 gene mutation, writes that the woman "may take drastic but unnecessary action." What is the author implying?

   a. The woman may decide to ignore the information and continue on with her life.
   b. The woman may threaten the doctor for giving her the information.
   c. The woman may start exercising and following a healthy diet.
   d. The woman may choose to have a mastectomy even if she currently doesn't have breast cancer.

15. The author explains the challenges of WGS in order to _____ .

   a. convince the reader that it's not an effective technology
   b. encourage further research into and debate about its use
   c. persuade students to study genetics so they can research these issues
   d. impress the reader with his depth of knowledge on the subject

B. **Read the section again. Check your answers and add details to your notes.**

C. **Using your notes, write a 100-word summary of the essay. Try to use the words from the box.**

accuracy	counseling	diagnose	ethical
physician	privacy	screening	symptom
treatment	whole genome sequencing (WGS)		

THINKING CRITICALLY

Look back at your notes and answers in Check What You've Learned. Answer the questions.

For more about identifying facts and opinions, see Bioethics, Part 2, Skills 1 and 2, pages 145 and 151.

1. Imagine that all medical exams included WGS. How might that affect patients? What about medical workers?

2. Think about the benefits of WGS. Think about the challenges. Which are greater? Why? Explain.

3. Based on the essay, what advice would you give someone planning to get WGS?

◆ Go to MyEnglishLab to complete a critical thinking activity.

THINKING VISUALLY

A. Look at the timeline about key events in the history of genetic research. From the information, what can you infer about this field?

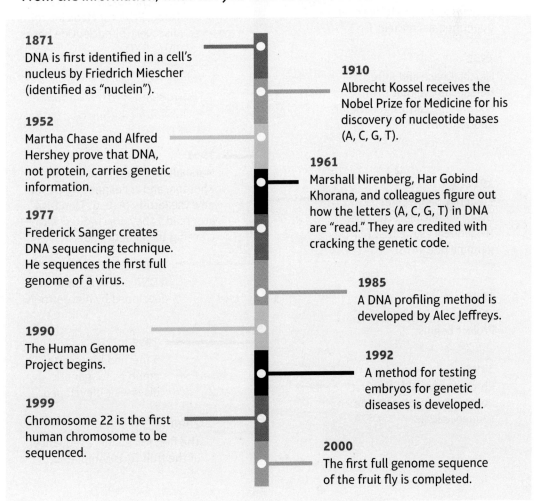

1871
DNA is first identified in a cell's nucleus by Friedrich Miescher (identified as "nuclein").

1910
Albrecht Kossel receives the Nobel Prize for Medicine for his discovery of nucleotide bases (A, C, G, T).

1952
Martha Chase and Alfred Hershey prove that DNA, not protein, carries genetic information.

1961
Marshall Nirenberg, Har Gobind Khorana, and colleagues figure out how the letters (A, C, G, T) in DNA are "read." They are credited with cracking the genetic code.

1977
Frederick Sanger creates DNA sequencing technique. He sequences the first full genome of a virus.

1985
A DNA profiling method is developed by Alec Jeffreys.

1990
The Human Genome Project begins.

1992
A method for testing embryos for genetic diseases is developed.

1999
Chromosome 22 is the first human chromosome to be sequenced.

2000
The first full genome sequence of the fruit fly is completed.

B. Add to the timeline, using your notes and the events from the box. Note years when possible. Compare timelines with a partner.

> Based on Quake's DNA, counselors inform him of their medical insights.
> ~~Crick and Watson discover the double helix structure of DNA.~~
> Quake sequences his own DNA.
> WGS becomes a routine part of medical exams.
> Doctors use DNA tests as part of some medical decisions.
> The first WGS of a human's DNA is made.
> Sanger receives Nobel Prize.
> Nirenberg, Khorana, colleagues receive Nobel Prize.
> The Human Genome Project is completed.

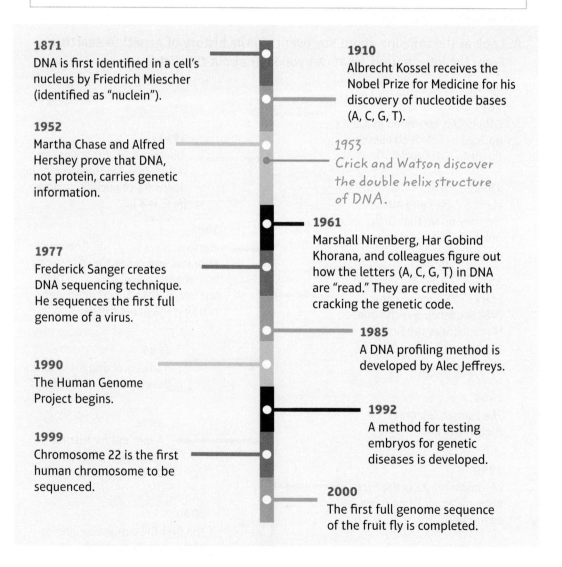

1871
DNA is first identified in a cell's nucleus by Friedrich Miescher (identified as "nuclein").

1952
Martha Chase and Alfred Hershey prove that DNA, not protein, carries genetic information.

1977
Frederick Sanger creates DNA sequencing technique. He sequences the first full genome of a virus.

1990
The Human Genome Project begins.

1999
Chromosome 22 is the first human chromosome to be sequenced.

1910
Albrecht Kossel receives the Nobel Prize for Medicine for his discovery of nucleotide bases (A, C, G, T).

1953
Crick and Watson discover the double helix structure of DNA.

1961
Marshall Nirenberg, Har Gobind Khorana, and colleagues figure out how the letters (A, C, G, T) in DNA are "read." They are credited with cracking the genetic code.

1985
A DNA profiling method is developed by Alec Jeffreys.

1992
A method for testing embryos for genetic diseases is developed.

2000
The first full genome sequence of the fruit fly is completed.

THINKING ABOUT LANGUAGE
CHOOSING EFFECTIVE SEARCH TERMS

A. Read this excerpt from "Whole Genome Sequencing: Uses and Challenges." Imagine that you want to find out more about Stephen Quake, the person who sequenced his own genome.

1. Underline the content words you could use in an online search.

2. What other words might you add? Write them.

3. Write three possible search terms.

4. Using a search engine, try your search terms and see how many results you get with each one.

5. Compare results with a partner.

TIP

When writing search terms, choose content words (objects, actions) that best describe your research focus. Avoid function words (articles, pronouns).

For help with choosing effective search terms, go to MyEnglishLab, Bioethics, Part 1, Language Skill.

In 2003, a human's DNA was "sequenced" for the first time in history. It had taken over a decade and cost about $500 million. By 2008, Stanford University's Stephen Quake sequenced his own DNA in a few weeks for about $100,000. By 2017, a person's genome could be sequenced for about $1,500, roughly 0.0003 percent of the price from less than 15 years earlier. Tomorrow's price, though never $0, will be lower still.

Other words: ....

....

3 search terms: ....

....

....

EXAMINING LANGUAGE FOR SUBJECTIVITY

B. Read the editorial about whole genome sequencing.
Underline words that signal subjectivity.
Then complete the chart.

TIP

Subjective language reflects the attitudes, thoughts, or feelings of the writer. It cannot be verified or proven. Certain adjectives (comparatives and superlatives), modals (*should, ought, had better, have to, must not*), and other words (*think, believe, in my opinion*) can signal a writer's opinion.

For help with examining language for subjectivity, go to MyEnglishLab, Bioethics, Part 2, Language Skill.

BUYER BEWARE: DO YOUR RESEARCH

Editorial   *Nancy J. Benjamin*

Whole genome sequencing (WGS) is the latest craze to hit. Although WGS is typically ordered by a doctor, you can have your genome sequenced if you are willing to pay. Most companies selling this service advertise their ability to predict terrible genetic diseases and to give the best medical information so that you the patient can understand your health. However, you had better research what these companies are actually selling. Are they promising to test and provide well-informed counseling so that you know what to do with all this genetic information? In addition, what kind of genetic testing are they providing? Does it just give information about where your ancestors come from? Or does it give you a complete explanation of your genome? Also, be sure to find out about their privacy rules. How do they guarantee to safeguard the privacy of your results? Before ordering a test, you must do your research to make sure that the company you choose knows how to accurately interpret, share, and protect your genomic results.

Adjective	Modal	Other Subjective Language

🔊 Go to MyEnglishLab for more practice reading an extended text and using your reading skills.

SMALL GROUP PRESENTATION

A. RESEARCH In 2015, President Barack Obama announced his Precision Medicine Initiative (PMI). Its goal was to use advances in genome sequencing to develop a more individualized approach for disease prevention and treatment. Work with a small group to find out more about this initiative. Use these questions to guide your research.

Precision Medicine Initiative (PMI)	
How does precision medicine differ from "traditional" medicine?	
What are the objectives of the Precision Medicine Initiative?	
How is it funded? Does this change depending on who the US president is?	
What is the "All of Us" Research Program? (a part of the PMI program)	

B. FOCUS Discuss your research. Take a position: Do you think the government should continue to fund the Precision Medicine Initiative? Or are you in favor of closing down the program? Support your ideas.

C. PRESENT Prepare and present your research and position to the class. Use visuals to help explain your ideas.

D. DISCUSS After the presentations, have a class discussion about the uses, benefits, and challenges of the Precision Medicine Initiative. Talk about what researchers hope to achieve with whole genome sequencing. Ask if anyone would volunteer their genome for the All of Us Research Program and why.

◗ Go to MyEnglishLab to complete a collaborative activity.

BUSINESS AND DESIGN

Best Practices

UNIT PROFILE

In this unit, you will read about a business model: what it is, how it is used, and which tools are used to design it. You will also learn about branding and how to create a strong brand.

You will research the business model of an existing company and present changes to the model that would help attract new customers.

EXTENDED READING

BEFORE YOU READ

Think about these questions before you read the essay "So What Is a Business Model?" Discuss them with another student.

1. What is the value of a well-thought-out plan—whether you are starting a business or writing a research paper?

2. A business model is a tool used to help design or build a business and / or evaluate how an existing business is working. Here are some words often found in a business model. Predict and write three more. Explain.

   - customers
   - product
   - profit
   - ....
   - ....
   - ....

3. Read this excerpt from the first paragraph of the essay and predict the last word of each sentence.

   > A business model, at its very essence, is a set of assumptions that ultimately lead to a representation of what your business does and how it makes (1) .... It is how the *inputs* (investments you make in your business and its activities) create the *outputs* (value for the customers you (2) ....). A business model describes the big picture and component parts of what makes your business run and (3) .... It represents the choices you make about who your customers are, what product you will create to bring them value, and how you will produce and distribute your (4) ....

READ

Skim Paragraphs 1–3. Look at the title and the image. Use the hierarchy diagram that follows to write the topic and main ideas. Then read the passage, annotate, add details to the diagram, and answer the questions in Check What You've Learned.

So What Is a Business Model?

by Juli Sherry

1   A business model, at its very essence, is a set of assumptions that ultimately lead to a representation of what your business does and how it makes money. It is how the *inputs* (investments you make in your business and its activities) create the *outputs* (value for the customers you serve). A business model describes the big picture and component parts of what makes your business run and succeed. It represents the choices you make about who your customers are, what product you will create to bring them value, and how you will produce and distribute your product. All of these choices are related. For example, if you decide to create a luxury product, you will probably need to provide a high level of customer service because your customers will expect it. Or if you decide to start a delivery-service business, you will have to hire logistics professionals to make it run efficiently.

2   A business model is a tool you can use to help build a business from scratch or a framework to evaluate how your business works today and how you can assure it continues into the future. While a business model is part of an overall business strategy, it does not take the place of one. It typically does not consider the external forces in the marketplace. That is something a good strategy assesses. A business model is used and designed to understand the operations of a business and the reason behind how it creates value. You can think of a business model as a way to tactically execute a larger business strategy.

3 Describing a business model can be tricky because there are many ways to approach designing one and communicating it to others. These experts define it simply and elegantly: "Management writer Joan Magretta defined a business model as 'the story that explains how an enterprise works,' harking back to Peter Drucker, who described it as the answer to the questions: Who is your customer, what does the customer value, and how do you deliver value at an appropriate cost?" (Casadesus-Masanell / Ricart) While these definitions can be worthwhile to explore and help us to realize the importance of having a business model and being able to communicate it, it is useful to break a business model down into its component parts in order to begin designing one.

CULTURE NOTE

Peter Drucker (1909–2005) was an Austrian-born, American business consultant, writer, and professor. His writings are credited with contributing to the principles of the modern business corporation and its management.

Glossary

Assumption: an understanding that something is true, but without proof

Logistics: the daily steps in making a business work

Efficiently: using time or money well without waste

From scratch: from nothing

Framework: a set of ideas or rules to guide a business

Evaluate: to judge the value of something

Enterprise: an organization or business

Component: a small part of a whole

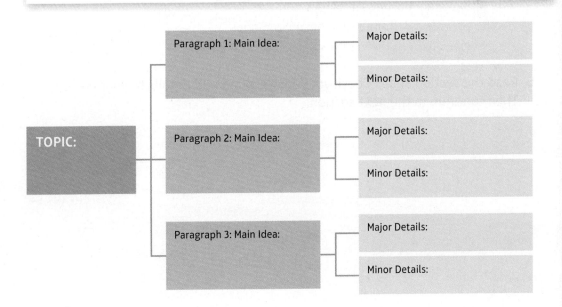

TOPIC:

Paragraph 1: Main Idea:
- Major Details:
- Minor Details:

Paragraph 2: Main Idea:
- Major Details:
- Minor Details:

Paragraph 3: Main Idea:
- Major Details:
- Minor Details:

CHECK WHAT YOU'VE LEARNED
PARAGRAPHS 1–3

A. Think about the section you just read and refer to your notes.
Answer these questions.

1. What do you think is the main purpose of the essay?
   a. to evaluate the effectiveness of a business plan
   b. to give the definition of a business model
   c. to compare a business model to a business strategy
   d. to analyze how to design a business model by studying its parts

2. What is NOT an example of an input?
   a. providing excellent service to customers
   b. hiring administrative help
   c. renting or buying office space
   d. attending professional development conferences

3. The relationship between a business model and a business strategy is the model shows how to _____ the strategy.
   a. evaluate
   b. put into practice
   c. replace
   d. outline

4. Why does the author cite Magretta, Drucker, and Casadesus-Masanell / Ricart?
   a. to persuade the reader of her expertise on the subject
   b. to explain a business strategy
   c. to provide a definition of a business model
   d. to give credit to the creators of the business model

B. Read the section again. Check your answers and add details to your notes.
Then continue to the next section.

"SO WHAT IS A BUSINESS MODEL?" CONTINUED

PARAGRAPHS 4–6

Read, annotate, and use a hierarchy diagram or other organizer to take notes.

TIP

Create your own graphic organizer or find one online by searching for "graphic organizer" or a specific kind, such as "hierarchy diagram."

Business Model Components

4 There are many tools available that can help you describe your business model. Some use fill-in-the-blank paragraphs. Others use writing-based exercises. But the best representations tend to be visual. The most popular of the visual-representation tools for business model design is the Business Model Canvas, created by Alex Osterwalder. This tool allows the user to quickly show and tell the different parts of the model and how they are interrelated. The concrete nature of quickly visualizing ideas helps to make this tool easy to share with others, and the layout helps signify the relationships and necessity of all the components.

5 The Business Model Canvas was created by analyzing the many definitions of business models and synthesizing them down to their essence. After years of research while completing a PhD in management information systems, Osterwalder and his advisor discovered, through testing with entrepreneurs, that a visual representation worked best. So he created a map of the nine components he had distilled from his research. (Greenwald) They are as follows:

Key Partners	Key Activities	Value Proposition	Customer Relationships	Customer Segments
Key Resources			Channels	
Cost Structure			Revenue Streams	

6 It should be noted that each component is located near the other components that are related to it. While developing an idea or hypothesis about one component, you can see which other components will likely be affected just by noting its location on the layout. All of the externally facing components are on the right side of the map while all of the internally facing components are on the left. Having all of the parts of your business in your visual field helps you to quickly notice the effects of your design decisions.

(Continued)

Value Proposition

The value proposition is the heart of the business model. It answers the question, "What does your customer segment need?" or "What problem are you solving in the world?"

Customer Segments

Your choice about customer segments is directly related to your value proposition. It answers the question, "Who are you solving a problem for?" This can be one group of people or a few.

Customer Relationships

This is how you communicate with your customers. It's related to who your customers are and how much assistance they expect throughout the product experience. It can range from high-touch (in-person consulting) to low-touch (automated order-taking and shipping).

Channels

Channels are your choices about how to reach new and existing customers and market your offering. Different ideas about advertising and selling would fall into this component.

Key Activities

These are choices about how to create your product and other necessities needed to run your business. Some examples are outsourcing, internal production, and equipment maintenance.

Key Resources

This component includes choices about supply chain and where you will acquire what you need to create your product. This includes human resources especially if you are creating a service-based business.

Key Partners

This component describes who you may need to partner with in order to bring your product to market.

Cost Structure

Will you compete with a low-cost product or a high-cost product? You will have to make a choice about pricing and relate it to your customer's price sensitivity. Your cost structure is directly related to the next component, revenue streams.

Revenue Streams

How will you make money? You can make choices to have multiple revenue streams or just one. It will depend on what your value proposition is and how many customer groups you are serving as well as your internal resources.

CULTURE NOTE

Management information systems is the study of the relationships between people, technology, and organizations. Students with a degree in MIS will be able to use information systems to collect and analyze data that is useful internally for a business.

Glossary

Tool: a resource useful for doing your job

Interrelated: related to one another

Concrete: (adj) definite and clear

Entrepreneur: a person who starts a new business

Externally: out, outside

Internally: within, inside

Outsourcing: sending work outside of a company, to another company

Supply chain: the series of organizations that are involved in passing products from manufacturers to the public

Acquire: to get something, especially by buying it

Human resources: in a company, the department that deals with employing, training, and hiring people; abbreviated as HR

CHECK WHAT YOU'VE LEARNED

PARAGRAPHS 4–6

A. Think about the section you just read and refer to your notes. Answer these questions.

5. What does the author believe is the best tool to help explain a business model and why?

6. How did Osterwalder come up with his nine components in a business model?

7. What is the difference between externally facing components and internally facing components?

8. Why is a value proposition the heart of the business model?

9. Which component do decisions about hiring employees fit into?

B. Read the section again. Check your answers and add details to your notes. Then continue to the next section.

Read, annotate, and use a hierarchy diagram or other organizer to take notes.

Target Corporation's Business Model

7 Now that you have an understanding about the different components of a business model and how they are generally related to one another, let's dive into an example: low-cost retail. How would this traditional model be described using the Business Model Canvas framework? Let's look at an example of a business using the low-cost retail model: Target Corporation.

8 The first two components to work with are Value Proposition and Customer Segments. Target's value proposition is, "We fulfill the needs and fuel the potential of our guests … [through] continuous innovation and exceptional experiences—consistently fulfilling our Expect More. Pay Less.® brand promise." ("Purpose & Beliefs") This can be simplified by saying that Target meets its customers' needs by offering a large assortment of low-cost everyday products with a high standard of design. Target's typical customer persona is described as a 41-year-old female who is likely to have children, with a median household income of $63,000, who has attended college. ("Target Corporation") An easier-to-manage description of this customer persona is a "minivan mom." So the heart of Target's business model (Value Proposition + Customer Segments) is providing low-cost, high-design utilitarian products of a large assortment to minivan moms across the US.

9 In order to provide this value to customers, Target has a lot of work to do. Target has made choices about its channels, which are an assortment of brick and mortar stores as well as an online marketplace. It also spends on advertising through print ads in daily newspapers and TV commercials, as well as online ads and billboards. In terms of customer relationships, Target provides mid-level customer service within stores through store employees. Target is not completely hands off but is not high-touch like a boutique or customized luxury brand.

10 The internally-facing components of its model (Key Activities, Key Partners, and Key Resources) are chosen with the intent to deliver its product at the cost and service level described previously. Target has many distribution centers across the US to keep its stores stocked efficiently. This is one of Target's key activities—distribution. It has some "house brands" that it manufactures internally and distributes through its stores, but Target's main activity is sourcing products and working with many manufacturers to find products that meet customers' expectations. Target also makes its store experience pleasant and maintains the real estate that it owns.

11 The key resources Target needs to keep the business running are its employees, logistics systems, computer equipment, shipping, and real estate. Key partners for Target are the manufacturers it purchases its products from, and its produce partners (it doesn't use its own distribution for perishable products). This helps keep costs down by not having to invest in more infrastructure. Target also has many other partners such as architects and advertising firms that it works with to manage its variable resources.

12 Target's cost system is based on all of these activities. It keeps costs low by being efficient at sourcing products and negotiating with manufacturers. It also makes larger profits by selling gift cards and dominating the gift card market. Target's revenue streams come directly from selling physical products but also through a few other outlets like its sourcing services and financial and retail services that were created to manage its REDcard® finance offering.

CULTURE NOTE

Target, first started by George Draper Dayton and known as Dayton Dry Goods Company in Minnesota, US, has been in the retail business since 1902. In 1962, it was renamed Target with the goal of offering retail goods at a good price, with good service and a commitment to the community. At that point, the bull's-eye logo, which is still synonymous with its name, was developed. From those days, Target has grown and now has over 1,800 stores in the United States with 323,000 employees.

Glossary

Retail: the sale of products from a store

Innovation: the creation of something new; new ideas

Median household income: average amount of money that the people in one house earns in one year

Minivan: a box-shaped automobile with seats for six to eight people

Utilitarian: practical, but maybe not attractive

Brick and mortar store: a business with a physical store, not online

Hands off: giving people freedom to make their own decisions

Source: (v) to find materials or other resources

Produce: (n) fruits and vegetables

Perishable: not lasting, becoming rotten after some time

Infrastructure: the basic system a business needs to function

CHECK WHAT YOU'VE LEARNED

PARAGRAPHS 7-12

A. Think about the section you just read and refer to your notes. Answer these questions.

10. From the description of a "minivan mom" in Paragraph 8, you can infer that Target's typical customer _____ .

    a. is employed
    b. owns a small automobile
    c. cares about pricing
    d. is divorced

11. In Paragraph 9, Sentence 2, *channels* most likely means _____ .

    a. TV networks that Target advertises on
    b. Target's employees
    c. the prices of Target's products
    d. the places where Target's products are sold

12. From Paragraph 10, you can infer that _____ .

    a. most of Target's products are manufactured by outside companies
    b. Target is responsible for manufacturing the majority of its products
    c. distribution is not a major part of Target's key activities
    d. Target does not consider the interior design of its stores to be important

13. From the information in Paragraph 11, you can infer that _____ .

    a. someone shopping at Target could buy food as well as other household goods
    b. Target's business model is poorly designed
    c. Target needs to cut its distribution costs
    d. Target does too much advertising

14. What is an example of how Target keeps costs low?

    a. It hires the best employees and offer great benefits.
    b. It negotiates prices with the manufacturers of its products.
    c. It purchases updated equipment on a regular basis.
    d. It makes its stores a visually pleasing place to shop.

B. Read the section again. Check your answers and add details to your notes. Then continue to the next section.

TIP

Inferences are educated guesses made from facts, observations, and logic. Inferencing is using what you know about a text to understand information not directly stated. Predicting is when you use the facts and ideas in a text, as well as your inferences, to make a guess about what will come next.

For more about making inferences and predictions, see Business and Design, Part 2, Skills 1 and 2, pages 171 and 176.

"SO WHAT IS A BUSINESS MODEL?" *CONTINUED*
PARAGRAPHS 13–16

Read and use your organizer to take notes.

Iterating to Create a Business Model That Works

13 A best practice if you are creating a new business is to use the business model framework to manage your assumptions about how your business could work. By going through this thought experiment and iterating on your ideas for each component, you can build a business model that works.

14 The best way to start is to sit down with the Canvas and sketch out what choices you would make for each component. Then compare each choice you make with the other components to test if it is logically sound. Once you have a draft, you can start to test your assumptions by building experiments around each component. For example, if you believe that your customer segment—college students—has a need to acquire course books faster, you can meet with college students and ask them about their experience buying books for their classes. If that assumption holds true and they have a need for faster acquisition of books, then you can start to take orders for next-day delivery. Through this test you will learn the key activities and resources you will have to partake in to meet the college student need that you have discovered.

15 Once you verify your assumptions about value proposition and customer segment, you can experiment with a cost structure, such as having students pay in advance or on delivery of their books. If one of your assumptions doesn't hold true, it is appropriate to try out another approach and to think through the effect it will have on the other parts of your business. Once you have worked through all of the components and tested and verified your assumptions for each, you have created a working business model. While building your business, your model will evolve and become stronger as you grow and try different ideas. Because business models are never quite done, it's important to always be thinking about each component and how it can be changed or improved to meet the changing needs of your customers.

16 There is never one "right" business model. A business model is always changing and being innovated upon. But there are great tools out there to help you manage and understand what your business model is and how to continually improve it.

Sources

1. Casadesus-Masanell, Ramon, and Ricart, Joan E. "How to Design a Winning Business Model." *Harvard Business Review.* N.p., 07 Oct. 2014. Web. 31 Mar. 2017.

2. Osterwalder, Alex. "Strategyzer: Business Model Canvas." *Strategyzer: Business Model Canvas.* N.p., n.d. Web. 31 Mar. 2017.

3. Greenwald, Ted. "Business Model Canvas: A Simple Tool For Designing Innovative Business Models." Forbes. *Forbes Magazine,* 31 Jan. 2012. Web. 31 Mar. 2017.

4. "Purpose & Beliefs." *Target Corporate.* N.p., n.d. Web. 31 Mar. 2017.

5. "Target Corporation." Wikipedia. Wikimedia Foundation, 28 Mar. 2017. Web. 31 Mar. 2017.

Glossary

Iterate: to repeat or do again

Best practice: a good rule or behavior that a business follows

Acquisition: receipt of something

Partake: to participate in

Verify: to decide if something is true

Evolve: to change slowly over time

CHECK WHAT YOU'VE LEARNED

PARAGRAPHS 13–16

A. Think about the section you just read and refer to your notes. Answer these questions.

15. In Paragraph 14, why does the author give an example of a college student who has a need for the faster acquisition of books?

   ....

   ....

16. In Paragraph 15, the author writes that "While building your business, your model will evolve and become stronger as you grow and try different ideas." What can you infer about what those different ideas might be? Why do you think the essay doesn't list specific ideas?

   ....

   ....

17. The final paragraph of the essay says, "There is never one 'right' business model. A business model is always changing and being innovated upon. But there are great tools out there to help you manage and understand what your business model is and to continually improve it." What inferences about creating a business model can you draw from this information?

   ....

   ....

18. What is the main idea of the essay? Use your own words. Does the title state the main idea? If so, how? If not, what would be a better title?

   ....

   ....

B. Read the section again. Check your answers and add details to your notes.

C. Using your notes, write a 100-word summary of the essay. Try to use the words from the box.

business model	component	customer	evaluate
framework	product	tool	

THINKING CRITICALLY

**Look back at your notes and answers in Check What You've Learned.
Answer the questions.**

1. Peter Drucker explains that a business model is the answer to "Who is your customer, what does the customer value, and how do you deliver value at an appropriate cost?" How does Drucker's explanation relate to the Business Model Canvas?

2. Think about what it takes to start and run a business. Do you think it's necessary for all businesses to have a business model? Why? Explain.

3. What advice would you give someone planning to create a business model?

◐ Go to MyEnglishLab to complete a critical thinking activity.

THINKING VISUALLY

A. Look at the Business Model Canvas for Target. From the information, what can you infer about Target?

Key Partners	Key Activities	Value Proposition	Customer Relationships	Customer Segments
• Manufacturers Target purchases its products from, and its produce partners	•	• "We fulfill the needs and fuel the potential of our guests … [through] continuous innovation and exceptional experiences—consistently fulfilling our Expect More. Pay Less.® brand promise." ("Purpose & Beliefs.") Author's paraphrase: Target meets customers' needs by offering a large assortment of low-cost everyday products with a high standard of design.	• Provide mid-level customer service within Target's stores through store employees	• a 41-year-old female who is likely to have children, with a median household income of $63,000, who has attended college ("Target Corporation") Author's paraphrase: "minivan mom"

Key Resources	Channels
•	•

Cost Structure	Revenue Streams
•	• Come directly from selling physical products but also through Target's sourcing services and financial and retail services created to manage Target's REDcard® finance offering

**B. Using your notes, complete the Business Model Canvas about Target.
Compare Canvases with a partner.**

THINKING ABOUT LANGUAGE

USING SYNONYMS AND EQUIVALENT EXPRESSIONS

A. Read the excerpt from "So What Is a Business Model?" Use synonyms from the box to replace the bold words. Change the form if necessary. More than one correct answer may be possible.

TIP

Writers use synonyms—words with the same or similar meaning to another—to add variety and to make their writing more engaging.

For help with synonyms and equivalent expressions, go to MyEnglishLab, Business and Design, Part 1, Language Skill.

carry out	add	evaluate	make
plan	process	outline	usually

A business model is a tool you can use to help (1) **build** a business from scratch or a (2) **framework** to evaluate how your business works today and how you can assure it continues into the future. While a business model is a part of an overall business (3) **strategy**, it does not take the place of one. It (4) **typically** does not consider the external forces in the marketplace. That is something a good strategy (5) **assesses**. A business model is used and designed to understand the (6) **operations** of a business and the reason behind how it (7) **creates** value. You can think of a business model as a way to tactically (8) **execute** a larger business strategy.

INTERPRETING HEDGING LANGUAGE

B. Read each sentence. Write the hedging language.

TIP

Hedging language is used by authors when making a claim to protect themselves in case of a mistake, to indicate the limits of their findings, or to express modesty or "soften" criticism. Noticing hedging language allows readers to better evaluate the strength of an author's claim.

For help with hedging, go to MyEnglishLab, Business and Design, Part 2, Language Skill.

1. It's possible that the Business Model Canvas is the best graphic organizer for visually presenting a business model.

   Hedging language: ....

2. Target may be able to increase its online sales by 2020 by pursuing a more robust online advertising strategy.

   Hedging language: ....

3. Target will probably expand its physical presence to more overseas markets in the coming years.

   Hedging language: ....

4. Some analysts think that brick and mortar stores will soon disappear and that shopping will only be done online.

    Hedging language: ....

5. Target's customer segment, the "minivan mom," generally looks for the best value before purchasing a product.

    Hedging language: ....

6. Looking at the happy expressions on Target's customers' faces, it appears that Target is achieving its value proposition and meeting its customers' needs.

    Hedging language: ....

⓵ Go to MyEnglishLab **for more practice reading an extended text and using your reading skills.**

SMALL GROUP PRESENTATION

A. RESEARCH Work in a small group. Think of an existing company whose business model you would like to evaluate (similar to the example of Target in the reading.) Do research to learn more about the company. Then create and fill out a Business Model Canvas to evaluate the company.

B. FOCUS Imagine that you have been asked by the company to change its customer segment to reflect the people in your class. Discuss your research. Decide if this will change the company's current plans. If so, come up with an updated Business Model Canvas reflecting that change.

C. PRESENT Prepare and give your presentation with the goal of persuading your classmates that this company is right for their needs.

D. DISCUSS After the presentations, have a class discussion on the uses, benefits, and challenges of the Business Model Canvas. Discuss what other tools could be useful for a company hoping to evaluate and grow.

⓵ Go to MyEnglishLab **to complete a collaborative activity.**

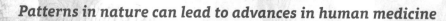
Patterns in nature can lead to advances in human medicine

ZOOLOGY

Elephant Behavior

UNIT PROFILE

In this unit, you will learn about elephant social organization and behavior, and the important role of matriarchs. You will also read about rituals in male elephant culture.

You will research female-led and male-led animal societies and present your findings.

EXTENDED READING

BEFORE YOU READ

Think about these questions before you read the essay "For Elephants, Being Social Has Costs and Benefits." Discuss them with another student.

1. Think about what you already know about elephants. For them, what are the costs and benefits of being social animals—for example, of living in a group? In your opinion, do the costs outweigh the benefits, or vice versa?

2. In elephant society, some members are higher-ranking than others. What might cause an elephant to have more importance than another? How does this compare to human society, with groups of friends, students, or coworkers?

3. The reading discusses elephant communication. What words do you associate with the idea of "elephant communication"?

READ

Read and annotate Paragraphs 1–4. Use the mind map that follows to write the main ideas and details. Then answer the questions in Check What You've Learned.

> **TIP**
>
> As you read, make associations, or try to recall experiences with the topic. Try to relate the text to yourself, to other things you have read, or to things in the world. Synthesize the information with other information to have a fuller understanding of the text.
>
> For more about making associations and synthesizing, see Zoology, Part 1, Skills 1 and 2, pages 55 and 62.

For Elephants, Being Social Has Costs and Benefits

by Professor Caitlin O'Connell-Rodwell

Dr. Caitlin O'Connell-Rodwell is the author of several books about elephants including the science memoir The Elephant's Secret Sense. *She's also a a consulting assistant professor at Stanford University School of Medicine and co-founder and CEO of Utopia Scientific, a nonprofit dedicated to research and science education.*

1 **African elephants are long-lived social mammals that grow up within a tightly bonded family group led by an older female family member called a** *matriarch.* **The matriarch is usually a mother, aunt, sister, cousin, great-aunt, grandmother, or often a great-grandmother—or, depending on how old she is, even a great-great-grandmother. Within an average elephant family, a new calf is born into a very social environment with mom, siblings, cousins, aunts, and many elder females of varying relatedness.**

2 A female calf is born into her core family for life, whereas a male calf leaves the family between the age of 12 and 15 and forms relationships within a network of associated adult males. Both male and female calves rely on others within the family not only for protection from predators, such as lions and hyenas, but also for the opportunity to learn what kinds of plants are safe to eat by watching and

(Continued)

sampling what the others are eating. Since an elephant isn't born with the knowledge of what plants are safe to eat, it has to learn from others, and a very practical way to achieve this goal is to place one's trunk in another's mouth to see what the other elephant is eating.

3 Ritual plays an important role in reinforcing bonds within the family, and calves learn these rituals at a very young age. One of the most important and striking rituals in elephant society is the trunk-to-mouth greeting. In this behavior, one elephant approaches another and places his or her trunk within the other elephant's mouth, akin to our handshake. Its origin stems from the very functional behavior of learning what another is eating, a behavior that was ritualized over time into a greeting.

Another example of functional behavior evolving into a greeting ritual is the wolf's face-licking greeting. This behavior had also evolved from the act of determining what another wolf had been eating by licking its mouth. Other examples of normal behaviors that have evolved into ritualized behaviors include stretching behaviors in some birds that evolved into ritualized mating dances, most famous being the bird of paradise, but there are many other showy examples such as the flamingo.

4 The trunk-to-mouth greeting ritual in elephants comes in many forms—some subtle, and some very overt. Often times the gesture is exhibited at a distance or at close range but without actually touching the other's mouth. Other times, the trunk is placed within the open mouth of another, usually while the other is drinking. The act places the individual in a very vulnerable position, as the receiver of the signal could easily bite the signaler.

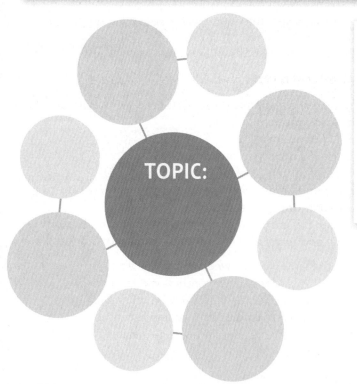

TOPIC:

Glossary

Mammal: any animal that drinks milk from its mother as a baby

Predator: an animal that kills and eats other animals

Trunk: an elephant's long nose

Ritual: a social practice or habit

Evolve: to change slowly over time

Overt: very open, clear to see

Vulnerable: easily hurt

CHECK WHAT YOU'VE LEARNED

PARAGRAPHS 1–4

For more about classifying information and distinguishing points of view, see Zoology, Part 2, Skills 1 and 2, pages 197 and 203.

A. Think about the section you just read and refer to your notes. Answer these questions.

1. The author says that elephants are born into a matriarchal family structure. Based on what you know about being raised in a family, what benefits would this bring to a calf (baby elephant)?

   ....

   ....

2. How do young elephants learn what is safe to eat? How is this like or unlike human behavior?

   ....

   ....

3. In Paragraph 4, the author says that there are two basic categories of trunk-to-mouth greetings. What are the two categories? What examples does she give? Complete the T-chart.

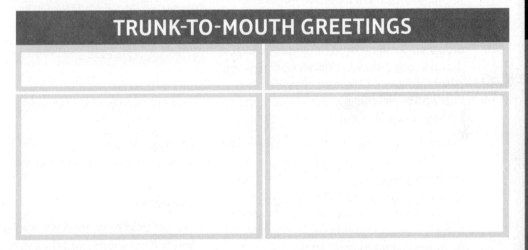

TRUNK-TO-MOUTH GREETINGS

4. Why does the passage include a sidebar about wolves' practice of face-licking and the stretching / mating dance of certain birds? How are these behaviors related to those of the elephant?

   ....

   ....

B. Read the section again. Check your answers and add details to your notes. Then continue to the next section.

PART 3

"FOR ELEPHANTS, BEING SOCIAL HAS COSTS AND BENEFITS," *CONTINUED*

PARAGRAPHS 5-7

Read, annotate, and use a mind map or other organizer to take notes.

TIP

Create your own graphic organizer or find one online by searching for "graphic organizer" or a specific kind, such as "mind map."

5 On signals of a more remote nature, elephants are masters of long-distance acoustic communication and generate low-frequency vocalizations called *rumbles* in the range of 20 hertz and below, which is below the range of human hearing. Rumbles are produced at such a high-sound pressure level (120 decibels) that they couple with the ground and travel along the surface of the ground as vibrational cues that are detectable by other elephants as meaningful signals.

6 Elephants generate rumble vocalizations at a very young age. These vocalizations, emitted by elder females within the group, tell other elephants things such as when it is time to leave an area and where members of the group are located if the group is foraging in a densely vegetated environment. Rumbles are also used in ritualized greeting ceremonies, telling the group the location of an extended family group in the distance, or alerting the group to some danger. Olfactory cues are often combined with acoustic cues to share information remotely, whereas visual and tactile cues are used at close range to convey status or intent.

CULTURE NOTE

Joyce Poole, an elephant researcher at Kenya's Amboseli National Park, has catalogued more than 70 vocalizations and 160 visual and tactile gestures that elephants use to communicate. These are detailed on the website Elephant Voices, the site for the nonprofit organization that Poole and her husband, Petter Granli, started in 2002.

7 The matriarch often employs rumble vocalizations to signal when and where the family spends its time in any one place. She assesses safety and environmental conditions to determine things like where it is safe to forage and drink, and which families to meet up with and maybe share a drink with at a waterhole. Depending on an individual matriarch's character, decisions might also include vocal input and assessment from several other older females within the group. Studies have shown that older matriarchs are better able to discern risk and make better decisions than younger matriarchs.

Glossary

Acoustic: relating to sound and hearing

Vocalization: a sound made by a voice

Vibrational: related to motion in the air or ground that is felt

Detectable: noticeable

Forage: to search for food

Olfactory: related to the sense of smell

Tactile: related to the sense of touch

Discern: to notice or figure out

CHECK WHAT YOU'VE LEARNED
PARAGRAPHS 5–7

A. Think about the section you just read and refer to your notes. Answer these questions.

5. Which of the following best summarizes the main idea of this section?

   a. Elephants communicate through visual, olfactory, tactile, and acoustic cues, including rumble vocalizations.
   b. Rumble vocalizations are an effective means of long-distance communication for elephants.
   c. Matriarchs are skilled at using rumble vocalizations to signal safety conditions.
   d. Humans are unable to hear the rumble vocalizations of elephants.

6. In Paragraph 6, the author says that elephants use olfactory and acoustic cues to share information remotely. What can we infer about these elephant senses?

   a. An elephant has a poor sense of smell but weak sense of hearing.
   b. An elephant has a good sense of smell and hearing.
   c. An elephant enjoys smelling and listening at long distances.
   d. An elephant uses its trunk to warn of danger, and its ears to hear those warnings.

7. What is NOT mentioned as a way that an elephant matriarch uses rumble vocalizations?

   a. to tell the herd the location of extended family
   b. to let the herd know when it is time to leave an area
   c. to warn her members of danger
   d. to challenge another elephant to a fight

B. Read the section again. Check your answers and add details to your notes. Then continue to the next section.

Read, annotate, and use a mind map or other organizer to take notes.

8 Elephant matriarchal family groups make up the core subunits of a fission-fusion society, where extended families that stem from matriarchal groups form larger bond groups that form subunits of even more distantly related units called clans. As is the case for social animals in general, dominance hierarchies form within and between family groups to minimize conflict over access to resources such as food and water and even mates.

9 The term "pecking order" has become synonymous with the idea of a linear dominance hierarchy. Watch birds at a bird feeder or a flock of guinea fowl move across a clearing in the early morning, and you will see the squabbles that quickly ensue over the discovery of a seed-ridden elephant dung ball. This pecking behavior reminds low-ranking individuals of their place in the hierarchy, i.e., "Get in line!" And at the head of the line stands the most dominant individual—or family.

10 The concept of linearity within a dominance hierarchy is illustrated by the idea that individual A always wins in contests with individual B, who always beats C, who beats D, etc. When the linearity of a hierarchy breaks down, C might beat A on occasion, or D might beat C or B, giving circuity to the hierarchy rather than linearity. In the end, the general pattern remains—at any point in time, there is a dominant family and dominant individuals within that family.

11 The elephant matriarch is usually the oldest family member, and as the eldest, she is the repository of the most knowledge in the group, which has important implications for the group's overall fitness and survival. For example, researchers have shown that elephants are not territorial but remain within a large home range, and matriarch age and status matter within the larger elephant community. One study showed that during a severe drought, families with older matriarchs survived better and had higher reproductive fitness than families with younger matriarchs simply because the elders had experienced such a severe drought in their distant past and knew where to go to find water under such extreme conditions.

12 In another study, matriarchs of known rank were tracked via satellite collars to reveal that dominant families had access to the best food resources within their home range. Better food led to higher reproductive fitness, where dominant families had more calves and a higher calf survival rate than lower-ranking families with restricted access and lower quality food. This would imply that there is a bloodline-driven advantage to being born into one family versus another.

CULTURE NOTE

Satellite collars are an effective approach to study and track elephants in the wild. Satellite collars are used not only to track the migratory behavior of elephants but also to detect if an elephant becomes immobile, which may signify a poaching situation. When this occurs, wildlife management and enforcement can arrive at the scene, respond to the situation, and hopefully deter future poaching.

Glossary

Fission-fusion society: a group whose members come together (fusion) and leave (fission) as they travel, changing over time

Dominance: having power or importance over other members

Pecking order: a social system in which each member of the group has a known position

Hierarchy: a system of organization that identifies members by level of importance

Squabble: (n) a noisy argument about something unimportant

Fitness: the level of preparedness for an occasion

Repository: a place of information

Territorial: protective of an area, wanting to prevent others from using it

Drought: a long period of dry weather that threatens the lives of plants and animals

CHECK WHAT YOU'VE LEARNED

PARAGRAPHS 8–12

A. Think about the section you just read and refer to your notes. Answer these questions.

8. In Paragraph 8, the author defines a fission-fusion society. Draw a basic diagram showing a fission-fusion society. Label the parts.

> **TIP**
>
> Try to notice how information is classified, or sorted into groups by similar characteristics. This will help you see how things are similar or different. Try also to understand the author's point of view. Consider what may influence it, such as the author's background, the kind of publication, and the purpose of the text.

9. The author gives the example of birds at a bird feeder to explain the concept of linear dominance hierarchy. What is another example in the animal kingdom that demonstrates a linear dominance hierarchy?

....

....

10. How does an older elephant matriarch differ from a younger elephant matriarch?

....

....

11. Why is being a member of a dominant family better for an elephant?

....

....

12. Why is the author a credible source to speak about elephant behavior? What factors might shape her point of view? (Hint: Read the bio at the beginning of the essay.)

....

....

B. Read the section again. Check your answers and add details to your notes. Then continue to the next section.

"FOR ELEPHANTS, BEING SOCIAL HAS COSTS AND BENEFITS," *CONTINUED* PARAGRAPHS 13–17

Read, annotate, and use a mind map or other organizer to take notes.

13 Studies within families have shown that the passing of the matriarch position goes to the next oldest female rather than the daughter of the matriarch, which would imply that there isn't a "queen ethos" in elephants. Similar studies have found that dominance rank is not a predictor of female reproductive fitness.

14 Although there isn't yet evidence to indicate that high-ranking female elephants can suppress low-ranking females from ovulating—called hormonal suppression—reproductive suppression is well known in baboons, mandrills, and marmosets as well as in African wild dogs, dwarf mongooses, and other species, either through endocrine or behavioral mechanisms or both.

15 Reproductive suppression might need to be revisited in elephants in the context of limited resources, as intolerance of low-ranking females by more dominant females is not uncommon and would best be explained by optimal foraging theory. Optimal foraging theory predicts that there is an optimal group size that needs to be maintained in order to maximize fitness, particularly in a resource-poor environment. Smaller group sizes would require less forage, and therefore individuals would be more likely to retain their fitness than if they were to travel in a larger group where there wouldn't be as much forage to go around. This intolerance, or behavioral suppression, could cause early terminations of pregnancies or reduced calf fitness if the mother is too stressed to produce enough milk.

16 In addition, aggressive behavior toward these low-ranking females could cause these females and their young calves to get displaced far enough away from family that they risk attracting the attention of predators. It is much harder for a single adult female to protect her calf from predators than it is for a large group of adult elephants to do so.

17 Although being social has many benefits for elephants, for the low-ranking family or individual within a family, it can also have drawbacks. Two questions will help address how elephants, social animals by nature, survive the pressures of a resource-poor environment. Do similar-aged female elephants within the family have the same number of calves on average, regardless of their rank, or do lower-ranking females have reduced reproductive fitness? And are lower-ranking adult females more distantly related to the matriarch?

Glossary

Imply: to suggest an idea indirectly

Suppress: to keep something from growing naturally

Ovulate: when a woman or female animal produces eggs inside her body

Endocrine: relating to the production of hormones

Intolerance: unwillingness to accept ways of thinking and behaving that are different from your own

Optimal: ideal, the best

Displace: to force to move

Drawback: a disadvantage, con

CHECK WHAT YOU'VE LEARNED
PARAGRAPHS 13–17

A. Think about the section you just read and refer to your notes.
   Answer these questions.

13. In Paragraph 15, why does the author mention optimal foraging theory?

    a. to explain how elephant matriarchs look for food
    b. to tell why dominant matriarchs of large groups may try to stop pregnancies in low-ranking females
    c. to show how group size does not affect reproductive fitness
    d. to demonstrate how elephant hierarchies are important for an elephant's survival

14. What is NOT mentioned as a benefit of belonging to a smaller elephant family?

    a. more available food
    b. less reproductive stress
    c. better availability of food for calves
    d. better ability to fight off predators

15. The purpose of including two questions in the concluding paragraph might be _____ .

    a. to demonstrate a lack of knowledge about the topic
    b. to suggest the focus of possible future research
    c. to show the complex nature of elephant behavior in the African savanna
    d. to support the theory of reproductive suppression because of optimal foraging theory

16. The author's point of view on elephant behavior is probably most influenced by _____ .

    a. her work in the field
    b. who she works for
    c. where she attended school
    d. her personal background

B. Read the section again. Check your answers and add details to your notes.

C. Using your notes, write a 100-word summary of the essay. Try to use the words from the box.

dominance	drawbacks	forage	hierarchy
intolerance	matriarch	predator	reproductive fitness
rumble vocalizations	survival	trunk	

THINKING CRITICALLY

Look back at your notes and answers in Check What You've Learned. Answer the questions.

1. What does the author believe are the costs and benefits of being social for elephants? Were any of these similar to the ones you came up with for Question 1 in Before You Read (p. 319)? Has your opinion changed on whether the benefits outweigh the costs or vice versa?

2. Research has shown that groups with older, more experienced elephants have better fitness and survival rates than those with younger, less experienced matriarchs. Why is this? Are age and experience always advantages for all animals? Explain.

3. How credible is the information in this essay? What is your opinion based on? How could you check the information in the essay?

⬆ Go to MyEnglishLab to complete a critical thinking activity.

THINKING VISUALLY

A. Work with a partner. Look at the images. Talk about what you know about the social behaviors of wolves and elephants, including greetings. What behaviors do these animals share? Fill in the blue circle (Wolves), yellow circle (Elephants), and green area of the diagram.

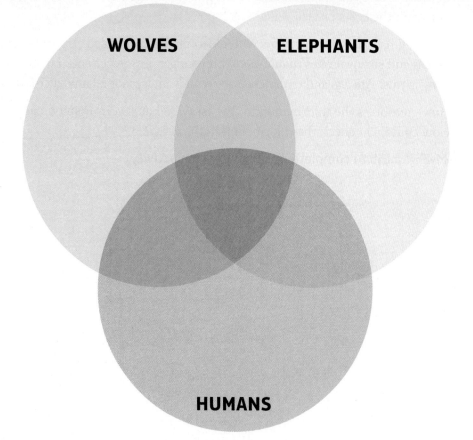

B. What social behaviors do humans share with wolves and with elephants? What human behaviors are unique? What behaviors do all three species have in common? Complete the diagram.

THINKING ABOUT LANGUAGE
EXPRESSING CONTRAST AND CONCESSION

A. Complete the sentences. Use the words and phrases from the box to make expressions of contrast or concession. Add punctuation as needed. More than one correct answer may be possible.

> **TIP**
>
> Expressions of both contrast and concession are used to show differences. However, expressions of concession signal a slightly unexpected or surprising result.

For help with expressing contrast and concession, go to MyEnglishLab, Zoology, Part 1, Language Skill.

even though	unlike	and yet	while
whereas	but	however	despite

1. A female calf will remain in the family for life .... a male calf will leave his birth family at adolescence.

2. .... appearing strange to some onlookers, when a young elephant places its trunk in the mouth of another, it may be learning what plants are edible or greeting an elder.

3. .... some of an elephant's rumble vocalizations may not be detectable to a human, elephants can communicate a great deal of information seismically.

4. Hormonal suppression has been studied in some mammals, including baboons and African wild dogs .... there is not yet enough evidence to support it in elephants.

5. At times a matriarch will consult with other older females within her family to assess the risk of a situation .... being the leader.

6. The elephant is a social animal .... if resources are scarce, there may be intolerance of certain low-ranking females, which may result in their displacement.

7. .... a younger matriarch who may not have an expansive knowledge repository, an older matriarch will use her experience to her group's reproductive and survival advantage.

8. Being born into an elephant herd has considerable benefits for a calf .... its survival may depend on the rank of its mother.

IDENTIFYING THE LANGUAGE OF PARTS AND WHOLES

B. Read each sentence. Follow these steps:

- Find and write the subject.
- Circle *Part* or *Whole*.
- Then write the verb phrase that signals part or whole.

> **TIP**
>
> Certain nouns in English represent parts, others represent wholes. Examples of parts nouns include *father, students,* and *elephant.* Examples of whole nouns include *family, class,* and *herd.*
>
> For help with identifying the language of parts and wholes, go to MyEnglishLab, Zoology, Part 2, Language Skill.

1. The elephant family was composed of 40 animals: 33 adult females and 7 juvenile males.

   The elephant family   Part / (Whole)   Verb phrase: *was composed of*

2. The seven juvenile males who were part of the herd were younger than ten years old.

   ....   Part / Whole   Verb phrase: ....

3. The matriarch, who was part of the family, had been the leader of the group for over 15 years.

   ....   Part / Whole   Verb phrase: ....

4. Elephant communication consists of a variety of acoustic, visual, olfactory, and tactile cues.

   ....   Part / Whole   Verb phrase: ....

5. An extended elephant family is made up of subunits of smaller groups, each headed by a matriarch.

   ....   Part / Whole   Verb phrase: ....

6. Rumble vocalizations, which are part of the acoustic communication of elephants, may sometimes be undetectable to the human ear.

   ....   Part / Whole   Verb phrase: ....

⊙ Go to MyEnglishLab for more practice reading an extended text and using your reading skills.

PAIR PRESENTATION

A. RESEARCH   Elephants organize themselves in family groups led by a matriarch. With a partner, research other animals that live in a matriarchal society. Then research patriarchal societies—what are some animals with that social structure?

B. FOCUS   Imagine that you and your partner have been asked to create a short (5–7 minutes) "documentary" about your findings. Discuss your research. Choose two animals that you researched. Compare and contrast their social structures. Argue why one structure is better than the other. Film your documentary.

C. PRESENT   Present your documentary. Take questions from the audience. Support your position.

D. DISCUSS   After the presentations, have a class discussion about the similarities and differences, and pros and cons, of matriarchal and patriarchal societies.

🔊 Go to MyEnglishLab to complete a collaborative activity.

The past is full of new discoveries

HISTORY

Changing History

UNIT PROFILE

In this unit, you will read about accidental and purposeful archaeological discoveries—specifically, the Rosetta Stone and the ruins at Pompeii. You will also read about the intentional discoveries of the cities of Nineveh and Akrotiri.

You will research Egyptian and Roman cultures around the beginning of the 1st century and present on an aspect of life during this time.

EXTENDED READING

BEFORE YOU READ

Think about these questions before you read the essay "Changing History by Accident: How Accidents Can Uncover Important Archaeological Finds." Discuss them with another student.

1. What do you think determines where archaeologists plan a dig? Once at the dig site, what do you think archaeologists need to do to find artifacts and document their recovery?

2. How is history learned? How is the field of history different from that of archaeology? What is the relationship between the two fields?

3. The essay discusses the discovery of the Rosetta Stone and the ruins at Pompeii. What do you already know about those two archaeological discoveries? Why are they considered important?

READ

Read and annotate Paragraphs 1–3. Use the timeline that follows to write dates and events. Then answer the questions in Check What You've Learned.

> **TIP**
>
> As you read, don't stop to look up words. Instead guess their meaning from context. To be sure you are understanding and remembering the information, take your time. Notice keywords and take clear notes.

For more about increasing smoothness and pace, see History, Part 1, Skill 1, page 87.

Changing History by Accident: How Accidents Can Uncover Important Archaeological Finds

by Dr. Patrick N. Hunt

1 How many important archaeological discoveries have been accidental? The basic answer is that accidental discovery happens fairly frequently, especially in the early stages of archaeology. Archaeology is the systematic study of the remains of the past and is a fairly young discipline, only developed within the last few centuries. This new approach to antiquity was because new historians began to look underneath their feet instead of only in books and texts. Thus, typical approaches to history can be divided into two main searches: first textual and then material. And the process has evolved in that order. Because some of the earliest important discoveries predate the actual formal discipline, it is only reasonable that quite a few of these discoveries were accidental.

2 Early on around 1700, the word *archaeologia* only meant "old words and texts." But by the end of the 18ᵗʰ century and the beginning of the 19ᵗʰ century, *archaeology* had changed to include the study of materials, otherwise known as *artifacts*.

(Continued)

These were the fragmentary remnants of the past surviving in ancient remains like architectural structures, pottery, and other objects, large and small. These fragmentary remnants of the past were often buried under modern civilizations where they were mostly invisible. Samuel Johnson, compiler of the first *Dictionary of the English Language* in 1755, summarized the first approach of textual history. He said that "all we know about the past we know from books." But subsequent archaeological remains have made this idea obsolete since so many archaeological discoveries proliferated after Samuel Johnson, many of them accidental.

3 How archaeological discoveries actually happen can be divided into two main categories: accidental and purposeful. Regardless of the cultures and when ancient people flourished in those cultures, many important discoveries have been made accidentally by amateurs not looking for anything archaeological or historical. Instead, their activities while farming, digging trenches, moving stones, or doing like enterprises have uncovered vital information, which they may not have even understood. Accidental archaeological discovery will also likely continue into the future as more and more of the Earth's surface is disturbed. Two early important archaeological discoveries that were found by accident have had immense ramifications for history. They are known today as the Rosetta Stone and the ruins of Pompeii, and they greatly changed perceptions and processes of historical recovery.

CULTURE NOTE

The *Dictionary of the English Language* contained 40,000 words and took eight years for Samuel Johnson and six helpers to complete. It was the first English dictionary that defined words and also provided quotations from other works that showed the use of each word. Although best known for his work on the dictionary, Johnson also wrote poems and essays, and published a collection of Shakespeare's plays.

Glossary

Antiquity: ancient times

Remnant: a small remaining piece of something

Obsolete: outdated, no longer useful

Proliferate: to increase quickly

Flourish: to grow and be very successful

Amateur: a person who does something as a hobby not as a profession

Ramification: consequence or result

Perception: how people see or think about something

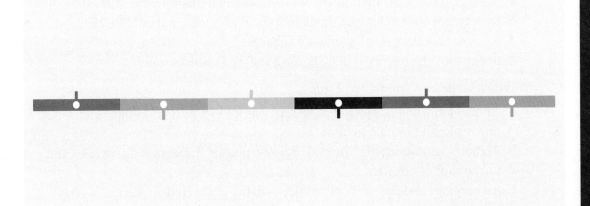

CHECK WHAT YOU'VE LEARNED

PARAGRAPHS 1–3

A. Think about the section you just read and refer to your notes. Answer these questions.

TIP

Try to answer the questions without looking back at the reading.

For more about developing accuracy, see History, Part 1, Skill 2, page 93.

1. In Paragraph 1, Sentence 2 suggests that many archaeological discoveries _____ .

   a. are the result of many years of careful study

   b. are not significant

   c. involve a systematic study of relics

   d. are accidental

2. In Sentence 3 of Paragraph 1, how does the author explain the idea of archaeology?

   a. by giving an example

   b. by giving a synonym

   c. by giving a definition

   d. by giving an antonym

3. What does the author mean by "typical approaches to history can be divided into two main searches: first textual and then material"?

   a. Students can study history from books and then go to museums to look at artifacts (materials).

   b. Archaeologists no longer do research before they begin a dig.

   c. Understanding history is a two-step process: reading and then looking for related artifacts.

   d. History can best be learned from reading books and looking at the materials used to make up those books.

4. Why does the author mention Samuel Johnson?

    a. to support the point that history was once learned mainly by textual information

    b. to persuade the reader that the definition of *archaeology* should be changed

    c. to show how the meaning of words changes

    d. to examine the history of the *Dictionary of the English Language*

5. Which is the best summary of this section?

    a. Samuel Johnson once said that history was known only by books. Archaeology now makes it possible to know more.

    b. Archaeology can best be divided into two phases: accidental discoveries and purposeful discoveries.

    c. Archaeology and the study of artifacts—many uncovered accidentally—has helped to expand our understanding of history, once known only through books.

    d. Artifacts are often first discovered accidentally by people who are working in their fields.

B. Read the section again. Check your answers and add details to your notes. Then continue to the next section.

"CHANGING HISTORY BY ACCIDENT," *CONTINUED*
PARAGRAPHS 4–6

Read, annotate, and use a timeline or other organizer to take notes.

> **TIP**
>
> Create your own graphic organizer or find one online by searching for "graphic organizer" or a specific kind, such as "timeline."

4 First, the Rosetta Stone was uncovered accidentally in 1799 by a French officer looking to rebuild a harbor fort on the Nile. Because the Napoleonic War was unfolding in the Mediterranean, the British Navy planned to blockade French forces around the mouths of the Nile. One French engineering officer, Lieutenant Pierre-François Xavier Bouchard, was digging up and reusing old stones around the ancient port in order to build up defenses against the British forces, especially at Fort St. Julien near Rashid (then called Rosetta). Many stones were left over from ruined Egyptian buildings that surrounded the area several thousand years earlier. Some were broken into fragments and others were almost complete blocks.

5   Bouchard knew that the old stones were already shaped and carved for prior use, eliminating the need to carve all new stone. In the process of digging, Bouchard found one particular stone—dark gray, shaped, and partly broken. This one—now famously named the Rosetta Stone—was carved flat on two sides but missing about a third at the top. When his workers prized the stone out of the earth and turned it over, Bouchard suddenly noticed an unusual inscription on the side now facing up: a text that was virtually buried for millennia and therefore unreadable until then. He knew this stone could be very important because it was written in three different scripts. While no one at the time could decipher and read Egyptian hieroglyphs, Bouchard observed that the top one of the three texts was that exact ancient hieroglyph language. With engineering training that included the use of mathematical symbols derived from Greek letters, Bouchard also observed that the bottom text was in ancient Greek. He recognized none of the letters of the middle text (which later turned out to be a sort of cursive shorthand of hieroglyphs called Demotic). But his question was brilliantly logical: What if the three texts all said the same thing? Bouchard brought the stone to Cairo where it became a sensation around the world to scholars and laypersons alike.

6   After only two decades of painstaking decipherment by competing linguists— including the British polymath scholar Thomas Young (1773–1829), who was also a mathematician and scientist, and the French scholar Jean-François Champollion (1790–1832)—it turned out that Bouchard was exactly right. Scholars used the Ptolemaic Greek—a language dating to around 300 BCE, when Greeks ruled Egypt and their scribes had to be bilingual—to help decode the ancient Egyptian hieroglyphs at the top, which repeated the ancient Greek text at the bottom. In the Greek text, Young recognized Egyptian hieroglyph cartouches (inscribed ellipses) that set apart and enclosed royal Greco-Egyptian names like *Ptolemy* and *Cleopatra*. These two names alone shared enough common consonants and vowels (*p, t, l, o, e*) in the right order to test Young's hypothesis. By employing critical thinking and problem solving from his mathematical training, Young could then hypothesize about the other letters (*c, m, a*). Champollion soon built on Young's Greco-Egyptian name observations. He had the advantage of being able to read the language of Coptic, which had preserved these ancient Egyptian words in the modified Greek letters of the Coptic alphabet. Linguists still use this template of working from known to unknown languages to decode ancient writing systems. Bouchard may have been an intelligent amateur who made a discovery by accident, but the Rosetta Stone is one of the most important historical discoveries ever made. One of the ironic discovery questions we can ask is: What would have happened if nobody had noticed the text or if it hadn't landed face-up? There are only a few triple inscriptions surviving in all of Egypt, and the other main one was found around a century later. We can only guess how long such an oversight would have delayed decipherment of Egyptian hieroglyphs.

Glossary

Unfold: to happen slowly

Blockade: (v) to stop or block

Mouth: where one body of water spills into another body of water

Prize: (v) to extract, using a level

Decipherment: the process of figuring out the meaning of something

Polymath: a person with a lot of knowledge on many subjects

Decode: to figure out the meaning of a message

Face-up: with the front looking toward the sky

TIP

Academic essays are full of advanced language. When you see a word you don't recognize, look at the context (the surrounding words, phrases, and sentences) to try to understand the meaning. Also use logic and your knowledge of word parts to guess the meaning.

For more about finding definitions and explanations, see History, Part 2, Skill 1, page 227.

CHECK WHAT YOU'VE LEARNED

PARAGRAPHS 4–6

A. Think about the section you just read and refer to your notes. Answer these questions.

6. Why is Lieutenant Pierre-François Xavier Bouchard an important figure in archaeology?

7. What three languages were written on the Rosetta Stone?

8. How would you define *laypersons*, based on the context at the end of Paragraph 5? What type of context clue does the text provide? (definition, synonym, contrast / antonym, example, logic)

9. How do you think being a mathematician helped Thomas Young decipher hieroglyphs?

10. Why is the Rosetta Stone one of the most important historical discoveries ever made?

....

....

B. Read the section again. Check your answers and add details to your notes. Then continue to the next section.

"CHANGING HISTORY BY ACCIDENT," *CONTINUED*
PARAGRAPHS 7–11

Read, annotate, and use a timeline or other organizer to take notes.

7 Pompeii was a Roman city, buried and forgotten after the volcanic Mount Vesuvius erupted in 79 CE. The city was discovered accidentally around 1750 by farmers who had gradually moved back into the region, which had been completely covered by volcanic debris even earlier—around 1800 BCE. We can only imagine how surprised the farmers were

when they dug down and found giant heads and bodies of marble. Most of Pompeii had been deeply buried under around 25 feet of ash and volcanic debris. While digging wells and basements in this rich soil of the old volcanic landscape above ancient Pompeii, the farmers also found other large sculptures and intact treasures, often a few meters under the surface. The locals were not alone in realizing that these objects could be valuable. After learning of the discovery, the Bourbon King of Naples began systematic searches of the area. He hired engineers and teams of workers to bring more objects to light. Soon, the king's filling of his palace with excavated objects caught the attention of the world.

(Continued)

8 Trained archaeologists excavated Pompeii over the next century and a half as the discipline of archaeology formally took over such sites and improved techniques were pioneered. One of the most fascinating yet macabre discoveries at Pompeii went unnoticed for decades until a keen observer realized that some of the hollow spaces near the original ground level looked familiar. It turned out they were almost exact "negatives" of human bodies. One archaeologist had the idea of filling them with fluid gypsum, or plaster of Paris, and then digging around them. The result: The whole shape of humans and even dogs could be "seen" at their moment of death.

9 Ultimately, the best Roman wall paintings in the entire Roman world came out of Pompeii and are our most complete examples of Roman art to date. They are now described as four distinct Pompeiian styles, based on dates and different clues about their stylistic differences found in Pompeii. One of the interesting last styles of Roman wall painting can even be dated to the earthquake of 63 CE, when many Pompeiian structures were rebuilt and repainted in a new phase. Additionally, much of what is known about Roman villas and houses also derives from surviving Pompeiian house foundations and walls with divided rooms and courts. We can apply names to those Roman room types based on Latin texts like Vitruvius's *De Architectura* and other literature, contemporary writing that explains how the Romans built at Pompeii, just as Vitruvius describes. There are whole blocks of neighborhoods at Pompeii called *insulae*, translatable from Latin as "islands" surrounded by paved roads. The roads are generally constructed out of blocks of basalt lava and are slightly raised in the middle with a "camber" so that water flows down the roadside edges bordered by ancient sidewalks. While there were no street signs, the districts were divided with recognizable landmarks and distinct fountains often in the middle of cross-streets, and many of the Roman houses were fronted with shops. From an urban city center called the Forum—the hub of commercial, administrative, legal, and religious activity—there were two main opposing streets that joined near the Forum. One main street was called the *Cardo Maximus*, running north to south. Its opposing main street was the *Decumanus Maximus*, running east to west. We can imagine that visitors to Pompeii looking for a particular house in a known district might have been instructed something like this, by a local: "Head north toward Vesuvius down the Cardo Maximus. After the Forum, pass six corners, then look for the wine shop just around the corner from the lion fountain, and count down four doors. The one with the fish mosaic in front is the House of Sextus."

10 Because modern farms and houses still surround portions of Pompeii, it has not yet been fully excavated. Archaeologists and historians think about 25,000 people lived in Pompeii, based on the number and size of the houses and projections about other residences within the known walls. A rule of thumb is to count the average two-level urban house as having around 10 residents. In a wealthy city like Pompeii, there would be parents, children, an elder or two, plus other relatives and possibly a few servants. If there are around 2,500 houses of varying size at Pompeii (averaging

in villas and smaller domiciles at both ends), it is not difficult to extrapolate such a population. While caution must qualify this assumption, things like contemporary texts, the volume of trade in and out of the adjacent port, tax records, and census records all support this demographic estimate of Pompeii. We can only imagine the terror and confusion of trying to escape Pompeii during the eruption of Vesuvius over several days. The sky was darkened with ash, and rocks would have been falling everywhere in every size. This is exactly how Pliny the Younger describes the eruption in his letters. Many locals thought it was the end of the world. Sadly, their misfortune turns out to be our fortune by providing so much information about an ancient city and how its people lived—and in some instances died—in 79 CE in a fairly sudden cataclysmic event.

11 In conclusion, both the Rosetta Stone and Pompeii are keys to understanding ancient cultures in ways never before imagined. Ancient Egyptian hieroglyphs could finally be deciphered after a hiatus of more than a thousand years because of the discovery and decipherment of the Rosetta Stone. Roman material culture could be fleshed out in great detail as thousands of daily objects came to light within their proper contexts—showing where and how these objects were used by Romans. Thus, accidental discovery in both cases has yielded enormous results for archaeology and has changed history dramatically for understanding those ancient cultures of Egypt and Rome. In these specific cases, the discoveries have also enormously changed the pioneering process of archaeology itself as a new discipline and the methods of how we attempt to recover the past.

CULTURE NOTE

Pliny the Younger (61–113 CE) was born into an aristocratic family during the Roman Empire. He wrote extensively—in the form of letters—about a variety of topics. He and his uncle, Pliny the Elder, both witnessed the explosion of Vesuvius in 79 CE, but his uncle did not survive. Pliny the Younger's letters, two of which describe the event, are rich in detail, capturing the explosion and providing an extensive picture of life at that time.

Glossary

Erupt: to explode

Debris: pieces of material after an explosion

Bring to light: to make known

Excavated: (adj) dug up from the earth

Site: a place where something important or interesting happened

Urban: related to a city

Extrapolate: to conclude something based on facts

Cataclysmic: violent, sudden, and destructive

Hiatus: a break in time

Yield: (v) to produce, result in

CHECK WHAT YOU'VE LEARNED

PARAGRAPHS 7–11

TIP

Every discipline—history, economics, physics, engineering, computer science—has vocabulary specific to itself. To understand specialized terms, use context clues, marginal glosses, footnotes, and your dictionary.

For more about dealing with specialized vocabulary, see History, Part 2, Skill 2, page 234.

A. Think about the section you just read and refer to your notes. Answer these questions.

11. In Paragraph 7, what can be inferred about the "giant heads and bodies of marble" that the farmers found?

    a. They were bodies of ancient Pompeiians.
    b. They were the remains of giants made out of stone.
    c. They were oversized statues.
    d. They were large marbles.

12. From the description of the neighborhoods and streets in Paragraph 9, it is evident that _____ .

    a. city planning did not exist in ancient Pompeiian times
    b. ancient roads were often impassable because of flooding
    c. people often got lost because of the absence of street signs
    d. ancient Pompeiians were skilled engineers and builders

13. Why was the Forum an important part of Pompeiian city life?

    a. It was the area for shopping.
    b. It contained government offices.
    c. It was a place for religious worship.
    d. all of the above

14. From the first sentence of Paragraph 10, we can infer that present-day inhabitants of the area around Pompeii _____ .

    a. may not support excavation because it would ruin their homes
    b. would welcome an archaeological dig
    c. believe that enough ancient Pompeiian artifacts have been discovered
    d. dislike the field of archaeology

15. What is the best meaning for the word *domiciles* in Paragraph 10?

    a. servants
    b. homes
    c. palaces
    d. addresses

B. Read the section again. Check your answers and add details to your notes.

C. Using your notes, write a 100-word response to the following question, an online discussion prompt. After you have written your first draft, review it against the checklist. Then exchange responses with a classmate and comment on his or her response. In your comment, be sure to state whether you agree or disagree and explain why.

For more about responding in an online forum, see History, Part 2, Integrated Skills, page 240.

Question: The author outlines the discoveries of the Rosetta Stone and the ruins at Pompeii. In your opinion, which one is more historically significant? Use evidence from the essay as well as your own opinion to support your answer.

- ☐ I identified the question type as ....
- ☐ I used academic English.
- ☐ My tone is polite.
- ☐ I checked for grammar, punctuation, and spelling.
- ☐ I supported my opinion and cited the source.
- ☐ My ideas relate to the question.
- ☐ My ideas are clear and concise.
- ☐ This represents what I believe.

THINKING CRITICALLY

Look back at your notes and answers in Check What You've Learned. Answer these questions.

1. In the essay the author explains that approaches to history can be divided into two main searches: textual and material. First, explain those two approaches and then compare those two ways of studying history. What are the advantages and disadvantages of each one? Explain.

2. Using the Rosetta Stone and ruins at Pompeii as examples, explain how accidental discoveries occur and then hypothesize how purposeful discoveries happen.

3. How does the author view the explosion of Mount Vesuvius as it relates to the field of archaeology? What textual evidence expresses his point of view?

⬆ Go to MyEnglishLab to complete a critical thinking activity.

THINKING VISUALLY

A. Look at the map of Pompeii, 79 CE. What can you say about life in Pompeii at that time?

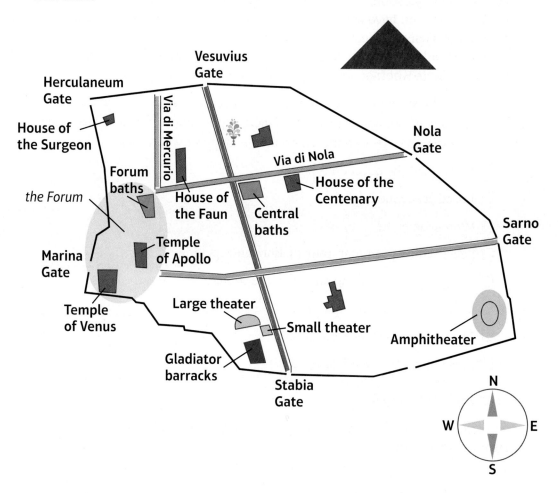

B. Using information from Paragraph 9, label the map with the places from the box. Then imagine you have to give the map to the person looking for the House of Sextus, as mentioned in the text. Identify the House of Sextus and put an X on it.

Mount Vesuvius	Cardo Maximus	Decumanus Maximus

THINKING ABOUT LANGUAGE
IDENTIFYING THOUGHT GROUPS

A. Read the excerpt from the reading "Changing History by Accident." Then read it aloud to a partner. Pause briefly at each single slash (/). Pause longer at each double slash (//).

How archaeological discoveries actually happen / can be divided / into two main categories // accidental and purposeful // Regardless of the cultures and when ancient people flourished / in those cultures / many important discoveries / have been made accidentally / by amateurs / not looking for anything / archaeological or historical // Instead their activities while farming / digging trenches / moving stones / or doing like enterprises / have uncovered vital information / which they may not have even understood // Accidental archaeological discovery / will also likely continue / into the future / as more and more / of the Earth's surface / is disturbed // Two early important archaeological discoveries / that were found by accident / had immense ramifications for history // They are known today / as the Rosetta Stone / and the ruins of Pompeii / and they greatly changed perceptions / and processes / of historical recovery //

DEMONSTRATING CIVIL DISCOURSE ONLINE

B. Read the online discussion question. Then read the responses on the next page. Check (✓) the responses that use civil discourse.

Question: In the essay, the author writes, "Because modern farms and houses still surround portions of Pompeii, it has not yet been fully excavated." Do you think that the Italian government should force these people to move by taking over their land by eminent domain (government takeover of private property for public use) so that archaeologists can continue excavating those lands and learn more about the history of ancient Romans? Explain.

1. ☐ **Italia4eva:** 6 hours ago

No way!!! I'd tell the government "HANDS OFF!" my land if they tried to take it. There's already enough old stuff from Pompeii to look at … what else do we need to learn about that time?? GO TO A MUSEUM, already.

[like] [comment]

2. ☐ **Pompeii79:** 6 hours ago

Although I wouldn't recommend the Italian government taking over anybody's land by eminent domain, I think it should offer those owners a considerable amount of money for their land and explain the historical significance of what may be underneath their property.

[like] [comment]

3. ☐ **HistoryRocks:** 5 hours ago

Italia4eva needs to chill out and check her keyboard … it seems like her CAPS key got stuck when she was writing her post. I think the Italian government is within its right to take over those lands by eminent domain if it wants to expand our knowledge of history, which will benefit the world, and not just an individual.

[like] [comment]

4. ☐ **RomaRules:** 4 hours ago

This is a tricky question. On one hand, I, personally, would be curious if I owned that land to know if anything from ancient Pompeii was buried under my property; however, if my house, which I had lived in for many years, was directly over the ground in question, I wouldn't want to destroy my house or have to move. Perhaps there is technology, like some sort of radar, that could detect if anything is buried underneath, and if so, then I'd allow the government to buy the land, at a fair cost, as long as it's guaranteed that I could still live nearby.

[like] [comment]

○ **Go to MyEnglishLab for more practice reading an extended text and using your reading skills.**

PANEL DISCUSSION

A. **RESEARCH** The author describes two main accidental archaeological discoveries: the Rosetta Stone from the Ptolemaic dynasty of Egypt, 196 BCE and the ruins at Pompeii from the Roman Empire, 79 CE. With a small group, research one of those eras to find out more about life at that time.

B. **FOCUS** Imagine that you have been asked to hold a panel discussion before a student audience interested in archaeology. From the era you researched, choose one part of life to focus on: language, gender roles, social class, employment, entertainment, religious beliefs, etc. Do further research as needed.

C. **PRESENT** Prepare and participate in the panel discussion. Include visuals and other aids, such as handouts or artifacts, to help explain your ideas to the audience. Invite and answer questions.

D. **DISCUSS** After the presentations, have a class discussion. Compare and contrast the people and the history of the time period between 200 BCE and 80 CE. Was information about one group more complete than information about the other? If so, why?

⊙ Go to MyEnglishLab to complete a collaborative activity.

CHEMICAL ENGINEERING

Chemical Connections

UNIT PROFILE

In this unit, you will read about why a candle's flame flickers (moves) and how this can explain actions like lake flow and continental drift. You will also learn about molecular behavior and its application in modern design.

You will research how gravity affects things like snow, soil, and magma, and present your findings.

EXTENDED READING

BEFORE YOU READ

Think about these questions before you read the essay "Physics of Scale: How Are Candle Flames, Lake Flow, and Continental Drift Related?" Discuss them with another student.

1. What do you think causes a candle's flame to flicker (move) or water in a lake to move from the surface to the bottom (lake flow)?

2. What do you think happens to water when the air temperature changes? For example, when the season changes from winter to spring, what happens to a lake?

3. Consider the example above, about the seasons and the lake. Did the example help you answer the question? What can a professor or writer do to help explain a complex topic? What can a student or reader do to better understand it?

READ

Read and annotate Paragraphs 1–4. Use the process diagram that follows to explain what causes the candle's flame to flicker. Then answer the questions in Check What You've Learned.

> **TIP**
>
> An **effect** is the result of an action. The action or circumstance that led to that result is the **cause**. Look for cause-and-effect signals. They will help you to recognize that two events are related and understand how one action made another happen.

For more about identifying cause and effect, see Chemical Engineering, Part 1, Skill 1, page 117.

Physics of Scale: How Are Candle Flames, Lake Flow, and Continental Drift Related?

by Professor Andrew Spakowitz

1   Our everyday experiences offer us innumerable opportunities to observe how physical forces lead to unexpected and intriguing phenomena. The foundational principles that govern our physical world are developed to a point where we are able to establish connections between seemingly disparate observations. Such connections serve to strengthen our fundamental understanding of nature and provide a roadmap for predicting the behavior in other areas where our basic understanding has not been established. In this regard, there is value in stepping away from those problems that have immediate or personal significance to consider the range of related problems that may inform us of basic governing principles.

(Continued)

2 While watching a candle flame, for example, you may be mesmerized by the natural beauty of the glow and the dancing flicker of the flame. Upon closer inspection, you may notice that the air within the flame forms a smooth jet near the wick, and farther above the wick, the flow pattern breaks down into a chaotic, swirling pattern that causes the flame to flicker. The air rises above the flame. You can move your hand next to it without being burned, but placing your hand above would be painful. Tilting the candle leads to the flame reorienting itself in the direction away from the floor.

3 All of these observations point to physical principles that are responsible for the behavior of the candle. The fact that the flame always orients away from the floor and that the hot air rises above the flame suggests that gravity is a critical contributor. You are probably familiar with the experience of pushing a ball below the surface  of pool water, leading to the ball pushing back against your hand. The air within the ball has a lower density (or mass per volume of the ball) than the water in the pool. Therefore, the gravitational force on the air is smaller than the force on the water. Since the ball is displacing the water, there is a net physical force that drives the ball upward to replace the volume of air with water. This same effect causes a hot-air balloon to rise, but in this case, the higher temperature air within the balloon has a lower density than the cooler air surrounding the balloon.

4 A candle flame heats up the air near the wick, which reduces the density of that air relative to the density of the surrounding air. In this regard, the candle flame is akin to a hot-air balloon without the balloon. The hot air in the flame rises, and cooler air above and to the sides of the flame circulates downward and back into the flame. This spontaneous flow pattern results in the hot air that rises being replenished with cooler air, and the candle continues to burn.

Glossary

Phenomenon: something that happens or exists, especially something that is unusual or difficult to understand

Disparate: different, varied

Flame: a bright moving yellow or orange light that you see when something is burning

Glow: (n) a soft, warm light

Wick: the string in a candle that you light

Tilt: (v) to turn at an angle

Reorient: to change direction

Gravity: the force that makes objects fall to the ground

Density: the relationship between an object's weight and the amount of space it fills

Displace: to force something out of its place

Circulate: to move around within a system

Spontaneous: happening without planning, by itself

Replenish: to resupply

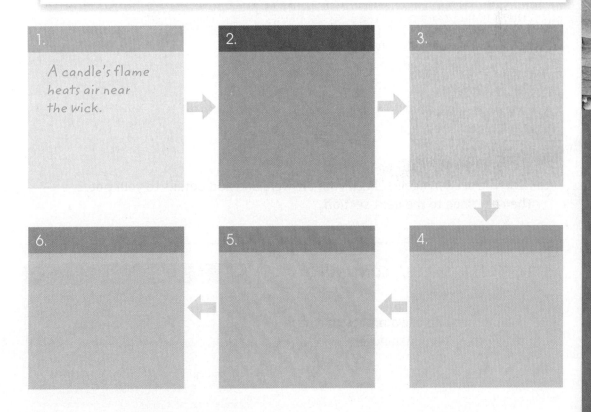

1.

A candle's flame heats air near the wick.

2.

3.

6.

5.

4.

CHECK WHAT YOU'VE LEARNED
PARAGRAPHS 1–4

A. Think about the section you just read and refer to your notes. Answer these questions.

1. What causes a candle flame to flicker?

   a. a person blowing on it
   b. the air flow around the candle
   c. the density of the candle
   d. the pull of gravity on the wick

2. The author's example of _____ shows gravity's role in the behavior of a flame.

   a. a ball in a pool
   b. a hot-air balloon
   c. a tilted candle
   d. a hand near a hot flame

3. The air just above a candle flame has _____ than the air around the flame.

   a. less density
   b. lower temperature
   c. less air flow
   d. more mass

> **TIP**
>
> Examples help writers explain ideas—especially difficult ones. Look for phrases like *for example, you are probably familiar with the experience of,* and *is akin to* to find helpful examples in this essay.

> For more about examining examples, see Chemical Engineering, Part 1, Skill 2, page 123.

B. Read the section again. Check your answers and add details to your notes. Then continue to the next section.

"PHYSICS OF SCALE," *CONTINUED*
PARAGRAPHS 5–7

Read, annotate, and use a process diagram or other organizer to take notes.

> **TIP**
>
> Create your own graphic organizer or find one online by searching for "graphic organizer" or a specific kind, such as "process diagram." As you read, continue to add to your notes or graphic organizer. For example, in this section, add details to your organizer about what makes a candle's flame flicker.

5 Many fluid-flow problems are governed by two physical effects that influence the behavior of the flow and the patterns that are formed. *Friction* is the resistance that arises when a surface of a material rubs against the surface of another material. Fluids also experience friction in flow when fluid regions are moving at a speed different from that of neighboring regions, causing these fluid regions to effectively rub against each other. The strength of friction in a fluid is measured by the viscosity. Fluids with large viscosity, such as honey, exhibit a large resistance to flow due to friction, and their flow is typically very sluggish in comparison to less viscous fluids such as air. *Inertia* is the force associated with accelerating or decelerating an object while moving it from one position to another. This is the force that you experience in a car when you slam on the brakes, carrying you forward as the car decelerates to a stop. Fluids also experience inertial forces as they accelerate from a resting state to a flowing state, and vice versa. As in a decelerating car, fluid elements in motion experience inertial forces that resist their deceleration.

6 The jet of heated air within a candle flame accelerates at the bottom of the flame, rises through and above the flame, and then decelerates far above the flame as the temperature reduces back to its ambient value. The inertial forces acting on the fluid above the flame tend to carry the fluid upward with the fluid momentum, and at some point above the flame, the additive contribution from the inertial forces dominate the  flow behavior over the frictional forces. At that position above the flame, the air flow begins to exhibit a chaotic behavior that is called *turbulence*. Note, this is not the same as turbulence in an airplane, which is so-named from the chaotic motion of the plane and not the chaotic motion of the air itself. The chaotic eddies from turbulent motion cause the flame to randomly dance or flicker. Air, which has a very low viscosity, tends to exhibit turbulent motion more readily than more viscous fluids, since turbulence is caused by inertial forces and resisted by frictional forces.

(Continued)

7 The candle flame is a valuable example of a system that exhibits buoyancy-driven flow or flow that is driven by differences in density in a gravitational field. The basic physical principles discussed in the previous paragraphs are also relevant to other important examples of buoyancy-driven flow, and identifying the dominant mechanisms for flow in a candle is essential to predicting behavior in other systems. The water in a lake undergoes seasonal changes in temperature. A lake that is located in a climate with subfreezing temperatures in the winter freezes in the winter and thaws in the spring. As the ice thaws in the spring, the lake undergoes a process called *lake turnover*, where warmer water at the lake surface spontaneously exchanges with colder water at the bottom of the lake. This process is essential to the ecosystem in the lake, as the surface water contains oxygen that replenishes the depleted oxygen at the lake bottom. Lake turnover is an example of buoyancy-driven flow.

Glossary

Fluid flow: a liquid moving in a smooth steady way

Influence: (v) to change how something acts

Viscosity: how thick a liquid is

Sluggish: slow moving

Accelerate: to go faster

Resist: to fight against

Eddy: a circular movement of air or water

CHECK WHAT YOU'VE LEARNED
PARAGRAPHS 5–7

A. Think about the section you just read and refer to your notes.
   Answer these questions.

4. What are the two physical effects that influence the behavior of flow?

   ....

5. What is friction?

   ....

   ....

6. In your own words, explain viscosity. What example does the author give of a fluid with large viscosity?

   ....

   ....

7. What is buoyancy-driven flow? What example does the author use to explain it?

....

....

8. Why is lake turnover important?

....

....

B. Read the section again. Check your answers and add details to your notes. Then continue to the next section.

"PHYSICS OF SCALE,"
CONTINUED

PARAGRAPHS 8–10

Read, annotate, and use a process diagram or other organizer to take notes.

TIP

To describe a process, writers explain it in steps. Look for words of time or sequence (*after, eventually, first, finally, then*) and space (*above, below, beside, on top, under*) to follow a description. In this section, focus on the process that causes lake flow.

For more about analyzing time and space descriptions, see Chemical Engineering, Part 2, Skill 1, page 259.

---

8 Water is a very complex substance. Perhaps this is a surprising statement. Water is pervasive in our everyday experience, and since water is flavorless and odorless, we frequently consider water to be very plain and mundane. However, scientists have spent and will continue to spend their entire careers studying the physical properties of water in a variety of settings.

9 One example of a curious property of water is the complex relationship between temperature and density. Unlike air, which expands with increasing temperature, water exhibits a narrow range of temperatures (between 0°C and 4°C at atmospheric pressure) where it actually contracts with increasing temperature. This contraction leads to a larger density with increasing temperature in this narrow range. The molecular-level cause of this behavior lies in the fact that water molecules form hydrogen-bonded networks that push the molecules apart. Increasing the temperature leads to more disorder in the water, and the hydrogen-bonded network is weakened to allow the water molecules to rotate and translate more freely. As the network breaks apart, the water contracts slightly, leading to larger densities.

(Continued)

10 Water at the lake surface in the spring heats up to temperatures slightly above the freezing point of water (0°C), and this warmer water is more dense than the water at the bottom of the lake. Thus, the heavier water on the surface experiences a larger gravitational force than the water at the lake bottom, and the lake water will turn over.

Since water is much more viscous than air, the flow behavior is much more sluggish than the flow in a candle flame and is more difficult to directly see at timescales of observation. Nonetheless, the basic driving forces involved in the flow patterns around a candle flame govern the spontaneous turnover of lake water in the spring.

Glossary

Complex: (adj) with lots of details or parts
Pervasive: found everywhere
Odorless: without smell
Mundane: plain, boring
Curious: interesting and unusual
Rotate: to turn, spin
Contract: (v) to get smaller and usually denser

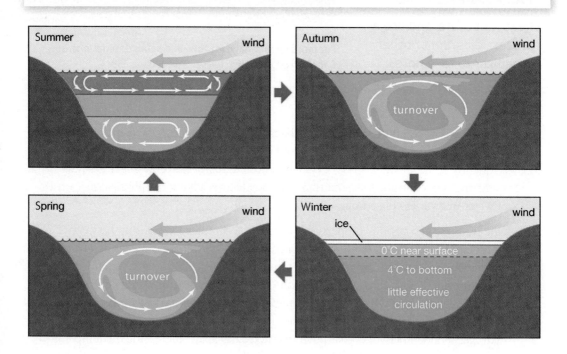

CHECK WHAT YOU'VE LEARNED
PARAGRAPHS 8–10

A. Think about the section you just read and refer to your notes. Answer these questions.

9. Between 0°C and 4°C, with increasing temperature, how do air and water behave?

   a. Both expand.

   b. Both contract.

   c. Air expands and water contracts.

   d. Air contracts and water expands.

10. In the example in Paragraph 9, what's "curious" about water's behavior as the temperature rises?

    a. It contracts.

    b. It becomes less dense.

    c. It melts.

    d. It turns to ice.

11. Which best explains why lake water turnover occurs?

    a. Cooler water is denser than warmer water, so the gravitational force is stronger on cooler water.

    b. Water at the surface is less dense than water at the bottom and is affected more by gravity.

    c. Water is more viscous than air and therefore flows more slowly.

    d. The gravitational force on warm water is greater than the force on cold water.

12. According to the essay, why is it more difficult to observe flow behavior in a lake than in a candle flame?

    a. because water is less viscous than air

    b. because water is more viscous than air

    c. because flow behavior in a candle is more sluggish

    d. because flow behavior in a candle is easier to measure

B. Read the section again. Check your answers and add details to your notes. Then continue to the next section.

"PHYSICS OF SCALE,"
CONTINUED

PARAGRAPHS 11–13

Read, annotate, and use a process diagram or other organizer to take notes.

TIP

When describing a process, a writer will usually explain the conditions that are necessary for something to occur. Look for signals like *If …* , *then* and *as long as*. Notice other conditional sentence structures. In this section, focus on the conditions that cause continental drift to occur.

For more about conditions, see Chemical Engineering, Part 2, Skill 2, page 266.

11 Earth's mantle lies between the surface crust and the core. Earth's core maintains a very high temperature due to nuclear reactions that occur within the core, and the temperature of the magma within the mantle gradually varies from the high temperature of the outer core region to the cooler temperature of the crust. The density of the magma is higher at the lower temperature, leading to larger gravitational forces on magma that is further from the core. As in a candle flame and in a lake during the spring, the magma will spontaneously flow from the upper mantle toward the core, and less dense magma near the core flows toward the crust. The resulting flow within Earth's mantle exerts forces on plates within the crust of Earth, and motion of the plates is dictated by the flow patterns of the magma within Earth's mantle.

12 The buoyancy-driven flow within Earth's mantle is responsible for tectonic drift and the formation and dynamics of land masses on Earth. The magma behaves as an extremely viscous fluid, resulting in flow that is so sluggish that it can only be observed on geological timescales (millions of years). Thus, the physical principles that are responsible for tectonic drift would be hard to identify by direct measurement of the motion of the plates and the magma within the mantle. In this regard, it is critical to use our fundamental understanding of the behavior of other systems in order to identify and characterize the driving forces for flow in the mantle.

13 These three related examples of buoyancy-driven flow demonstrate that the basic physical principles governing natural phenomena are transferable from one problem to another. Certainly, some physical effects are more significant in one system versus another. For example, inertial forces play a significant role in the flickering motion of a candle flame, whereas frictional forces dominate the behavior of the extremely viscous flow in the mantle. However, our fundamental understanding of the basic physical laws of nature provides a roadmap for understanding a range of physical phenomena and for predicting behavior in new research areas.

Glossary

Mantle: the layer of Earth between the central core and outer crust

Crust: the hard outer surface of Earth

Core: the very center of Earth

Magma: hot, melted rock

Vary: to change based on the situation

Exert: to push with force

Dictate: to control

Fundamental: basic and important

Transferable: able to be moved from place to place

CHECK WHAT YOU'VE LEARNED

PARAGRAPHS 11–13

**A. Think about the section you just read and refer to your notes.
Answer these questions.**

13. Label the parts of Earth using the words from the box.

surface crust	mantle (containing magma)	solid inner core	liquid outer core

14. Why does magma flow from Earth's upper mantle toward the core?

....

....

15. What is responsible for the formation and movement of Earth's land masses?

....

....

16. How does knowing about candle flames help our understanding of tectonic drift?

....

....

17. What are the three related examples of buoyancy-driven flow, and why do you think the author uses them to explain buoyancy-driven flow?

....

....

....

....

B. Read the section again. Check your answers and add details to your notes.

C. Using your notes, write a description of buoyancy-driven flow, using an example from the essay to help explain the process. Try to use the words from the box.

| candle flame | continental drift | density | flow | fluid |
| gravity | lake turnover | magma | sluggish | viscous |

THINKING CRITICALLY

Look back at your notes and answers in Check What You've Learned. Answer the questions.

1. Why is it important to be able to make connections between events in our physical world as the author did with his examples of candle flame, lake flow, and continental drift?

2. In each of the examples of buoyancy-driven flow, gravity is mentioned as having an effect on the fluid. What effect does gravity have on air (in the candle), on water, and on magma?

3. How did your understanding of candles, lakes, and continents change from reading this essay?

❶ Go to MyEnglishLab to complete a critical thinking activity.

THINKING VISUALLY

A. Look at the diagram about the combustion process of a candle. Combustion is a chemical activity that uses oxygen to produce light and heat. From the diagram, what can you tell about how combustion produces light and heat in a candle? How does temperature affect the state of wax? Where is the heat most intense and why?

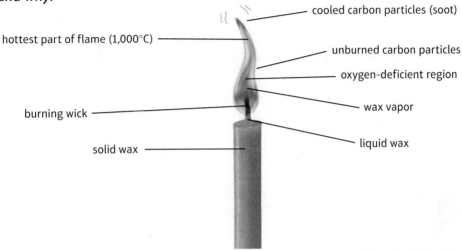

cooled carbon particles (soot)

hottest part of flame (1,000°C)

unburned carbon particles

oxygen-deficient region

wax vapor

burning wick

solid wax

liquid wax

B. Use your notes to complete the diagram to explain buoyancy-driven flow. Use the labels from the box. How can a diagram help students understand the idea of buoyancy-driven flow?

turbulence	less dense air	cooler air circulates down	denser air

THINKING ABOUT LANGUAGE
WORKING WITH PRO-FORMS

A. Read each sentence and identify the pro-forms and their referents.

1. Air rises above a candle's flame but not beside it.

    Pro-form: ....

    Referent: ....

2. Tilting a candle will result in its flame re-orienting itself away from the floor.

    Pro-form: ....   Referent: ....

    Pro-form: ....   Referent: ....

> **TIP**
>
> A pro-form is a word that can be substituted for other words and phrases and whose meaning is understood from the context. The most common pro-forms are pronouns, but other words may also be used, such as *this* or *there*. Pro-forms are useful to writers and readers because they link ideas while reducing repetition of the original term, or referent.
>
> For help with pro-forms, go to MyEnglishLab, Chemical Engineering, Part 1, Language Skill.

3. The author believes connections can be made among many things in the natural world. In fact, he has written an essay about how candle flames are connected to continental drift.

Pro-form: .... Referent: ....

4. Gravitational force helps pull dense water to the bottom of a lake. Similarly, this force acts on magma but on a slower timescale.

Pro-form: .... Referent: ....

5. The water at the bottom of a lake is much colder than the water at the surface, where the sun helps to heat it.

Pro-form: .... Referent: ....

Pro-form: .... Referent: ....

6. Honey has a higher viscosity than air. Because of that, honey acts more sluggishly in its fluid state.

Pro-form: .... Referent: ....

Pro-form: .... Referent: ....

MAKING USE OF CONDITIONALS

B. Complete the sentences. Use the words in parentheses to form conditionals. More than one correct answer may be possible.

1. When a candle .... (burn), it .... (melt) the wax, which helps to produce a flame.

2. If you .... (go) into space and .... (light) a candle, the flame .... (not flicker) because there is no gravity.

3. If gravity .... (exist) on the moon, scientists .... (research) buoyancy-driven flow on that surface.

4. If the surface of the lake water .... (not warm up) this past spring, the plants at the bottom .... (die).

5. If magma .... (have) a viscosity like air, then continents .... (move) on a visible scale.

> **TIP**
>
> Conditionals are often used in academic language to express hypotheticals. Real conditionals talk about things that actually happen; unreal conditionals describe imaginary or hypothetical situations. Conditionals generally have two clauses—the *if*-clause expresses the condition, and the main clause expresses the result.
>
> For help with using conditionals, go to MyEnglishLab, Chemical Engineering, Part 2, Language Skill.

🔊 **Go to MyEnglishLab for more practice reading an extended text and using your reading skills.**

SMALL GROUP PRESENTATION

A. RESEARCH   The essay "Physics of Scale: How Are Candle Flames, Lake Flow, and Continental Drift Related?" explains gravity density flow as a "flow that is driven by differences in density in a gravitational field." It includes examples of a candle flame, lake turnover, and continental drift. Gravity density flow can also be explained with avalanches, landslides, mudslides, and lava flows. In a small group, research how gravity density flow can be explained using one of these examples. Consider the viscosity of the fluids involved in each natural event, as well as the fluids involved in the author's examples.

B. FOCUS   Decide which example you want to focus on in your presentation. Include a comparison of your example to an example from the essay. Imagine that you have to explain the example to a group of middle school students. How can you explain it so that they understand terms like *gravity, density, fluid,* and *flow?*

C. PRESENT   Give your presentation. Use visuals or realia (real objects) to help explain your ideas.

D. DISCUSS   After the presentations, have a class discussion comparing the viscosity of fluids involved in avalanches, landslides, mudslides, and lava flows, as well as the fluids involved in the essay. What application does viscosity have in our daily lives?

◑ Go to MyEnglishLab to complete a collaborative activity.

Index

Page numbers followed by f and t indicate figures and tables, respectively. Page numbers followed by ⊙(LS) refer to terms found in Language Skill presentations in MyEnglishLab referenced on those pages.

Credits

Page viii (top): Eric Isselee/123RF; viii (bottom): Alila Medical Media/Shutterstock; ix: Peter Hermes Furian/Shutterstock; x (top): Galina Yashina/123RF; x (center, right): Aksanaku/Shutterstock; x (center, right): DK Images; x (bottom): Alex Popov/123RF; xi: Pearson Education, Inc.; Page 1: (multiple uses): Budai Romeo Gabor/Fotolia (gold coins); Nik_Merkulov/Fotolia (green leaf with drops of water); Scisetti Alfio/Fotolia (old letter); Vichly4thai/Fotolia (red molecule/DNA cell); Tobkatrina/123RF (hands holding Earth); orelphoto/Fotolia (honeycomb background); Page 2: Kheng Ho Toh/123RF; 5: Designua/123RF; 15: Heiti Paves/123RF; 24: Deco Images II/Alamy Stock Photo; 30: Gajus/123RF; 33: Ronstik/123RF; 39: Weedezign/123RF; 44: Julia Henze/Shutterstock; 50: Darren Michaels/Netflix/Everett Collection; 54: Villiers Steyn/Shutterstock; 56: Christopher Nuzzaco/123RF; 59: Jez Bennett/Shutterstock; 66: Jonathan Pledger/Shutterstock; 67: Michael Cuthbert/Alamy Stock Photo; 73: Premusa Dilenge/123RF; 82: Stockbyte/Getty Images; 86: Fedor Selivanov/123RF; 90: Alex Popov/123RF; 96: Photos.com/Getty Images; 101: Gianni Dagli Orti/REX/Shutterstock; 111: Reklamer/Shutterstock; 114: Beholdereye/123RF; 116: NikoNomad/Shutterstock; 120 (Earth and Moon, center): Darius Turek/123RF; 120 (astronaut): Khunaspix/123RF; 120 (man in black shirt): Nicholas Piccillo/123RF; 125: CTK/Alamy Stock Photo; 130 (avalanche, top): Med_ved/Getty Images; 130-131 (sand dune, bottom): Tamara Kulikova/Shutterstock; 139: Designua/123RF; 140: Designua/123RF; 144: Molekuul_be/Shutterstock; 146: MARKA/Alamy Stock Photo; 148: Jim Rogash/Getty Images; 149 (top): Leezsnow/Getty Images; 149 (bottom, left): Belchonock/123RF; 149 (bottom, center): Lightspring/Shutterstock; 149 (bottom, right): Semenenko Stanislav/Shutterstock; 166: Newzulu/Alamy Stock Photo; 170: Cathy Yeulet/123RF; 173: Amble Design/Shutterstock; 184: Mark R Cristino/EPA/Newscom; 196: Eric Isselee/123RF; 207: Alila Medical Media/Shutterstock; 212: Peter Hermes Furian/Shutterstock; 213 (top): Martyn Colbeck/Photodisc/Getty Images; 213 (bottom): Walter Stein/Shutterstock; 220: Galina Yashina/123RF; 226: Steve Hamblin/Alamy Stock Photo; 230: AF archive/Alamy Stock Photo; 237: Piero Oliosi/Polaris/Newscom; 244: David Cole/Alamy Stock Photo; 249: Piero Oliosi/Polaris/Newscom; 250: Paul Lawrence/123RF; 253: Pietro Scozzari/age fotostock/Alamy Stock Photo; 258: Don Mennig/Alamy Stock Photo; 262: Balint Roxana/123RF; 268: Designua/Shutterstock; 269: Designua/123RF; 273: Blueringmedia/123RF; 277: Anna Om/123RF; 282: Fouad A. Saad/Shutterstock; 286: Alanphillips/E+/Getty Images; 288: Designua/123RF; 302: Alphaspirit/123RF; 304: Alphaspirit/123RF; 318: Meinzahn/123RF; 330 (left): Tierfotoagentur/Alamy Stock Photo; 330 (right): Gerry Pearce/Alamy Stock Photo; 334: Alex Popov/123RF; 338: Photos.com/Getty Images; 341: Dogstock/123RF; 350: 123dartist/Shutterstock; 352: Tim Tadder/Corbis/Getty Images; 355: Everything I Do/Shutterstock; 358: Universal Images Group North America LLC/Alamy Stock Photo; 361: Simone Brandt/Alamy Stock Photo; 363: Serg V/123RF.